GAME SOUND

GAME SOUND

An Introduction to the History, Theory, and
Practice of Video Game Music and Sound Design

KAREN COLLINS

The MIT Press • Cambridge, Massachusetts • London, England

MIT Press books may be purchased at special quantity discounts for business or sales promotional use. For information, email special_sales@mitpress.mit.edu or write to Special Sales Department, The MIT Press, 55 Hayward Street, Cambridge, MA 02142.

This book was set in Melior and MetaPlus on 3B2 by Asco Typesetters, Hong Kong, and was printed and bound in the United States of America.

Library of Congress Cataloging-in-Publication Data

Collins, Karen, 1973–.
Game sound : an introduction to the history, theory, and practice of video game music and sound design / Karen Collins.
    p. cm.
Includes bibliographical references (p.) and index.
ISBN 978-0-262-03378-7 (hardcover : alk. paper)
1. Video game music—History and criticism. I. Title.
ML3540.7.C65   2008
781.5′4—dc22   2008008742

10 9 8 7 6 5 4 3 2

TO MY GRANDMOTHER

Contents

PREFACE

When I first began writing about video game audio in 2002, it seemed somehow necessary to preface each article with a series of facts and figures about the importance of the game industry in terms of economic value, demographics, and cultural impact. It is a testament to the ubiquity of video games today that in such a short time it has become unnecessary to quote such statistics to legitimize or validate a study such as this. After all, major newspapers are reporting on the popularity of Nintendo's Wii in retirement homes, Hollywood has been appropriating heavily from games (rather than the other way around), and many of us are pretending to check our email on our cell phone in a meeting when we are really playing *Lumines.*

Attention to game audio among the general populace is also increasing. The efforts of industry groups such as the Interactive Audio Special Interest Group (IAsig), Project Bar-B-Q, and the Game Audio Network Guild (GANG) have in recent years been advancing the technology and tools, along with the rights and recognition, of composers, sound designers, voice actors, and audio programmers. As public recognition rises, academia is slowly following: new courses in game audio are beginning to appear in universities and colleges (such as those at the University of Southern California and the Vancouver Film School), and new journals—such as *Music and the Moving Image* published by University of Illinois Press, and *Music, Sound and the Moving Image* published by the University of Liverpool—are expanding the focus beyond film and television.

In some ways, this book began when my Uncle Tom bought me one of the early forms of *Pong* games some time around 1980, and thus infected me with a love for video games. I began thinking about game audio more seriously when I was completing my Ph.D. in music, and began my research the day after my dissertation had been submitted. The research for the book continued during my time as postdoctoral research fellow at Carleton University in Ottawa, funded by the Social Sciences and Humanities Research Council of Canada, under the supervision of Paul Théberge, who provided encouragement and insight. It was finished in my current position as Canada Research Chair at the Canadian Centre of Arts and Technology at the University of Waterloo, where I enjoy support from the Government of Canada, the Canadian Foundation for Innovation, and the Ontario Ministry of Economic Development and Trade.

The years of research and writing could not have been possible without the support of family and friends (special thanks to Damian Kastbauer, Jennifer Nichol, Tanya Collison, Christina Sutcliffe, Parm and Paul Gill, Peter Taillon, Ruth Dockwray, Holly Tessler, Lee Ann Fullington, and my brother James): Your kindness and generosity are not forgotten. The Interactive Audio Special Interest

Group and the folks at Project Bar-B-Q provided guidance, thought-provoking conversation, and friendship (special thanks to Brad Fuller, Peter Drescher, Simon Ashby, D. B. Cooper, Guy Whitmore, and Tom White), as did the Game Audio Network Guild. My "unofficial editors" for portions of the book were Kenneth Young (sound designer at Sony Computer Entertainment Europe), Damian Kastbauer (sound designer at Bay Area Sound), and Chung Ming Tam (2Peer), who volunteered to proofread and fact check without any hope of reward. Thanks also to Doug Sery at MIT Press and to the book's anonymous reviewers, who gave valuable feedback. Appreciation to all who have provided academic challenge and support, including my colleagues at Waterloo, Philip Tagg and his students at Université de Montréal, Anahid Kassabian (Liverpool), John Richardson (Jyväskylä), and Ron Sadoff and Gillian Anderson at New York University. Elements of this book were previously published, including parts of chapter 2 in *Twentieth Century Music*, *Soundscapes: Journal of Media Culture*, and *Popular Musicology Online*, most of chapter 6 in *Music and the Moving Image*, and parts of chapter 7 in the book *Essays on Sound and Vision*, edited by John Richardson and Stan Hawkins (Helsinki: Helsinki University Press).

GAME SOUND

CHAPTER 1

INTRODUCTION

San Jose, California, March 2006: I am in line to a sold-out concert, standing in front of Mario and Samus. Mario is a short Italian man, with sparkling eyes and a thick wide moustache, wearing blue overalls and a floppy red cap, while his female companion, Samus, is part Chozo, part human, and wears a sleek blue suit and large space helmet. They get their picture taken with Link, a young elflike Hylian boy in green felt, and we are slowly pushed into the Civic Auditorium. In the darkness that follows our entrance from the California sunshine, the murmur of the crowd is building. It is the first time I have seen so many people turn up for an orchestra; every seat is filled as the show begins. This was, however, no ordinary performance: the orchestra would be playing classics, but these were classics of an entirely new variety—the songs from "classic" video games, including *Pong*, *Super Mario Bros.*, and *Halo*.

The power of video game music to attract such an enthusiastic crowd—many of whom dressed up in costumes for the occasion—was in many ways remarkable. After all, symphony orchestras have for years been struggling to survive financially amid dwindling attendance and increasing costs. *Video Games Live*, along with *Play!* and other symphonic performances of game music, however, have been bringing the orchestra to younger people, and bringing game music to their parents. While some of the older crowd was clearly bemused as we entered the auditorium, many left afterward exclaiming how *good* the music was. I expect that after that night, some of them began to see (or hear) the sounds emanating from the video games at home in an entirely different light.[1]

Video games offer a new and rather unique field of study that, as I will show throughout this book, requires a radical revision of older theories and approaches toward sound in media. However, I would argue that at this stage, games are so new to academic study that we are not yet able to develop truly useful theories without basic, substantial empirical research into their practice, production and consumption. As Aphra Kerr (2006, p. 2) argues in her study of the games industry, "How can we talk with authority about the effects of digital games when we are only beginning to understand the game/user relationship and the degree to which it gives more creative freedom and agency to users?" Twenty years ago, Charles Eidsvik wrote of film a phrase that may be equally appropriate for games at this early stage:

> The basic problem in theorizing about technical change ... is that accurate histories of the production community and its perspectives, as well as of the technological options ... must precede the attempt to theorize.... It is not that we do not need theory that can help us understand the relationships between larger social and cultural developments, ideology, technical practice, and the history of cinema. Rather it is that whatever we do in our attempts to theorize, we need to welcome all the available sources of information, from all available perspectives, tainted or not, and try to put them in balance. (Eidsvik 1988–1989, p. 23)

The fact that game studies is such a recent endeavor means that much of the needed empirical evidence has not yet been gathered or researched, and what is available is very scattered. The research presented in this book has come from a disparate collection of sources, including those involved with the games industry (composers, sound designers, voice-over actors, programmers, middleware developers, engineers and publishers of games), Internet articles and fan sites, industry conferences, magazines, patent documents, and of course, the games.[2] Although I have tried to include examples from the Japanese games industry whenever appropriate, my study is unfortunately biased toward the information to which I had access, which was largely North American and British.

As a discipline, the study of games is still in its infancy, struggling through disagreements of terminology and theoretical approach (see, e.g., Murray 2005). Such disagreement—while creating an exciting academic field—I would argue, has at times come at the expense of much-needed empirical research, and threatens to mire the study of games in jargon, alienating the very people who create and use games. It is not my intent here, therefore, to engage in either the larger debates over such terminology or with the theoretical discords within the study of games in general. As such, whenever possible, I use the terminology shared by those in the industry. There are, however, a few terms that are increasingly used to refer to many different concepts, which require some clarification in regard to my usage here. I prefer Jesper Juul's definition of a *game*: "a rule-based system with a variable and quantifiable outcome, where different outcomes are assigned different values, the player exerts effort in order to influence the outcome, the player feels emotionally attached to the outcome, and the consequences of the activity are negotiable" (Juul 2006, p. 36). I use the term *video game* here to refer to any game consumed on video screens, whether these are computer monitors, mobile phones, handheld devices, televisions, or coin-operated arcade consoles.

There are also a few terms that require some small engagement with the debates surrounding their usage, as they have particular relevance to audio in games; specifically, *interactivity* and *nonlinearity*. Interactivity is a much-critiqued term; after all, as Lev Manovich (2001, p. 56) suggests in his book on new media, "All classical, and even more so modern, art is 'interactive' in a number of ways. Ellipses in literary narration, missing details of objects in visual art, and other representational 'shortcuts' require the user to fill in missing information." Indeed, used in the sense Manovich describes, reading this book's endnotes is an example of the reader interacting with the material. Juha Arrasvuori, on the other hand, suggests that "a video game cannot be interactive because it cannot anticipate the actions of its players. In this sense, video games are active, not interactive" (Arrasvuori 2006, p. 132). So, either all media can be considered interactive, or nothing that yet exists can be. It seems safe to say that interactivity is something that can occur on many levels, from the physical activity of pushing a button to the "psychological processes of filling-in, hypothesis formation, recall, and identification, which are required for us to comprehend any text or image at all" (Manovich 2001, p. 47). Granted that interactivity does take place on many levels, I use the term *interactive* throughout this book much as it is used by the games industry, and as defined by theorist Andy Cameron (1995), to refer not to being able to read or interpret media in one's own way, but to physically act, with agency, with that media (see also Apperley 2006).

Playing a video game involves both *diegetic* and *extradiegetic* activity: the player has a conscious interaction with the interface (the diegetic), as well as a corporeal response to the gaming environment and experience (extradiegetic) (Shinkle 2005, p. 3). This element of interactivity distinguishes games from many other forms of media, in which the physical body is "transcended" in order to be immersed in the narrative space (of the television/film screen, and so on). Although the goal of many game developers is to create an immersive experience, the body cannot be removed from the experience of video game play, which has interesting implications for sound. Unlike the consumption of many other forms of media in which the audience is a more passive "receiver" of a sound signal, game players play an active role in the triggering of sound events in the game (including dialogue, ambient sounds, sound effects, and even musical events). While they are still, in a sense, the receiver of the end sound signal, they are also partly the transmitter of that signal, playing an active role in the triggering and timing of these audio events. Existing studies and theories of audience reception and musical meaning have focused primarily on linear texts. Nicholas Cook, for instance, claimed his goals were to "outline as much of a working model as we need for the purposes of analysing musical multimedia" (Cook 2004, p. 87), but his approaches rely largely on examples where we can tie a linear shot to specific durations of musical phrasing, and so on. We cannot apply the same approaches to understanding sound in video games, because of their interactive nature and the very different role that the participant plays.

To complicate matters further, the term *interactive* is often used in discussions of audio, sometimes interchangeably or alongside terms such as *reactive* or *adaptive*. Rather than add to the confusion, I draw my terminology here from that used by Athem Entertainment president Todd M. Fay and Xbox Senior Audio Specialist Scott Selfon in their book on DirectX programming (2004, pp. 3–11). *Interactive audio* therefore refers to those sound events that react to the player's direct input. In *Super Mario Bros.*, for instance, an interactive sound is the sound Mario makes when a button has been pushed by the player signaling him to jump. Another common example is footsteps or gunshots triggered by the player. Music, ambience, and dialogue can also be interactive, as will be shown later on. *Adaptive audio*, on the other hand, is sound that reacts to the game states, responding to various in-game parameters such as time-ins, time-outs, player health, enemy health, and so on. An example from *Super Mario Bros.* is the music's tempo speeding up when the timer set by the game begins to run out. I use the more generic *dynamic audio* to encompass both interactive and adaptive audio. Dynamic audio reacts both to changes in the gameplay environment, and/or to actions taken by the player.

The most important element of interactivity, and that which gives interactivity meaning, argues Richard Rouse, is *nonlinearity*, since "without nonlinearity, game developers might as well be working on movies instead" (Rouse 2005, chapter 7). Going back to the very first mass-produced computer game, *Computer Space* (1971), it is evident that this aspect of games is important, since nonlinearity was advertised as a unique, differentiating feature of this games machine: "No repeating sequence. Each game is different for a longer location life" (see the online Arcade Flyers Archive, http://www.arcadeflyers.com). I use the term *nonlinear* to refer to the fact that games provide many choices for players to make, and that every gameplay will be different. Nonlinearity serves several functions in games by providing players with reasons to replay a game in a new order, thereby facing new challenges, for example, as well as to grant users a sense of agency and freedom, to "tell their own story" (Rouse 2005 chapter 7). It is the fact that players have some control over authorship (playback of audio) that is of particular relevance here. I discuss the impact this nonlinearity has on audio throughout this book, since nonlinearity is one of the primary distinctions between video games and the more linear world of film and television, in which the playback is typically fixed.[3]

GAMES ARE NOT FILMS! BUT ...

Scholars Gonzalo Frasca and Espen Aarseth, among others, warn that we must be wary of theoretical imperialism and the "colonisation of game studies by theories from other fields" (cited in Kerr 2006, p. 33). Indeed, games are very different from other forms of cultural media, and in many ways the use of older forms of cultural theories is inappropriate for games. However, there are places where distinctions between various media forms—as well as parallels or corollaries—highlight some interesting ideas and concepts that in some ways make games a continuation of linear media, and in other ways distinguish the forms. In particular, there are theories and discussions drawn from film studies throughout this book, as there are certainly some similarities between film and games. Games often contain what are called *cinematics*, *full motion video* (*FMV*), or *noninteractive sequences*, which are linear animated clips inside the game in which the player has no control or participation. The production of audio for these sequences is very similar to film sound production, and there are many other cases where the production and technology of games and film are increasingly similar. For instance, "The score can follow an overall arc in both mediums, it can develop themes, underscore action, communicate exotic locations, and add dimension to the emotional landscape of either medium using similar tools" (Bill Brown, cited in Bridgett 2005). Understanding how and why games are different from or similar to film or other linear audiovisual media in terms of the needs of audio production and consumption is useful to our understanding of game audio in general, and therefore I draw attention to these similarities and differences throughout the book.

The other major thread of the book is that of technology and the constraints it has placed on the production of game audio throughout its history. Technological constraints are, of course, nothing new to sound, although most discussions arising about the subject have focused on earlier twentieth-century concerns. Mark Katz, for instance, discusses how the 78 RPM record led to a standard time limit for pop songs, and how Stravinsky famously tailored *Sérénade en la* for the length of an LP (Katz 2004, pp. 3–5). Critiques of hard technological determinism as it relates to musical technologies have dominated this literature (see, e.g., Théberge 1997 or Katz 2004). In its place has arisen a softer approach, in which "traditional instrument technologies can sometimes be little more than a field of possibility within which the innovative musician chooses to operate. The particular 'sound' produced in such instances is as intimately tied to personal style and technique as it is to the characteristics of the instrument's sound-producing mechanism" (Théberge 1997, p. 187). In accordance with many other recent approaches to music technology, I argue that the relationship between technology and aesthetics in video games is one of mutual influence rather than dominance, what Barry Salt (1985, p. 37) refers to as a "loose pressure on what is done, rather than a rigid constraint." Although some compositional choices may have been predetermined by the technology, as will be shown, creative composers have invented ways to overcome or even to aestheticize those limitations.

As James Lastra notes in his history of film music, "Individual studies of specific media tell us ... that their technological and cultural forms were by no means historical inevitabilities, but rather the result of complex interactions between technical possibilities, economic incentives, representational norms, and cultural demands" (Lastra 2000, p. 13). To discuss the influences and pressures on the development of cultural forms, Lastra uses *device* (the material objects), *discourse* (their public reception and definition), *practice* (the system of practices in which they are embedded), and *institution* (the social and economic structures defining their use), a multifaceted approach upon which I draw here. As will be shown, the development of game audio can be seen as the result of a series of pressures of a technological, economic, ideological, social, and cultural nature. Audio is further constrained by genre and audience expectations, by the formal aspects of space, time, and narrative, and by the dynamic nature of gameplay. These elements have all worked to influence the ways in which game audio developed, as well as how it functions and sounds today. The first three chapters of this book focus on that historical development, from the penny arcades through the 8-bit era (roughly, the 1930s to 1985) in chapter 2; from the decline of the arcades to the rise of home games in the 16-bit era (roughly 1985 to 1995) in chapter 3; and the more recent and more rapid developments of the industry in chapter 4.

In chapter 5 I examine the various roles undertaken by those involved in the production of game audio, including composers (who write the music), sound designers (who develop and implement nonmusical sounds), voice talent (who perform dialogue), and audio programmers (who program how these elements all function together and with the game). I take the reader through the process of developing a game from start to finish, discussing these roles in the context of the variety of tasks that must be fulfilled. In examining these roles, the notions of author and text are questioned and discussed within the framework of game audio. Even further blurring notions of author and text is the growing role of licensed intellectual property (IP), such as popular music in games, taken up in chapter 6.

Chapter 7 examines the functions of audio in games, exploring how sound in games is specific to the game's genre and how different game genres require different uses of audio. In particular, I focus on a theoretical discussion of the drive toward immersion or realism in games. I finish the book with a focus on musical composition, discussing the variety of difficulties posed by nonlinearity and interactivity with which the composer must cope.

CHAPTER **2**

PUSH START BUTTON: THE RISE OF
VIDEO GAMES

If video games had parents, one would be the bespectacled academic world of computer science and the other would be the flamboyant and fun penny arcade, with a close cousin in Las Vegas. Many of the thematic concepts of the earliest video games (such as racecar driving, hunting, baseball, and gunfights) had first been seen in the mechanical novelty game machines that lined the Victorian arcades.[1] These novelty game machines date back to at least the nineteenth-century *Bagatelle* table, a kind of bumper-billiards. The *Bagatelle* developed into the pinball machine, first made famous by the *Ballyhoo* in 1931, created by the founder of Bally Manufacturing Company, Raymond Maloney. Within two years of the *Ballyhoo*, pinball machines were incorporating various bells and buzzers, which served to attract players and generate excitement. One early example of pinball sound was found in the Pacific Amusement Company's *Contact* (1934), which had an electric bell, designed by Harry Williams of Williams Manufacturing. Various electric bell and chime sounds were incorporated into the machines in the following decades, before electronic pinball machines became the fashion in the 1970s.

Related to the pinball and novelty arcades were gambling machines, notably the one-armed-bandit-style slot machine. The earliest slot machines, such as the *Mills Liberty Bell* of 1907, included a ringing bell with a winning combination, a concept that is still present in most slots today.[2] Playwright Noël Coward noted that sound was a key part of the experience in Las Vegas: "The sound is fascinating ... the noise of the fruit machines, the clink of silver dollars, quarters, nickels" (cited in Ferrari and Ives 2005). As in the contemporary nickelodeons, sound's most important early role was its hailing function, attracting attention to the machines (Lastra 2000, p. 98). More important is that sound was a key factor in generating the feeling of success, as sound effects were often used for wins or *near wins*, to create the illusion of winning.³ Indeed, the importance of sound in attracting players and keeping them interested was not lost on these companies when they later ventured into the video arcade games market. Many of the same companies that were influential in the development of pinball machines also made slots, or became associated with slots through the creation of *pay out* machines, a combination of slots and pinball, which was developed in the 1930s during the Prohibition (Kent 2001, p. 5). It was these companies—Williams, Gottlieb, and Bally, for instance—that would become among the first to market electronic video arcade games.

The very earliest electronic video games, including William Higinbotham's never published tennis game of 1958, *Tennis for Two*, and *Spacewar!* (1962, developed at the Massachusetts Institute of Technology), had no sound. However, the first mass-produced video arcade game, pinball company Nutting Associates' *Computer Space* (1971), included a series of different "space battle" sounds, including "rocket and thrusters engines, missiles firing, and explosions."⁴ A flyer advertising the machine highlights its sound-based interactions with the user: "The thrust motors from your rocket ship, the rocket turning signals, the firing of your missiles and explosions fill the air with the sights and sounds of combat as you battle against the saucers for the highest score."⁵ The first real arcade hit, however, would be Atari's *Pong* (1972), which led to countless companies entering the games industry. By the end of the year following its original release, Williams had introduced a version of *Pong* called *Paddle Ball*, Chicago Coin had launched a very similar game called *TV Hockey*, Sega of Japan had introduced *Hockey TV*, and Brunswick offered *Astro Hockey*. Midway had cloned *Pong* with *Winner*, and created a follow-up, *Leader*. As *Pong's* designer Al Alcorn explains, "There were probably 10,000 *Pong* games made, Atari made maybe 3,000. Our defense was . . . 'OK. Let's make another video game. Something we can do that they can't do'" (cited in Demaria and Wilson 2002, p. 22). The answer was *Space Race*, which would be cloned by Midway as *Asteroids* (1973). The video game industry had been born.

Pong was to some extent responsible for making the sound of video games famous, with the beeping sound it made when the ball hit the paddle. The *Pong* sound—as with many early games successes—was a bit of an accident, Alcorn recalls:

> The truth is, I was running out of parts on the board. Nolan [Bushnell, Atari's founder] wanted the roar of a crowd of thousands—the approving roar of cheering people when you made a point. Ted Dabney told me to make a boo and a hiss when you lost a point, because for every winner there's a loser. I said "Screw it, I don't know how to make any one of those sounds. I don't have enough parts anyhow." Since I had the

wire wrapped on the scope, I poked around the sync generator to find an appropriate frequency or a tone. So those sounds were done in half a day. They were the sounds that were already in the machine. (Cited in Kent 2001, pp. 41–42)

It is interesting to note, then, that the sounds were not an aesthetic decision, but were a direct result of the limited capabilities of the technology of the time.

Despite these humble beginnings, most coin-operated (coin-op) machine flyers of the era advertised the sound effects as a selling feature, an attribute that would attract customers to the machines, much as had been witnessed with pinball and slot machines. Drawing on their heritage, these early arcade games commonly had what was known as an *attract function*, which would call players to the machines when nobody was using them, and so games like *Barrel Pong* (Atari, 1972) or *Gotcha* (Atari, 1973) had "Electronic sounds ... [which were] always beckoning."[6] Also interesting was the proliferation of advertisements boasting "realistic" sounds (including that of *Pong*). It is not mentioned how players are to judge the realism of "flying rocket" sounds in Nutting's 1973 *Missile Radar*, or those of Project Support Engineering's 1975 *Jaws* tie-in *Man Eater*, which advertised a "realistic chomp and scream."[7] Of course, most players today would laugh at the attempts to describe these low-fidelity blips and bleeps as realistic. This drive toward realism, however, is a trend we shall see throughout the history of game sound.

In the arcades, sound varied considerably from machine to machine, with the sound requirements often driving the hardware technology for the game. A 1976 game machine programming guide described how the technical specificity drove the audio on the machines, and vice versa: "Sound circuits are one of several areas which show little specific similarity from game to game. This is a natural result of designers needing very different noises for play functions of games where the theme of the machines varies greatly. For example, a shooting game requires a much different sound circuit design than a driving game."[8] Indeed, genre sound codifications (discussed in chapter 7) began quite early, although the coin-op arcade games also developed in a particular way owing to the sonic environment of the arcade. Sound had to be loud, and sound effects and percussion more prominent, in order to rise above the background noise of the arcade, attract players, and then keep them interested.

Sound was difficult to program on the early machines, and there was a constant battle to reduce the size of the sound files owing to technological constraints, as Garry Kitchen, developer for many early games systems described: "You put sound in and take it out as you design your game.... You have to consider that the sound must fit into the memory that's available. It's a delicate balance between making things good and making them fit" (cited in Martin 1983). Typically, the early arcade games had only a short introductory and "game over" music theme, and were limited to sound effects during gameplay. Typically the

Box 2.1
Sound Synthesis in Video Games

(Note: There are ample excellent discussions of synthesis on the Internet, in journals, and in books on acoustics, computer music, synthesis, and so on. I will, therefore, only quickly summarize the main types relevant to video game audio here, with a note to their relevance.)

PROGRAMMABLE SOUND GENERATORS (PSGs) are sound chips designed for audio applications that generate sound based on the user's input. These specifications are usually coded in assembly language to engage the *oscillators*. An oscillator is an electric signal that generates a repeating shape, or wave form. *Sine waves* are the most common form of oscillator. An oscillator is capable of either making an independent tone by itself, or of being paired up cooperatively with its neighbor in a pairing known as a *generator*. Instrument sounds are typically created with both a waveform (tone generator) and an envelope generator. Many video game PSGs were created by Texas Instruments or General Instruments, but some companies, such as Atari and Commodore, designed their own sound chips in an effort to improve sound quality.

SUBTRACTIVE SYNTHESIS, common in PSGs, starts with a waveform created by an oscillator, and uses a filter to attenuate (subtract) specific frequencies. It then passes this new frequency through an amplifier to control the envelope and amplitude of the final resulting sound. Subtractive synthesis was common in analog synthesizers, and is often referred to as *analog synthesis* for this reason. Most PSGs were subtractive synthesis chips, and many arcades and home consoles used subtractive synthesis chips, such as the General Instruments AY-8910 series. The AY-8910 (and derivatives) found its way into a variety of home computers and games consoles including the Sinclair ZX Spectrum, Amstrad CPC, Mattel Intellivision, Atari ST, and Sega Master System.

FREQUENCY MODULATION (FM) synthesis was one of the major sound advances of the 16-bit era. FM synthesis was developed by John Chowning at Stanford University in the late 1960s, and licensed and improved upon by Yamaha, who would use the method for their computer sound chips, as well as their DX series of music keyboards. FM uses a modulating (usually sine) wave signal to change the pitch of another wave (known as the *carrier*). Each FM sound needs at least two signal generators (oscillators), one of which is the carrier wave and one of which is the

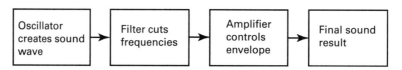

FIGURE B2.1
Subtractive synthesis method of sound generation.

Box 2.1
(continued)

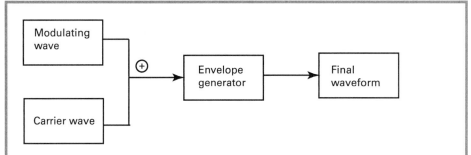

Figure B2.2
FM synthesis method of sound generation.

modulating wave. Many FM chips used four or six oscillators for each sound, or instrument. An oscillator could also be fed back on itself, modulating its original sound.

FM sound chips found their way into many of the early arcade games of the late 1970s and early 1980s, and into most mid-1980s computer soundcards. Compared with other PSG methods of the era, FM chips were far more flexible, offering a much wider range of timbres and sounds. Arcades of the 16-bit era typically used one or more FM synthesis chips (the Yamaha YM2151, 2203, and 2612 being the most popular).

WAVETABLE SYNTHESIS, also introduced in the 16-bit era, uses preset digital samples of instruments (usually combined with basic waveforms of subtractive synthesis). It is therefore much more "realistic" sounding than FM synthesis, but is much more expensive as it requires the soundcard to contain its own RAM or ROM. The Roland MT-32 used a form of wavetable synthesis known as *linear arithmetic*, or LA synthesis. Essentially, what the human ear recognizes most about any particular sound is the attack transient. LA-based synthesisers used this idea to reduce the amount of space required by the sound by combining the attack transients of a sample with simple subtractive synthesis waveforms.

GRANULAR SYNTHESIS is a relatively new form of synthesis (having begun with the stochastic method composers, such as Iannis Xenakis, in the 1970s), which is based on the principle of *microsound*. Hundreds—perhaps thousands—of small (10–50 millisecond) granules or "grains" of sound are mixed together to create an amorphous soundscape, which can be filtered through effects or treated with envelope generators to create sound effects and musical tones. Leonard Paul at the Vancouver Film School is currently working on ways to incorporate granular synthesis techniques into next-generation consoles (see Paul 2008 for an introduction to granular synthesis techniques in games).

music only played when there was no game action, since any action required all of the system's available memory.

Continuous music was, if not fully introduced, then arguably foreshadowed as one of the prominent features of future video games as early as 1978, when sound was used to keep a regular beat in a few popular games. In terms of *non-diegetic* sound,[9] *Space Invaders* (Midway, 1978) set an important precedent for continuous music, with a descending four-tone loop of marching alien feet that sped up as the game progressed. Arguably, *Space Invaders* and *Asteroids* (Atari, 1979, with a two-note "melody") represent the first examples of continuous music in games, depending on how one defines music. Music was slow to develop because it was difficult and time-consuming to program on the early machines, as Nintendo composer Hirokazu "Hip" Tanaka explains: "Most music and sound in the arcade era (*Donkey Kong* and *Mario Brothers*) was designed little by little, by combining transistors, condensers, and resistance. And sometimes, music and sound were even created directly into the CPU port by writing 1s and 0s, and outputting the wave that becomes sound at the end. In the era when ROM capacities were only 1K or 2K, you had to create all the tools by yourself. The switches that manifest addresses and data were placed side by side, so you have to write something like '1, 0, 0, 0, 1' literally by hand" (cited in Brandon 2002). A combination of the arcade's environment and the difficulty in producing sound led to the primacy of sound effects over the music in this early stage of game audio's history.

By 1980, arcade manufacturers included dedicated sound chips known as *programmable sound generators*, or PSGs (see box 2.1, "Sound Synthesis") into their circuit boards, and more tonal background music and elaborate sound effects developed. Some of the earliest examples of repeating musical loops in games were found in *Rally X* (Namco/Midway, 1980), which had a six-bar loop (one bar repeated four times, followed by the same melody transposed to a lower pitch), and *Carnival* (Sega, 1980, which used Juventino Rosas's "Over the Waves" waltz of ca. 1889). Although *Rally X* relied on sampled sound using a *digital-to-analog converter* (a DAC: see box 2.2, "Sampling"), *Carnival* used the most popular of early PSG sound chips, the General Instruments AY-3-8910. As with most PSG sound chips, the AY series was capable of playing three simultaneous square-wave tones, as well as white noise (what I will call a *3+1 generator*, as it has three tone channels and one noise channel; see box 2.3, "Sound Waves"). Although many early sound chips had this four-channel functionality, the range of notes available varied considerably from chip to chip, set by what was known as a *tone register* or *frequency divider*. In this case the register was 12-bit, meaning it would allow for 4,096 notes (see box 2.2). The instrument sound was set by an envelope generator, manipulating the attack, decay, sustain, and release (*ADSR*) of a sound wave. By adjusting the ADSR, a sound's amplitude and filter cut-off could be set.

Box 2.2
Sampling

A *bit*, derived from binary digit, is the smallest unit of information in computer language, a one (1) or zero (0) (also sometimes referred to as "on or off," or "white or black"). In referring to processors, the number of bits indicates how much data a computer's main processor can manipulate simultaneously. For instance, an 8-bit computer can process 8 bits of data at the same time.

Bits can also be used to describe sound fidelity or resolution. *Bit depth* is used to describe the number of bits available in a byte. Higher bit depths result in better quality or *fidelity*, but larger file sizes. 8 bits can represent 2^8 (binary being base 2), or 256 variations in a byte. Adding one bit doubles the accuracy, or number of levels. At 16 bits, there are 65,536 possible states ($2^{16} = 65,536$). When recording sound, 256 divisions are not very accurate, since the amplitude of a wave is rounded up or down to fit the nearest available point of resolution. This process, known as *quantization*, distorts the sound or adds noise. CD quality sound is considered 16-bit, although often the CDs are recorded in 24-bit and converted to 16-bit before release. Figure B2.3 simplifies the process, by showing a 4-bit sample (16 sample points along the positive and negative amplitudes), with amplitudes sampled at 16 times per second. The black wave line shows the original sound wave, and the gray line shows the sample points that would occur. As you can see from the gray line, the original sound is considerably changed by the *sampling* of the sound at a low rate.

A *sample* contains the information of the amplitude value of a waveform measured over a period of time. The sample rate is the number of times the original sound is sampled per second, or the number of measurements per second. Sample rate is also known as sample frequency: A CD quality sample rate of 44.1 KHz means that 44,100 samples per second were recorded. If the sample rate is too low, a distortion known as aliasing will occur, and will be audible when the sample is converted back to analog by a *digital-to-analog converter* (DAC). Analog-to-digital

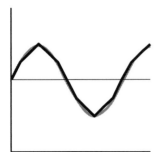

FIGURE B2.3
Bit depth, showing a 4-bit sample.

Box 2.2
(continued)

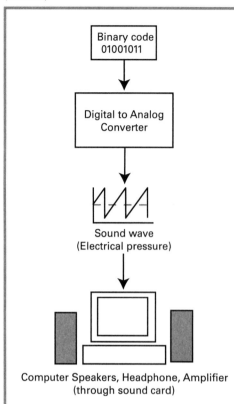

FIGURE B2.4
Digital-to-analog converter (DAC).

converters (ADCs) typically have an anti-aliasing filter that removes harmonics above the highest frequency that the sample rate can accommodate.

The recreation of a sound wave from sample data (binary code) to an analog current (an electrical pressure soundwave) is performed by a DAC (figure B2.4). DACs have bit depths and sample rates. The higher the bit rate and sample rate, the better the resulting sound. DACs most often work through *pulse code modulation* (PCM, otherwise known as raw, or AI2 synthesis), which refers to an analog sound converted into digital sound by sampling an analog waveform. The data is stored in binary, which is then decoded and played back as it was originally recorded. The downside of this method is the amount of space required to store the samples: as a result, most PCM samples in early games were limited to those sounds with a short envelope, such as percussion. 8-bit PCM samples commonly had an audible hiss because of resolution problems.

Box 2.2
(continued)

Adaptive differential PCM (also known as adaptive delta PCM, or ADPCM), is essentially a method of compressing a PCM sample. The difference between two adjacent sample values is quantified, reducing or raising the pitch slightly, to reduce the amount of data required. ADPCM uses only 4 bits per sample, therefore requiring only one quarter of the space of a 16-bit PCM sample. This works well for lower frequencies, but at higher frequencies can lead to distortion. ADPCM speech chips made their way into late 1980s coin-op machines, such as in the OKI Electric Industry Co.'s OKI 6295 chip, used in *Hit the Ice* (Williams, 1990, which used a YM 2203 and two speech chips, since it had a lot of voice parts, including announcers and crowds), and *Pit Fighter* (Atari, 1990, using a YM2151 and a speech chip).

The AY-3-8910 (and derivatives) found its way into a variety of home computers and game machines including the Sinclair ZX Spectrum, Mattel Intellivision, and the Sega Master System. Similarly, another popular arcade chip, the Texas Instruments SN76489, was shared with a few computers of the time, such as the BBC Micro, as well as consoles like the ColecoVision and the Sega Genesis. The SN76489 was also a 3+1 sound chip, although the frequency divider was limited to 10-bit, meaning only 1,024 possible pitches, and was, therefore, slightly inferior to the AY series.[10] Most of these chips were capable of playing short, low-fidelity samples, typically used for sound effects, or percussion, using *pulse width* or *pulse code modulation* (see box 2.2).

By 1980, most game systems had co-processors specifically to deal with sound, although the majority of games had yet to develop any continuous music. Roughly half of coin-ops were using DACs (such as Nintendo's original *Donkey Kong* of 1981) and half PSGs, usually the AY series (such as Atari's *Centipede* of 1980), the SN chip (such as Nintendo's *Sheriff* of 1980) or Atari's own custom chip, the Pokey (such as in *Battle Zone* or *Missile Command* [both Atari, 1980]). Soon it became increasingly common to use more than one sound chip in a coin-op game, as in *Front Line* (Taito, 1982), which used four AY chips and a DAC. The additional sound chips were typically used for more advanced sound effects, rather than increased polyphony for music. The likely reason for this was a combination of the arcade's atmosphere and the difficulty in programming music, as discussed above. Competing machines had to be loud, with short, simple, but exciting sounds that would attract players. The advantage of separate chips for music, however, meant that any music included could play without being interrupted by the sound effects having to access the same chip. As this idea became more common, an increasing number of games incorporated music, such as *Alpine Ski* (four AY chips and a DAC, Taito, 1983) and *Jungle Hunt* (four AYs and

Box 2.3
Sound Waves

Sound waves are described using three properties: wavelength, frequency, and amplitude (see figure B2.5). (The fourth, velocity [velocity = wavelength × frequency] is typically the same for all sound waveforms and so is not discussed here.)

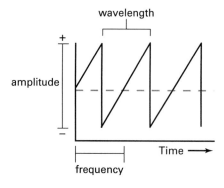

FIGURE B2.5
Anatomy of a sound wave.

Wavelength is the distance from one peak of a wave to the next, or the distance between maximum compressions. *Frequency*, the technical name for pitch, is a measure of the number of pulses (waves) in a given space of time. It is measured in Hertz, or CPS (cycles per second). For example, a note with a frequency of 440 Hz (A), means that in one second, 440 pulses occur. Shorter wavelengths result in higher frequencies. *Amplitude* is the measure of the amount of energy in a wave (technically, the amount of compression the wave is under), typically described as intensity, or loudness. The more energy a sound has, the more intense, or loud, the sound that results. Loudness is measured in decibels (dB).

Regular, or *periodic*, waveforms are considered pleasing to the ear, and can take several forms, including:

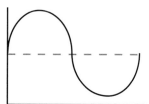

FIGURE B2.6
Sine wave.

Box 2.3
(continued)

Sine waves have only one frequency associated with them—they are "pure" in that they have no harmonics. They are also referred to as "pure tones." In games, sine waves are often used for certain sound effects (laser, alarm), or for flute-like melodic parts.

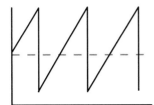

FIGURE B2.7
Ramp wave.

Sawtooth waves are so named because they resemble the teeth on a saw. They are also sometimes referred to as *ramp waves*. Sawtooth waves typically ramp upward and then drop sharply, although the opposite are also found (inverse/reverse sawtooth waves). Sawtooth waves contain both odd and even harmonics. Sawtooth waveforms in games are used to create bass parts, as it resembles a warm, round sound.

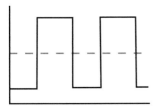

FIGURE B2.8
Pulse wave.

Pulse waves contain only odd harmonics, and are rectangular waveforms with "on" and "off" slopes, known as the *duty cycle*. When the duty cycle is of equal length in its "on" and "off" period, it is known as a square wave. Changing the duty cycle options (changing the ratio of the "on" to "off" of the waveform), alters the harmonics. At 50 percent (square wave), the waveform is quite smooth, but

Box 2.3
(continued)

with adjustments can be "fat," or thin and "raspy"). Square waves are often referred to as "hollow" sounding.

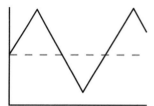

FIGURE B2.9
Triangle wave.

Triangle waves contain only odd harmonics, like pulse waves; however, in triangle waves, harmonics finish much faster, and so the resultant sound is much smoother, sounding similar to a sine wave.

FIGURE B2.10
Noise.

White noise is a sound that contains every frequency within the range of human hearing in equal amounts. In games, it is commonly used for laser sounds, wind, surf, or percussion sounds. Pink noise is a variant of white noise. Pink noise is white noise that has been filtered to reduce the volume at each octave. It is also commonly used for rain or percussion sounds in games, sounding like white noise with more bass.

a DAC, Taito 1983). Sometimes, as many as five synthesis chips and a DAC were used (such as *Gyruss*, Konami, 1983, which appears to use at least two chips for sound effects, one for percussion, and at least one chip to create a rendition of Bach's *Tocatta and Fugue in D minor*).[11]

Speech chips, which could be used for short vocal samples or for sound effects, also began to see more prominence in the early 1980s.[12] Atari included a Texas Instruments TMS5220 chip (which had been used in *Speak 'n' Spell*, the popular family electronic game) in several games, such as *Star Wars* (1983) and *Indiana Jones and the Temple of Doom* (1985). With a separate chip to handle sound effects and voice, the primary sound chip's noise channel could be freed up, allowing for more complex music and advanced sounding effects, such as in *Discs of Tron* (Atari, 1983), which was also one of the first games to use stereo sound.[13]

In a market driven by fierce competition, innovation was a key ingredient in the success of many early arcade games, as a manual for programming games describes as early as 1976: "Today, jaded players have become bored by the myriad of variations of these first games and increasingly more dramatic game action is required to stimulate the average player who might still play a fifteen year old pin ball machine, but is not at all interested in last year's video game" (Kush N' Stuff Amusement Electronics, Inc., 1976, p. 6). In addition to the technological hardware advances that distinguished arcade machines from their competitors, there were also some novel beginnings in the software programming of game audio in some of the very earliest arcade games. Although it was to some extent a response to the technological constraints of the time, looping was an aesthetic that developed in the early years of game music. There were a few early examples of games with loops (such as those discussed above), but it was not until 1984 that music looping in video games began to gain real prominence. This change to a looping aesthetic is most obvious when examining the ColecoVision games, where there is a clear division between the nonlooping games of 1982 and 1983 (e.g., *Tutankhamun*, *Miner 2049er*, *Jungle Hunt*, *Dig Dug*, *Congo Bongo*, and so on) and the games of 1984, most of which have loops (e.g., *Gyruss*, *Sewer Sam*, *Tarzan*, *Burger Time*, *Antarctic Adventure*, and *Up N Down*), despite the fact that the hardware remained the same. Such a change in aesthetic is also evident in Nintendo's home console games, where the very first games released in 1983 and 1984 (*Donkey Kong*, *Donkey Kong Jr.*, *Popeye*, and *Devil World*) had only very short one- or two-bar loops (*Popeye's* loop was eight bars, but it was the same two bars transposed into different pitches), but later games increased the number and length of looping parts.

There were also some nonlooping programming practices during this era that would go on to influence future developments in game music. *Frogger* (Konami, 1981) was one of the first games to incorporate dynamic music. The game, in which the player guides a frog past cars and over moving logs into a series of four safe-houses, used at least eleven different gameplay songs, in addition to "game over" and the level's start themes. The player began in the main gameplay theme, and when he or she successfully guided a frog into a safe-house, the song would switch to another quite abruptly, continuing until a new frog either was successfully guided into another safe-house (moving onto a new song), or died (returning to the gameplay song). Since the maximum time a gameplay could last before arriving at a safe-house or dying was about thirty seconds (much less as the levels increased), the songs did not need to loop. A similar approach was found in Jetsoft's *Cavelon* (1983). The player moved about the screen capturing various items and pieces of a door, and when the player captured a piece, the loop changed into a new sequence after a brief "win item" cue. Each time the player stopped moving, the music also stopped, an approach that was also seen in *Dig Dug* (Namco/Atari, 1983). These techniques are discussed further in chapter 8.

INVADERS IN OUR HOMES: THE BIRTH OF HOME CONSOLES

Although home game consoles had existed before their coin-operated counterparts, it was not until the success of video games in the arcades along with the decrease in the cost of microprocessors that home consumer versions were mass-produced. The Magnavox Odyssey, released in 1972 (in black and white, with no sound) had some success, but it was Atari, piggybacking on their arcade hit and releasing *Pong* on the Sears Tele-Games system in 1975, which really brought gaming home to the masses. By the following year, some seventy-five companies had launched a home version of *Pong*, nearly all using a General Instruments chip that had been made available to any manufacturer, which became known as the "*Pong* Chip" (i.e., the AY-3-8500: see Kent 2001, p. 94). Not only would the graphics of *Pong* be reproducible, but the *Pong* sound was carried into hundreds of versions of the game.

Although there would be other popular consoles, it was another Atari release, the Video Computer System, or VCS (later known as the 2600), relying on a cartridge system, that was to revolutionize home gaming and become the longest-running console ever, sold from 1977 until 1992. The Atari VCS saw limited success when it was first released, and the machine struggled during its first few years of production. In 1980, however, Atari licensed the popular arcade game *Space Invaders*, which became a best seller and helped to spur on the sales of the VCS. Eventually, over 25 million homes owned a VCS, and over 120 million cartridges had been sold.[14]

The sound chip in the VCS was manufactured specifically by Atari for sound and graphics, and was known as the Television Interface Adapter, or TIA chip. The audio portion had just two channels, meaning whatever music and sound effects were to be produced could only be heard on two simultaneous voices, mixed into a mono output. Each channel had a 4-bit waveform selector, meaning there were sixteen possible waveform settings, though several were the same or similar to others. Typically, the usable waveform options were two square waves (one treble, one bass), one sine wave, one saw wave, or several noise-based sounds useful for effects or percussion.[15] Sound effects were often reduced to simple sine wave tones of one volume, or noise. The trouble with the tonal sounds, however, was that each channel had a different tuning, so that in music, the pitch value would often be different between the bass and the lead voice.

The awkward tuning on the VCS was due to the TIA's 5-bit pseudo-random frequency divider, capable of dividing a base frequency of 30 KHz by 32 values. Starting with one base tone, that frequency was then divided between 1 and 32 to obtain the other notes in the *tuning set*, or note options available to the composer. To compound the problem, there were slight variations between the frequencies on the NTSC (the North American television broadcast standard) and PAL (the European format) versions of the machine. At times, pitches were off by as much as fifty cents (half a semitone) (Stolberg 2003). Depending on the random division, tuning sets could be quite variable, as some sets would allow for more bass notes, while others would allow for more treble, and since many sets would have conflicting tunings between bass and treble, they were useless for most tonal compositional purposes. Paul Slocum, creator of an Atari VCS sequencing kit for *chip-tunes* composers who incorporate the old sound chips into contemporary compositions, advises, "Although each set contains notes that are close to being in-tune, you can still end up with songs that sound pretty bad if you aren't careful" (Slocum 2003).

The tuning set example shown in table 2.1 gives us five tonal voices from which to choose our melody or bass. Pitches are given as closest to equal tuning temperament, but depending on whether or not the system is NTSC or PAL, the actual pitch can vary. For instance, A4 (440Hz) on the lead square-wave voice would be off by thirteen cents on an NTSC machine, and by twenty-seven cents on a PAL machine. Examining the tuning set, the most complete range in terms of a chromatic scale within any one octave is the square wave, which allows only six out of the twelve notes (A, B, C, D, E, and G in the fifth octave), though on a PAL machine these were nearly all very out of tune (tuning calculations are from Stolberg 2003).

The fact that the tuning was different between different voices (there may have been a G available in the bass, but only a G-sharp in the treble channel, for

TABLE 2.1

An example tuning set for the Atari VCS, showing a typical frequency selection, and distance in cents from equal tuning on NTSC and PAL formats.

Bass, Pitfall			Low Bass		
NOTE	NTSC	PAL	NOTE	NTSC	PAL
F#2	−6	−19	B0	−11	−22
F1	+16	+4	G#0	0	−13
D#1	+4	−9			
C1	0	−11			

Lead (square wave)			Saw			Square		
NOTE	NTSC	PAL	NOTE	NTSC	PAL	NOTE	NTSC	PAL
E8	−11	−25	C7	+2	−1	B8	−9	−23
E7	−11	−25	C6	+2	−1	E8	−11	−25
A6	−14	−27	F5	0	−1	B7	−11	−25
E6	−11	−25	C5	+2	−1	G7	+4	−9
C6	+2	−11	F4	0	−13	E7	−11	−25
A5	−14	−27	C4	+3	−11	B6	−9	−23
E5	−12	−25	A#3	−2	−15	A6	−13	−27
D5	−16	−29	F3	+1	−13	G6	+4	−9
C5	+2	−11	C3	+3	−11	E6	−11	−25
A4	−13	−27	B2	−3	−16	C6	+2	−11
F4	0	−13	A#2	0	−14	B5	−10	−23
E4	−11	−25	A2	+5	−8	A5	−14	−27
D4	−16	−29	F2	0	−12	G5	+4	−9
C4	+3	−11	D#2	−5	−18	E5	−12	−25
A3	−14	−27	C2	+3	−11	D5	−16	−29
G3	−17	−31				C5	+2	−11
F3	+1	−13				B4	−9	−23
E3	−11	−25						

FIGURE 2.1
Tapeworm (Spectravision, 1982).

instance) complicated programming in harmony, and it is little wonder that very few VCS games included songs with both bass and treble voices. These complications in programming songs for the Atari VCS (in addition to the awkward assembly language) meant that there was very little music, and what there was tended to use rather uncommon keys or notes. For instance, if a composer chose the saw wave sound from the figure 2.1 chart, the bass (say, the lower two octaves of the chart) is limited to C, D-sharp/E-flat, F, A, A-sharp/B-flat, and B, and he or she would be left without either a full diatonic or chromatic scale to play with. Such limitations meant that a composer may end up with something as peculiar as the theme song for *Tapeworm* (Spectravision, 1982) (figure 2.1).

Comparing Atari games with their arcade counterparts shows a clear distinction in the capabilities of the chips. The bass lines of the arcade versions were often abandoned when ported to the VCS, since there was little chance of finding compatible lead and bass voices on the TIA chip (such as *Burger Time*, Data East, 1982). More notably, the songs often have a distinctly different flavor. *Up N Down* (Sega, 1983) in particular suggests that the Atari's tunings may have played a significant role in the sound of the machine, as the tune changed from a bluesy F-sharp minor groove (figure 2.2) to a very unsettling version based in C minor with a flattened melodic second (figure 2.3; see Collins 2006 for a more detailed discussion of this phenomenon).

Home console sound would be improved by Atari's chief competitors, Mattel and Coleco. Mattel's answer to the Atari VCS was the Intellivision (Intelligent Television), which was significantly more advanced in sound and graphics.[16] Also important was its modular design, allowing for extensions such as the Entertainment Computer System, consisting of a music keyboard and second sound chip, leading to six simultaneous channels. The original Intellivision used a General Instruments PSG sound chip that had been popular in the arcades, an AY-3-8914. The chip meant that the Intellivision could create recognizable renditions of precomposed music, such as Bill Goodrich's use of "Flight of the Bumblebee" (Rimsky-Korsakov) in the game *Buzz Bombers* (Intellivision Productions, 1983). Indeed, since most programmers were not musicians or were under strict time constraints, precomposed songs were frequently used on the early machines (see chapter 6). By the late 1980s, music composition on the Intellivision became easier when a program was created by programmer–composer Dave

FIGURE 2.2
Up N Down—Arcade Version (Sega, 1983).

FIGURE 2.3
Up N Down—Atari VCS Version (Sega, 1983).

Warhol that could convert musical data (MIDI) files directly into Intellivision code; but by that time Intellivision had seen the peak of its success. (See chapter 3 for an explanation and discussion of the role of MIDI.)

Competing with Mattel and Atari was Coleco, who had experienced only moderate success with their earlier Telstar console. ColecoVision consoles, beginning in 1982, were shipped with the Nintendo arcade hit *Donkey Kong*, which helped spur on sales for the machine. The ColecoVision used the Texas Instrument SN76489 sound chip that had been common in arcade games.

Despite the moderate success of the ColecoVision and Intellivision, as well as the success of other companies entering the market during the early 1980s (e.g., General Consumer Electric's Vectrex, Emerson Radio Corp's Arcadia 2001), for a number of reasons the games industry saw a significant drop in sales by the mid-1980s.[17] It was the release of the Nintendo Entertainment System or NES (known in Japan as the Famicom) that would help to revive the games industry and secure its future. The Japanese company had previously barely been able to break into the North American market, at a time when "the American companies showed little interest. Game publishers such as Sierra On-Line, Brøderbund, and Electronic Arts were more interested in making games for computers than for consoles, and toy companies like Milton Bradley and Mattel had left the industry entirely" (Kent 2001, p. 307). Nevertheless, with hits like *Super Mario Bros.* (Nintendo, 1985) and *The Legend of Zelda* (Nintendo, 1986), as well as cunning business practices (see chapter 3), Nintendo was to capture the American market and prove to the public and to retailers that video games were here to stay.

FIGURE 2.4
Castlevania, "Boss Music: Poison Mind" (*Akumajō Dracula*, Kinuyo Yamashita, Konami, 1987), showing the use of the tone channels in arpeggiating one channel.

The NES's sound chip, invented by composer Yukio Kaneoka, used a custom-made five-channel PSG chip. There were two pulse-wave channels capable of about eight octaves,[18] with four duty cycle options to set the timbre (see box 2.3). As well, one of the pulse-wave channels had a frequency sweep function that could create portamento-like effects, useful for UFOs or laser-gun sound effects. A triangle wave channel was one octave lower than that of the pulse waves,[19] and was more limited in pitch options, having only a 4-bit frequency control. The fourth, the noise channel, could generate white noise, which was useful for effects or percussion.[20] The fifth channel was a sampler, also known as the delta modulation channel (DMC), which had two methods of sampling. The first method was pulse code modulation, which was often used for speech, such as in *Mike Tyson's Punch-Out!* (Nintendo, 1987) or Tengen's *Gauntlet 2* (1990), and the second was known as *direct memory access*. This form of sampling was only 1-bit, and was more frequently used for sounds of short duration, such as sound effects (see box 2.2).

The NES's three tone channels were typically used in a fairly conventional way, with one channel for lead, one for accompaniment, and one for bass (and noise or DMC for percussion). The two pulse channels commonly worked as a chord or solo lead, with the triangle channel as a bass accompaniment. The most obvious reason for using the triangle as bass was the limitations of the channel, which included lower pitch, reduced frequencies, and no volume control. These limitations meant that many of the effects that could be simulated with the pulse waves, such as vibrato (pitch modulation), tremolo (volume modulation), slides, portamento, echo effects, and so on were unavailable for the triangle wave. At times, all three channels were used as chords (as in *Ultima's* battle music, in which two pulse waves create a chordlike lead in the first two channels, and the triangle creates the bass of the chord), or with one channel arpeggiated (as in *Castlevania's* "Poison Mind," figure 2.4). The pulse channels also occasionally worked as counterpoint to each other, as in *Ultima's* "Overworld" music.

By altering the volume and adjusting the timing of the two pulse channels, phasing, echo effects, and vibrato could be simulated, as in *Metroid*'s "Mother Brain" and "Kraid" (Nintendo, 1987). *Metroid* also made other uncommon applications of the channels, such as the use of pulse wave for bass with triangle lead, in the "Hideout" music for the game. Indeed, *Metroid* represented a turning point in game music, as its composer Hirokazu "Hip" Tanaka explains:

> The sound for games used to be regarded just as an effect, but I think it was around the time *Metroid* was in development when the sound started gaining more respect and began to be properly called game music.... Then, sound designers in many studios started to compete with each other by creating upbeat melodies for game music. The pop-like, lilting tunes were everywhere. The industry was delighted, but on the contrary, I wasn't happy with the trend, because those melodies weren't necessarily matched with the tastes and atmospheres that the games originally had. The sound design for *Metroid* was, therefore, intended to be the antithesis for that trend. I had a concept that the music for *Metroid* should be created not as game music, but as music the players feel as if they were encountering a living creature. I wanted to create the sound without any distinctions between music and sound effects.... As you know, the melody in *Metroid* is only used at the ending after you killed the Mother Brain. That's because I wanted only a winner to have a catharsis at the maximum level. For [this] reason, I decided that melodies would be eliminated during the gameplay. By melody here I mean something that someone can sing or hum. (Cited in Brandon 2002)

The noise channel was nearly always employed as percussion in songs, although there were some interesting uses of it as sound effects in the music, such as radio static in *Maniac Mansion* (LucasArts, 1990), and a skipping record sound in the same game. The fifth channel (the DMC) was rarely used for music, but was instead used for sound effects in games, although there are a few examples of samples taking on the role of bass, such as in *Journey to Silius* (in which the triangle channel is used like Linn drum toms, Sunsoft, 1990), and more commonly as percussion, such as in *Contra* (Konami, 1988) and *Crystalis* (SNK, 1990). With the possibility of sampled sound, sound effects for the Nintendo system were far in advance of other 8-bit machines, and even included the occasional fuzzy vocal sample, as in *Mike Tyson's Punch Out!* Despite these advances in sound design, mixing was rarely if ever a consideration, and sound effects and music would often clash with each other aurally.

Nintendo games that were *ports* (copies) from early arcade games tended to use the same music and sound effects style, rather than to create their own songs.[21] This meant that these early Nintendo games, as in the arcades, had little in the way of song loops. *Donkey Kong* (1981 Nintendo for the arcade, 1983 for the Famicom), for instance, had short loops, only one or two bars long. By late 1984 to 1985, as arcade games and their music became more advanced, Nintendo's ports of these games followed suit, with longer looping gradually being incorporated into the games. Loop lengths were genre-specific, with the genres that had the longest gameplay (role-playing games and platform adventures) having the longest loops. These loops were made longer because players would spend more time on these levels than the levels of other games, as the games were designed to last for many hours. Shorter or more action-orientated genres (such as sports games or flight simulators) typically had very short loops or no music at all.

Unlike most popular music, the looping of the early game music did not typically follow a variation of a verse–chorus format. Rather, sections ranging from one to eight bars were typically found in the song-loop only once, one after the other, rarely returning to the original unless the entire loop was beginning anew. Loops were, however, often reused in other parts of a game, since system memory was always a concern. As Nintendo composer Koji Kondo states: "I should admit that for each sound, music was composed in a manner so that a short segment of music was repeatedly used in the same gameplay. I'm afraid that the current gamers can more easily get tired to listening to the repetition of such a short piece of music. Of course, back in those days that was all we could do within the limited capacity" (cited in MacDonald 2005).

A few looping examples can be broken down to see the looping structure in more detail. The sixteen-bar first level music of the action-adventure platformer *Castlevania* (table 2.2) had a one-bar intro (A) that repeated before moving on to the B section, which had a two-bar pattern (labeled here as B and B′) which also repeated once. The C and D sections also had two-bar patterns that repeated, followed by the repeating one-bar E section. This entire A–E song then repeated in a loop. The music for role-playing game *Ultima's* "Ambrosia" (table 2.3), however, had a much longer song. It began with an eight-bar A section that repeated once, followed by a four-bar B section that repeated, and a four-bar C section that was heard only once before the entire song loops.

TABLE 2.2
Castlevania "Level One" (*Akumajō Dracula*, Kinuyo Yamashita, Konami, 1987). Each block represents one bar.

Bar 1	2	3	4	5	6	7	8	9	10	11	12	13	14	15	16
A	A	B	B′	B	B′	C	C′	C	C′	D	D′	D	D′	E	E

TABLE 2.3
Ultima III: Exodus "Ambrosia" (Kenneth W. Arnold, Origin Systems, 1987).

Bars 1–8	9–16	17–20	21–24	25–28
A	A	B	B	C

These types of looping structures were fairly common in Nintendo games, though there were also games that used less conventional looping. The first-level overworld music to *Super Mario Bros.* (Nintendo, 1985), for instance, had four-bar sections with minor variations, and it alternated sections before looping the entire song. Looping was also dependent on the game state—whether a player was in battle, on an easy level, or entering a new area, for instance. Longer sections such as the *overworld* levels in adventure platform games tended to have more variation.[22] Battle music (or *boss music*) usually had much shorter loops than other songs in a game, with only one or two sections. This shorter looping in boss levels added to the tension, and since this part of the game usually lasted only a few seconds (or minutes at most), there was no need for longer loops.

At this stage in the development of game audio, the immersive power of audio was not yet understood, and music and sound effects were less responsive to action than they are today. Transitions between segments of music, for instance, would often cut abruptly without any regard for smoothness. Besides these *hard cuts*, transitions between sequences or loops were dealt with in several ways: either the loop was designed so that the last section would fit with the beginning of the loop, or a small transitional sequence was used in between looping. In *Castlevania's* Boss music (see figure 2.4), for instance, the fourth bar loops nicely back into the first. Transition segments typically used an effective glissando or rising scale of one or two bars. Another form of transition was akin to a break in a typical popular music song, in which the instrumentation would slow or pause briefly before returning to the start.

"WELL IT NEEDS SOUND": THE BIRTH OF PERSONAL COMPUTERS

Game consoles like the Nintendo were designed for gaming, although a few companies had tried to venture into business computer territory without much success (the Intellivision, for instance, "was seen as the heart of a computer system that would do family planning, stock analysis ...," according to designer Keith Robinson [cited in Demaria and Wilson 2002, p. 70]). Home computers like the IBM Personal Computer (PC), on the other hand, had been first designed as business machines, although games were often viewed as a way to make the machines more user-friendly. IBM introduced their PC in April of 1981. Intended largely for business use, the original PC had several advantages over its competitors in the personal computer market. IBM's upgradeability and open architecture—meaning the computer used standardized protocols and components—meant that third-party manufacturers could develop peripheral products (such as games, soundcards, or joysticks) for the PC system, and even build their own PC systems, called clones (such as COMPAQ, who was the first to introduce such a system in 1982). Microprocessor sound was slow to develop, however, since the technology for the earliest computers had been developed primarily for business applications, which had little use for audio. The first IBM PCs and clones contained only a tiny speaker that could produce simple tones of varying pitch but of a fixed volume, designed to indicate errors or other messages, sometimes referred to as a *bipper* or a *beeper*.[23] Later, add-on soundcards would be designed as upgrades for early PCs, such as Mindscape's Music Board of 1986, a six-voice soundcard (see chapter 3).

By 1983, seeing the success of its major competitors such as Commodore and Apple (see below), IBM realized that their business could be expanded into a wider market by making the PC more accessible to the needs of the home user. With this in mind, the IBM PCjr was launched in 1984. To better compete with the other home computers being marketed at the time, several changes were made to the original PC. In addition to the usual floppy disks that had to be booted by command lines in DOS, the PCjr used cartridge ports that could be loaded by sticking the cartridge into the port and turning the computer on, which was much easier for children. The PCjr's sound enhancement over the original PC was created by the Texas Instruments SN76496, a 3+1 chip used in arcade games. The enhanced graphics and sound illustrated the importance of video games to the home computer market.

In an effort to market the PCjr, IBM hired US games industry leader Sierra On-Line to produce a PCjr game that would show off these newly enhanced colors and sound capabilities. Sierra had previously created graphic and text adventures for the PC, such as *Ulysses and the Golden Fleece* (1982), *Mystery House* (1980), and *The Dark Crystal* (1982). Sierra's answer to IBM's assignment was *King's Quest* (1984), the first "3D" graphic adventure game. But Sierra went one step further, creating an Adventure Game Interpreter, or AGI game engine, which would become the standard for programming Sierra's popular graphic adventure series such as *Space Quest*, *Police Quest*, and the *Leisure Suit Larry* series. The games still had a text interface in which users would type commands, but now had the additional feature of a character to be moved about on-screen in a three-dimensional space, using the keyboard, joystick, or mouse. The AGI format was designed for and modeled around the PCjr's sound chip, using all available sound channels. The PCjr versions of the songs were made up of four parts: the melody, two accompaniment parts, and one noise (generally for sound effects). When the same games were played on the original PC, only the first channel (the melody) was heard.

Unlike the original IBM, the Apple II (first released in 1977) had been designed specifically for the casual home user and developed in part out of ideas borrowed from video games, as creator Steve Wozniak elaborates:

A lot of features of the Apple II went in because I had designed *Breakout* for Atari. I had designed it in hardware. I wanted to write it in software now. So that was the reason that color was added in first—so that games could be programmed. I sat down one night and tried to put it into BASIC … I got this ball bouncing around, and I said, "Well it needs sound," and I had to add a speaker to the Apple II. It wasn't planned, it was just accidental … So a lot of these features that really made the Apple II stand out in its day came from a game, and the fun features that were built in were only to do one pet project, which was to program a BASIC version of *Breakout* and show it off at the club. (Cited in Connick 1986, p. 24)

The original Apple II series had similar sound capabilities to those of the early PCs—a one channel bipper for warnings and errors. As with the PC, later versions of the Apple II improved sound capabilities, and third-party sound expansion boards were made available. Many, such as Sweet Micro Systems' Mockingboard, used the arcade chip AY-3-8912.[24] Some even used several of these chips, such as Applied Engineering's Phasor, which used four AY-3-8913 chips, creating a total of twelve tonal voices and four noise generators, in addition to a speech synthesis card. Such add-ons made programming music for games difficult, since several different versions of the code had to be included to accommodate each soundcard (see chapter 3).

In direct competition with Apple was Commodore, who had experienced great success with their VIC-20 computer, and who had topped all sales records with the Commodore 64 (C64). Like the Apple, the C64 was originally conceived as a game computer, and the advanced (for the time) graphics and sound were clear evidence of this. Appealing more to gamers, Commodore marketed the computers in department stores and toy stores, which were formerly the domain of home consoles, rather than PCs. In addition, the computer could be hooked up to a television set and played like a games machine. More directly targeting competing home game consoles, in 1983 Commodore offered a $100 rebate on the $400 machine to any customers who would send in their old game console ("Commodore Aims at Video Games," *New York Times*, April 12, 1983). It is interesting to note, then, that the Commodore 64 had been built around the concept of games, with games as a driving force in the technology, particularly in the area of sound.

The C64 sound chip (called the Sound Interface Device or SID) was a 3+1 chip, created by Robert Yannes in 1981, who had helped to engineer Commodore's earlier VIC-20, and who would later go on to create the sound chip for the Apple IIGS. Each tone on the chip could be selected from a range of waveforms—sawtooth, triangle, variable pulse, and noise. The noise channel could also operate as a simple pulse width modulation sampler. An independent ADSR envelope generator for each channel enabled the SID more accurately to imitate traditional instruments than previous chips, and each channel had a frequency range comparable to that of a piano. Each tone could also be subjected to a variety of effects and programmable filters including ring modulation.[25] One of the biggest problems for game composers was the SID's filters (low pass, high pass, band pass, and notch), which would act differently on different versions of the C64 machine.[26] Attempts to overcome the problem varied. One game, *Beach-Head 2* (1985), allowed the user to select the filter settings for the sounds, to prevent the screeching that would occasionally be heard with the wrong filter setting. Composer Ben Dalglish explained, "I tended to use 'static' filters as little as possible for exactly that reason—generally, I'd use filter sweeps, which were pretty much guaranteed to have the same effect irrespective of the start/end frequencies" (cited in Pouladi 2004). In other words, the computer's chips often drove the resulting sound.

The limitations of memory were another major problem for game developers. The games were distributed on three kinds of media: 5.25-inch floppy, data cassette tape, and cartridge. The data cassettes—the most popular storage medium for games—had built-in audio converters to convert the computer's digital information into analog sound, though the loading of games on cassette was slower than it was on floppy. The floppy disks, on the other hand, offered faster loading but less storage, providing a total storage capacity of 170 kB, of which music was usually limited to between 5 and 10 kB. The most common approach to the limitations of memory was to reuse sequences of music, as described by composer Dave Warhol: "I would talk with the game designer to figure out what type of music they were after. Then there were the architectural limitations, how much memory I had been allocated, and stuff like that. I often had to figure the structure of the composition (A:A:B:A) and only include copies of the portion that were unique, or have 'music subroutines' of a bar here and there" (cited in Carr 2002a).

As on other early machines, looping was commonly used when space was limited, as composer Martin Galway elaborates: "The [song conversion] was a nightmare since it's the tune right from the beginning of the movie [*Short Circuit*] with all the robotic short notes and arpeggios. The tune just built up so massive [*sic*] that the poor C64 was short of notes by about 30 seconds into it, so I had to fudge the end a bit and make it repeat, basically."[27] One composer, Rob Hubbard, partially overcame this limitation by arranging the music into a series of subroutines or *modules*.[28] Each module could contain title music, in-game music, and game-over music using the same source code to share instrument tables (that is, each different timbre used in the game was set out in the code in advance, and just called upon when needed). Each song typically had three tracks (one for each channel), and each track consisted of a list of patterns (sequences) in the order in which they were to be played. The code would refer to specific sections of the module to be called when necessary, reducing the need to repeat any coding that would take up valuable space.[29] This modular approach to song construction would go on to influence the MOD format on the Commodore Amiga (see chapter 3).

Some Commodore composers were quite adventurous with their music coding, and included random number generators into the code that could select from a group of sequence options. For instance, *Times of Lore* (Martin Galway, Microprose, 1988) used a selection of guitar solos that were repeated randomly for the eleven-minute duration of the song. In this way, the game's ten songs (over thirty minutes of music) could fit into just 923 bytes. A similar random generation was used in *Rock Star Ate My Hamster* (The Codemasters Software Company Limited, 1988), a rock management game. The music for the band's practice session was chosen from a random combination of sixteen sequences. Even more advanced randomization was developed at LucasFilm Games, in a soccer game called *Ballblazer* (1984), which incorporated fractal-based algorithmic music during gameplay. Programmer-musician Peter Langston designed a series of jazz sequences and a standard bass line. The lead was improvised on (algorithmically varied) by the computer. Another interesting approach was seen also in *Lazy Jones* (Terminal Software, 1984), which had twenty-one songs, one of which was selected when the character entered or left one of the "room" levels of gameplay. There were eighteen rooms in total, and each room had its own four-bar "song," which actually played like a segment of one greater song (the title music). Even if the character left the room at, say, bar twenty-one, the rest of the loop would play before it would transition back into the theme song. Most of the loops worked well together, in part because of the ragtime-like bass lines, the same timbres used, and the fact that the game used only two channels. These ideas are discussed further in chapter 8.

Cover songs were very popular on the Commodore 64, partly because its advanced sound chip enabled more recognizable renditions than other systems of the time, although a few composers for the C64 favored original tunes, such as Ben Dalglish: "Covers, on the whole [were more difficult], simply because I was a perfectionist when it came to things like getting fast guitar solos right note-for-note ... and also because of the arrangement challenge of fitting a 'real world' piece of music with drums and bass and strings and everything into three voices" (cited in Pouladi 2004). In other words, in many early cases of cover songs in games, the original music had to be significantly altered in order to suit the limitations of the technology. Classical music was common in Commodore 64 games, such as Chopin's *Funeral March* (*Sonata no. 2 in B-flat minor*) in *Zak McKracken* (Chris Grigg, LucasArts, 1988), or Holst's *Mars, Bringer of War* and Bach's *Prelude no. 2 in C Minor* in *Wicked* (Electric Dreams, 1989). More interesting, perhaps, was the mingling of popular and classical songs in games like *Frantic Freddie* (Commercial Data Systems, 1983), which used the Sylvers' "Boogie Fever," several Scott Joplin songs, Paul Simon's "Kodachrome," Beethoven's *Fifth Symphony*, "Crazy Little Thing Called Love" (Queen), and ELO's "Don't Bring Me

Down." Traditional American folksongs of the nineteenth century were also very common in games, including for instance *Buffalo Bill's Wild West Show*, which used the "Star Spangled Banner" (John Stafford Smith), "Oh Susanna" (Stephen Foster), "Yankee Doodle" (Richard Schuckburgh), and "Camptown Races" (Stephen Foster), among others. As well, many title themes were based on film music, such as *International Karate*'s (System 3, 1986) use of *Merry Christmas Mr. Lawrence* (Ryuichi Sakamoto, 1983), and *Super Pipeline*'s (Taskset, 1983) use of Miklós Rózsa and Walter Schumann's *Dragnet* theme (1967). Cover tunes seemed largely the result of the whims of the games' producers, and there was little or no concern for copyright infringements. As Martin Galway tells the story of one selection: "I was still freelancing when I worked on that music first in 1984, and I just said to [programmer] Tony Pomfret, 'what do you want for the music?' to which he replied 'I want the B-side from the Limahl single "Neverending Story" I bought the other day.'"[30] Composer Mark Cooksey elaborates, "I think I would have preferred to compose my own music most of the time, however the programmers reigned supreme when it came to many of the decisions especially where it concerned the lowly musician. A lot of the games were arcade conversions or licensed titles and hence the music was copied from the original source, when an original product was produced the programmer would often want some of their favourite music in the game (such as J. M. Jarre)" (cited in Carr 2002b).

It was rare to see the original composers credited in these games, however, and there was little credit given or information on licensing at the time, although there were some exceptions, such as Devo's "Some Things Never Change," used in *Neuromancer* (Electronic Arts, 1988) and *California Games'* use of the Kingsmen's "Louie Louie" (Chris Grigg, Epyx, 1987), both of which include a credit in the manuals.[31] As is discussed further in chapter 6, the music industry had not yet discovered the potentials of the medium as a form of promotion and sales, and there were apparently no lawsuits from these early covers.

By the late 1980s and early 1990s, facing more competition from home consoles, there were several Commodore games that clearly tried to copy the Nintendo aesthetic, such as *Mayhem in Monsterland* (Apex Computer Productions, 1993), or *The Great Giana Sisters* (Time Warp, 1987), which was so similar to *Super Mario Bros.* that Nintendo successfully sued to have it pulled from stores. Particularly notable is the fact that these games adopted a distinctly NES-style music and sound design. Each contained similar background loops for overworlds, underworlds, and boss music, in Nintendo style, with longer overworld music, and short boss music loops. *Mayhem in Monsterland*, for instance, followed Nintendo's looping style with a short four-bar boss music pattern. Sound effects were more "cheery" and "poppy" than Commodore's earlier games. This approach to game audio suggests that what had developed even in the 8-bit era was as much a result of aesthetic as it was technology.

CONCLUSION

The audio of the 8-bit era games represents an interesting tension between game sound aesthetics and the series of pressures and constraints exerted by technology, by industry, by genre, and by the very nature of games themselves. Each machine had a slightly different aesthetic that grew, in part, from the technology that was available. Explains composer Rob Hubbard of the sound of the C64, "Well, you know, part of that [sound aesthetic] is dictated by the fact that you have such limited resources. The way that you have to write, in order to create rich textures, you have to write a lot of rhythmic kinds of stuff ... it's easier to try to make it sound a lot fuller and like you're doing a lot more if you use much shorter, more rhythmic sounds."[32]

The persistent practice of looping is particularly illustrative of the tensions between technology and aesthetic. As was discussed, various approaches to looping were certainly available—and, at times, used—although straight short looping remained the most prominent response to limited memory. Looping was not the only choice, however, and other approaches such as random sequencing were also seen. Looping, then, appears to be as much an aesthetic choice as a predetermined factor led by technology.

The parallels between responses to these constraints of technology in games with those of early film sound are remarkable. Looping, for example, was also historically viewed as a way to get around certain problems in film sound. James Lastra (2000, p. 210), for instance, discusses W. A. Mueller's use of background loops to create smooth ambience and reduce the cost of production in film as early as 1935. Although the constraints in this case were financial rather than technical, it is interesting that both film and games turned to looping quite early on, and would later abandon the idea. Likewise, early transitioning between musical segments to accompany silent film often occurred in *hard cuts* (abruptly cutting between musical segments). Lastra examines Carl Dreher's criticism of early film audiences, who were not yet "sophisticated enough to complain about 'synchronized pictures in which, as the scenes [shots] change, one musical selection is abruptly broken off and another starts will [*sic*] full volume in the middle of a bar'" (Lastra 2000, p. 176). As Roy Prendergast indicates, in the era of silent film, when music was commonly played from composition cue sheets, "Sometimes single sections were played side by side with no transitions at all, although short modulations were written when the contrast of styles appeared too crude" (Prendergast 1977, p. 11).[33] Later, audiences would expect smoother transitions and a closer relationship between picture and image, but in the early stages of both film and games, music was more of an accompaniment than a true integration with the image.

The limitations imposed on early game composers and sound designers were not just limited to technology, however. The nature of gameplay and a game's genre also led to various constraints, as in the game *Frogger*, which had a specific time constraint in each level to which the music had to conform. It may also be the case that the prominence toward science-fiction or fantasy-oriented games (which do not depend on realistic sound effects or graphics, and which had not been common in mechanical games) was partially determined by the constrained nature of the technology. With no equivalent to realistic or naturalistic representation within our scope of experience, disbelief may be suspended regardless of the low-fidelity sound effects. In fact, despite the suggestion of flyers that professed a degree of realism, there were very few attempts during this time at creating a truly realistic sound design aesthetic. Rather, graphics developed toward cartoon-like figures, and audio responded with futuristic, alien, and obviously synthesized sounds. After all, in such cases "there is no need to conform to any performance standards. Is someone going to criticize your rendition of 'A Lawnmower Travelling through the center of the earth'?" (Righter and Mercuri 1985, p. 236).

The social constraints of specialized knowledge required to program the software—and to develop audio and write music—also influenced the developing aesthetic, with many composers lacking formal musical training, which is not to say lacking in talent. Even when musicians were involved, they were generally separated completely from the integration of the music; as Linda Law, manager of game composer George "The Fat Man" Sanger described, "Game music in those days was usually delivered as note lists or on manuscript paper. This resulted in the composer being completely at the mercy of the programmer (a scary notion). But the upside for the composer was that the skills he needed to create this music were solely conventional composing skills and the ability to work within very specific parameters. A composer needed no special software or recording gear. The boatload of labor involved in getting the sound into the game was all done by the programmer" (Law 2003).

The impact of this division between the specialized knowledge of music and programming could well be one of the reasons why sound effects were so prominent in these early games, and why some of the audio in the 8-bit era was unconventional in many ways, since many companies did not employ sound or music people but, rather, relied on programmers. Some games appeared to rely on merely copying music from piano sheet music.[34] Rather than their being detrimental to game audio's development, however, I would suggest that one of the reasons for some of the innovations in approaches to composition, such as the use of random generation and algorithmic composition, was the very fact that many of the game composers were often programmers. Many early games were produced by a single author who programmed gameplay, drew graphics, and designed the sound effects and music, and they were rarely specialists in any of these areas. Later, other innovative approaches, such as in the sound and music to *Metroid*, were in part driven by the industry and a desire to be distinguished from the growing codification of stylistic traits. The resulting approaches to composition, I would argue, directly affected the development of music not only in games, but electronic music in general, as Rob Hubbard's module format, taken up in the following chapter, was certainly a likely influence on later sequencing software.

As shown, games were also a driving force in the development of microprocessor-based sound technology. Advanced sound chips were developed for computers specifically for the purpose of games. This technology, of course, would spill over into the music instrument industry. As Bob Yannes, creator of the Commodore 64 SID chip, who would later leave to form Ensoniq, a music keyboard manufacturer, elaborates, "Actually, I was an electronic music hobbyist before I started working for MOS Technology (one of Commodore's chip divisions at the time) and before I knew anything at all about VLSI chip design. One of the reasons I was hired was [that] my knowledge of music synthesis was deemed valuable for future MOS/Commodore products. When I designed the SID chip, I was attempting to create a single-chip synthesizer voice which hopefully would find it's [*sic*] way into polyphonic/polytimbral synthesizers" (cited in Varga 1996).

Game audio was, then, to some extent, instrumental in developing techniques and technologies that would carry over into the popular music and audio production sphere. This important historical role of games has been remarkably absent from histories of musical instrument technology and popular music studies.[35] Indeed, the relationship between games and some other industries has always been quite closely knit. Not only did games cross over with the musical instrument industry, but, as shown, elements of games were marketed alongside popular music and film. These relationships and their impacts are taken up in chapter 6.

Many of the developments of the 8-bit era would help to define a video game audio aesthetic that is still present today. Certainly, games were not the first to see some of the more advanced ideas introduced in this chapter: random sequencing goes back to early musical dice games such as that of Mozart's *Musikalisches Würfelspiel*, and had more recently been used by the aleatoric and mobile form compositions of Stockhausen, Boulez, and others—an idea that is taken up in chapter 8. Similarly, repetition and the use of loops had been seen previously in film, had been a staple of the 1960s minimalist movement, and had coincided with the rise of disco and drum machine–based popular music. Thus, although few of the important concepts introduced in the 8-bit era were necessarily new, they did help to introduce many of these ideas (consciously or not) to a mass audience and laid the groundwork for the game audio of the 16-bit era.

CHAPTER 3

INSERT QUARTER TO CONTINUE: 16-BIT AND THE DEATH OF THE ARCADE

By the late 1980s, video games were no longer viewed as a novelty or passing fad. The Nintendo NES had sold over sixty million consoles, and the Commodore 64, whose success was built on games, had become the best-selling personal computer of all time, with over fourteen million units sold.[1] Games were big business, and competition was fierce. Notes Martin Campbell-Kelly in his history of the software industry, "A few hit products, such as Brøderbund's *Choplifter* and Sierra On-Line's *Frogger*, stayed on the best-seller lists for more than a year, but the average life of a computer game was about 3 months and the average sales were less than 10,000 units" (Campbell-Kelly 2004, p. 226). Games had a short life cycle, resulting in a constant desire for new titles coupled with very high risk. By the close of the decade, Atari had lost its grip on the industry, and responded by joining forces with Sega in an antitrust lawsuit against Nintendo, who by that time controlled more than 80 percent of the home console market (Oxford 2005). Nintendo held its developers under strict licenses that prevented them from developing for other systems, creating a monopoly atmosphere that shut out competitors. Nintendo ultimately lost the suit, and was forced to pay out over $25 million (Oxford 2005). It was not the first time game companies had ended up in court. One employee was cited as defining Nintendo's business as "games and litigation" (cited in Kline, Dyer-Witherford, and de Peuter 2003, p. 115). Part of the legal problem was the inability of the existing copyright laws to protect games, since in many countries, such as the United States, the law explicitly stated that it did not protect "games," "methods of operation" (and the method of play), "ideas," and "utilitarian" aspects of pictorial works.[2] Canada's first lawsuit, *Atari Inc. v. Video Amusements of Canada Ltd.*, came as early as

1982, and questioned whether copyright could in fact be applied to the source code of a game. Summarizes the Canadian law firm Davis and Company,

> The defendant's game units would flash the "Atari" logo, and when Atari sought an injunction the judge stated that there was clear evidence of copying. However, the defendant raised the issue as to whether existing Canadian copyright laws extended to game machines or pieces of equipment, EPROMS, source code or object code. Because this was a question of major importance to copyright law, and because damages would be an appropriate remedy should the plaintiff succeed at trial, the judge denied an injunction and stated that the issue of whether a video game was copyrightable should be sent to trial. [However] There is no record of this issue ever being sent to trial.[3]

The implications of the laws and the nature of the industry led to a climate of secrecy, protectiveness, and fear, made worse by the failing arcade coin-op industry. The arcades had previously been the first to launch new technologies, but the introduction of the next generation of games, the 16-bit machines, heralded an era of the home console and cast a near-fatal blow for the arcades. When Nintendo pulled out of the arcade market to focus on their console business in 1992, the coin-op industry was dealt another symbolic blow. In 1994, there were still some 860,000 arcade game units in the United States, earning $2.3 billion a year, but a decade later, those numbers would drop by more than half, to 333,000 and $866 million.[4] With significant advances made in the technology of home consoles, there was simply less of a reason for gamers to visit the arcades.

One of the major audio advances of the 16-bit era was the introduction of *Frequency Modulation* (*FM*) synthesis (see box 2.1, "Sound Synthesis"). FM synthesis had been developed by John Chowning at Stanford University in 1967–68, and licensed and improved on by Yamaha, who would use the method for a variety of computer sound chips, as well as their DX series of keyboards. FM used a modulating wave signal to change the pitch of a second sound wave. Many FM chips used four or six different *oscillators* (creating the waveforms) for each sound, to generate more realistic sounding instruments than previously heard on sound chips.[5] These chips found their way into many of the arcade games of the mid-1980s, and into most computer soundcards of the era. Compared to the subtractive synthesis PSG chips of the 8-bit games era, FM chips were far more flexible, offering a wider range of timbres and sounds. Moreover, they allowed for more realistic sounding sound effects. The attributes of FM synthesis were particularly well suited to organ and electric piano sounds, pitched percussion, and plucked instrument sounds, and, as shown below, these instrument sounds dominated those games machines that relied on FM synthesis.

Arcades of the 16-bit era typically used one or more FM chips, as well as pulse code modulation (PCM) voice synthesis chips.[6] Some companies, such as Nintendo and Konami, used custom-made speech chips for their arcade games. Walking around the arcade in the late 1980s, the machines would literally call out to players, begging to be played: SNK's *Guerilla War* (1987) had victims calling out, "Help me!" But these sounds were to be replaced with the new sounds for the next generation—the sounds of the home console.

NINTENDO AND SEGA: THE HOME CONSOLE WARS

The first 16-bit home console was released by the multinational communications corporation NEC in Japan in 1987 as the PC Engine. The PC Engine, or Turbo-Grafx16 as it became known in North America, was not true 16-bit, but rather had dual 8-bit processors. Nevertheless, it did have a 16-bit graphics chip as well as six-channel stereo sound, and was popular in Japan for a brief time. When it came time for a North American release, however, the TurboGrafx16 did not fare so well. Part of the reason for this lack of success was Nintendo's exclusive contracts, which restricted developers from producing games for other companies or console systems.[7] The TurboGrafx16 managed to sell close to one million units, but when true 16-bit systems were released, such as the Sega Genesis (or Mega-Drive as it was known in Europe), it was left far behind.[8] Sega had previously enjoyed some success in Europe with their 8-bit Master System, but could not compete with the NES in the North American market. Sega did, however, own a much bigger segment of the coin-op arcade market, and could rely on these games to sell its consoles. As David Sheff (1993, p. 352), author of a history of Nintendo's rise indicates,

> Sega's coin-op arcade games were key to the console's success; "[Nintendo's] Yamauchi underestimated Sega, whose executives understood the importance of software to drive hardware sales ... Sega had simply taken the design of its 16-bit arcade machines and adapted it for Genesis. It could therefore boast not only such 16-bit features as high-definition graphics and animation, a full spectrum of colors [512] ... two independently scrolling backgrounds that created impressive depth-of-field, the illusion of three dimensions, and near CD-quality sound, but also a proven software catalogue: Sega's arcade hits."

The Genesis produced many games ported from successful Sega arcade titles like *Space Harrier* (1985), *After Burner* (1987), and *Ghouls 'N Ghosts* (1988). The system originally came packaged with the arcade hit *Altered Beast* (1988), but soon took on Nintendo's popular *Mario* character head-to-head with their *Sonic the Hedgehog* (1991). The Genesis also had superior sound to the 8-bit NES. It had an equivalent PSG 3+1 chip to handle effects and the occasional music part (a Texas Instruments SN76489, which had been used in the ColecoVision), as well as a Yamaha FM synthesis chip, a YM 2612, which had six channels of digitized stereo sound, and one PCM 8-bit sample channel (the same chip used in the popular Yamaha DX27 and DX100 music keyboards).

The Sega Genesis was the most popular game console to employ FM sound. Although sampled vocals still sounded somewhat scratchy on the machines (rather like a detuned radio), they were a significant improvement over those of the NES, and along with the Genesis' advanced graphics there was a clear distinction for fans between the games of the 8-bit era and those of the 16-bit era. Sound on the Genesis was rather difficult to program, however, requiring assembly language code to engage the two chips. Masato Yakamura, composer of *Sonic the Hedgehog*, recalls, "Nowadays, you'd just be able to send the data through email, but at the time, I had to record onto cassette. *[laughs]* The sound engineer would then listen to them, and reproduce them for implementation on the Genesis. Then, they'd send me back a bare game chip, and then I'd listen to it and check it. It's sort of unthinkable, now, but at the time, we just did that over and over until we got to the finished product."[9]

Instrument sounds and sound effects had to be coded by hand in a cumbersome format,[10] and thus sounds and instruments were used many times in different games to save coding new ones. The *Genesis Technical Manual* described the most common instrument sounds (see table 3.1). Each FM channel had four *operators* (waveforms) assigned, each with a frequency and an envelope with which to modify the input. Operator One (the oscillator, or carrier wave) could feed back into itself, creating a more complex waveform, and thus, a different instrument sound. The other operators served as modulating waveforms (known as *slots*). The oscillator would produce a basic sine-wave tone, and the modulators could then affect the output waveform, altering the complexity of the waveform and therefore its timbre. There were eight different algorithmic configurations of these four operators, presented with suggested instrument uses (table 3.1). Although they could be used for other instrument sounds, these suggested sounds became the most common on the Genesis.[11]

The result of the assembly programming and the eight algorithms meant that many of the same types of sounds were used over and over in games. The same "fat square-wave-like organ sound" is used in the *Shadow of the Beast II* (Psygnosis 1992) game discussed below, as well as other Psygnosis games, like *Fatal Rewind* (1991), while the "flute-like sound" from the same game was also used in *Misadventures of Flink* (1993), and so on.

Once the instruments were developed, the musical routines (sequences) could be coded, often using loops and transpositions to save time and system memory. In the "Labyrinth" section of *Sonic the Hedgehog*, for instance, there is repeated use of various sequences that are transposed, which are part of an overall ABAC song pattern. Typically, one channel handled percussion, one bass, one the melody, and others were used for filler chords, or arpeggios. The multiple

TABLE 3.1

Eight algorithmic configurations of the FM chip's operators, from the *Sega Genesis Technical Manual*. Slots are indicated by shading.

Algorithm #	Layout	Suggested uses
0		Distorted guitar, "high hat chopper," bass
1		Harp, "PSG"-like sound
2		Bass guitar, electric guitar, brass, piano, woodwinds
3		Strings, folk guitar, chimes
4		Flute, bells, chorus, bass drum, snare drum, tom-tom
5		Brass, organ
6		Xylophone, tom-tom, organ, vibraphone, snare drum, bass drum
7		Pipe organ

channels were also used to create various effects, which were common on the Genesis. The most popular effect seen was a kind of *double-tracking*,[12] in which a slight delay between channels "fattens up" the instruments, creating a fuller sound. A more significant delay could be used to create phasing effects, or even a kind of flanging.

Song structures on the Genesis were not significantly different than those of its 8-bit predecessors or those of other 16-bit systems. Typically, level gameplay had the longest loops, while boss music had the shortest loops, often eight to ten bars, as in figure 3.1, which also used a double-tracking effect, and illustrates very typical usage of the YM chip's six channels.

Transitions between the loops on the Sega Genesis also did not significantly differ from those of the 8-bit games. The most common transitions were still hard cuts, although there were also some rapid fade-outs of the original cue before the

FIGURE 3.1

Boss music from *Sonic the Hedgehog* (Masato Nakamura, Sega, 1991), showing very typical use of the Genesis chip's channels.

new cue began. It could be argued, in fact, that apart from the increased quality of the sound (in terms of more "realistic" sounding instruments), and the extra channels, there was little significant change from the music of the 8-bit games. In terms of sound design, however, Sega's digital sample channel enabled a far more advanced repertoire. Sound effects became more realistic sounding, and vocal samples were far in advance of their 8-bit predecessors. A few Sega games managed to experiment with interactivity between the music and the player in some way. *Toejam and Earl: Panic on Funkotron* (Sega, 1992), a music side-scrolling platform game, for instance, allowed the player to select the initial game music (by John Baker), and had the player "jam out" to the percussion in the funky score in a simple *Simon*-type memory game at several stages in gameplay. In a few other games, the player had some minor interaction with the music, but the most interesting example came from the *Looney Tunes* game, *Desert Demolition* (Blue Sky, 1995). Reminiscent of *DigDug* discussed in chapter 2, the player selected a character to control (Wile E. Coyote or the Road Runner), and the sound then *mickey-moused* the character (that is, followed the character's movements), speeding up or slowing down, starting and stopping with the player's actions. The music was very simplistic, but nevertheless the game represented one of the most interactive soundtracks produced on the Genesis.

Perhaps the most distinguishing feature of Sega Genesis audio was the adoption of progressive-rock stylistic traits. Occasionally, graphics on the Sega made some reference to progressive rock, such as those of *Shadow of the Beast II*, which recalled the Roger Dean album covers for Yes. More significant, though, is that elements of progressive rock instrumentation entered the Genesis sound. Since the chip could somewhat accurately mimic the common progressive rock instruments, it is perhaps not surprising that a progressive rock sound was used. Rather than using a guitar lead sound like that common to the Commodore 64, the Genesis more commonly used keyboard instrument sounds, which had contributed significantly to the progressive aesthetic, used primarily for supplying background chords and for stating thematic material (Macan 1997, pp. 33–34). Providing the rhythm section were bass guitar and drums, and these were often accompanied by various percussion sounds (such as woodblocks, bells, chimes, and so on, "to create tone colours rather than emphasize the beat") (ibid., pp. 37–38). Flute and violin sounds were then used 'in an obbligato role (most often to supply instrumental commentary between vocal stanzas) or as an alternate lead instrument to the keyboards and guitar' (ibid., p. 37). A keyboard-like lead, organ sounds, and unusual wood-block or bell/chime percussion were staples of Genesis music, and flute and violin sounds were also quite common, particularly in epic role-playing games, like *Phantasy Star* (Sega, 1988). There were also examples in shoot-'em-ups, like *Vapour Trail* (Riot, 1991), puzzle games, such as *Fatal Rewind*'s Pink Floyd-esque beginnings (Psygnosis, 1991), and platform games like *Shadow of the Beast II*, which used a fat synth sound (slightly resembling an organ), a flute-like sound, and a bell, with unusual percussive accents (music by David Whittaker).

Song structure on the Genesis (and to some extent other platforms of the era), like progressive rock, deemphasized "full-blown tunes in favour of other types of melodic material. Large-scale structure in instrumental progressive rock results from the repetition of brief melodic ideas or chord progressions, and the combination of such fragments to produce larger, more complex units" (Macan 1997, p. 44). Indeed, it was a common element in some game music of the 16-bit era and beyond to avoid anything too "catchy" that might become annoying after many repetitions, in favor of various smaller melodic riffs which, collectively, could often be played like a longer epic soundtrack, with each tune thematically and instrumentally tied to each other. It was also quite common to use ground bass, a recurring bass line with variations overtop. As Macan (1997, p. 44) indicates in his study of progressive rock, these variations were commonly four- or eight-bar fanfare melodic riffs. On the Genesis, some games were entirely composed using this concept, such as *Pirates of Dark Water* (Sunsoft, 1994), in which each distinct level in the game had a different theme, but within each level, all the music shared one bass line, with two or three melodic variations, as in figure 3.2, which shows a simple sixteen-bar loop made up of two variations over the bass.

FIGURE 3.2
Pirates of Dark Water, "Citadel level" (Tom Chase and Steve Rucker, Sunsoft, 1994).

One final element worth noting common to both progressive rock and the music of the Sega Genesis was the use of modal harmony, exotic modes, and chromaticism. It is perhaps not surprising that progressive rock—with themes commonly drawn from science fiction, mythology, and fantasy—might use non-Western or archaic tonal elements to signify these "other" places and worlds in which the songs were set. Equally unsurprising, then, is the adoption of similar modal elements and chromatic notes in video games, which were also commonly set in fantasy realms, as can be seen in the examples above as well as, more clearly, in figure 3.3, from *Shadow of the Beast II*, which had several pentatonic melodies.

With the Genesis leagues ahead of the NES in capabilities, Nintendo realized that they would have to build a 16-bit system to compete. By 1991, they had developed their Super Famicom, or Super Nintendo Entertainment System (SNES). The SNES was arguably superior in graphics and sound capabilities to the Genesis, and managed to sell 46 million units over the course of the product's lifetime.[13] The SNES sound module consisted of several components, the most important of which was the Sony SPC-700. The SPC-700 was an 8-bit co-processor, with an attached 16-bit Sony *digital signal processor* (see box 3.1, "DSP"), and a 16-bit stereo DAC. The DSP was essentially a *wavetable synthesizer* that supported eight stereo channels at programmable frequency and

FIGURE 3.3
Shadow of the Beast II, "Prison level" (Tim Wright, Psygnosis, 1992).

Box 3.1
Digital Signal Processing (DSP)

DSP refers to the processing of a signal (sound) digitally. This subject is worthy of a book in itself (see Zölzer, Amatriain, and Arfib 2002 for a more detailed look at these effects). Common game sound effects processing includes:

ECHO   delayed signals of 50 milliseconds or above. Echo is useful for creating the effect of an enormous cavernous environment.

REVERBERATION (REVERB)   recreates the reflection of sound waves off a solid surface, typically with delayed signal of 50 ms or below. Reverb is used for creating indoor environments.

CHORUS   a delayed sound added to original with constant delay. Chorus may have one or more delayed sounds, resulting in the effect of multiple voices. Creates several "layers" of the same sound, adding depth.

TIME STRETCHING   altering the speed of a sound without adjusting the pitch.

COMPRESSION   reducing the dynamic range of a sound. Compressors make loud sounds quieter, and the quiet sounds louder. Compression has been used to extremes in games, although dynamic range is improving. See Bridgett 2008 for more information on dynamic range in games.

EQUALIZATION (EQ)   attenuating (reducing or eliminating) or amplifying various frequency bands in a sound; used in mixing.

FILTERING   specific frequency ranges can be emphasized or attenuated. Band-pass (reducing high and low frequencies) creates a "telephone voice" effect. Low-pass filters cut high frequencies, while high-pass filters cut low frequencies. Used in mixing, and for creating effects (such as the aforementioned telephone voice).

volume, effects such as reverb, filters, panning, and envelope generators, and had a preset stock of MIDI instruments (see below for an explanation of MIDI). Unlike previous synthesis models used in computer sound, wavetable synthesis used preset digital samples of instruments, usually combined with basic waveforms of analog synths (see box 2.1, pp. 10–12). It was, therefore, much more "realistic" sounding than FM synthesis,[14] and with the addition of software to convert MIDI data into files executable by the sound processor, it was much more user-friendly.

Despite appealing to the same market, Nintendo had cultivated an image quite different from that of Sega. The marketing practice of Sega has been summarized as "smearing its rival as infantile and boring and building it own 'cool' image" (Kline, Dyer-Witherford, and de Peuter 2003, pp. 130–131). Sheff (1993, p. 358) describes the differences, for instance, in the design of the visual style of the consoles: "The Genesis, in black, was the outsider, the heavy metal of video-game machines. The SNES, sleekly styled in gray, was commercial and pop." This distinction was similar to that of the music and sound effects, which typically had a different style between consoles. Even though the SNES had wavetable synthesis sound, it still maintained a distinctly "chip-tune" and poppy feel, relying on the aesthetic of the 8-bit era, for the most part using squarewave-like sounds rather than relying on more "traditional" musical instruments.[15] Whereas the Genesis had more progressive-rock stylistic traits, the SNES leaned toward more popular music of the early 1990s, including dance (such as *Adventures of Dr. Franken* [Elite, 1993]), hard rock, such as *Biker Mice from Mars* (Konami, 1994, which used three electric guitar sounds, three drumkit sounds, and a bass), and even hip-hop, such as *Barkley Shut and Jam* (Accolade, 1993, sound by Rudy Helm and Richard Kelly).

Sega's initial success in the home console market had been reliant to some extent on celebrity-endorsed games, such as *Michael Jackson's Moonwalker* (Sega, 1991) and *Joe Montana Football* (Sega, 1990). This marketing concept was not lost on Nintendo, who released many games with movie tie-ins (*Cliff Hanger* [Sony, 1993], *Demolition Man* [Acclaim, 1995], *Judge Dredd* [Acclaim, 1995], and so on).[16] This celebrity marketing also spilled over into the music, as the SNES relied on more cover songs and licensed music than its predecessors, employing various electronic music artists to write soundtracks (such as Eurodance band 2Unlimited's soundtrack for *Biometal* [European and US versions, Activision, 1993], and Psykosonik's soundtrack for the SNES game, *X-Kaliber 2097* [Activision, 1994]). *Ken Griffey Baseball* (Nintendo, 1994), even included a Jimi Hendrix–style American national anthem. Even classical music was more frequently used on the Super Nintendo, such as *Adventures of Dr. Franken*'s dance version of Beethoven's *Moonlight Sonata*, or *Air Cavalry*'s (Cybersoft, 1995) use of Wagner (a clear reference to *Apocalypse Now*, considering the setting of the game as a helicopter-war game), shown in figure 3.4.

Although there were clear differences in instrumentation, the channel usage on the SNES was quite similar to that of the Genesis. Chords (in octaves) were often simulated by adding an overtone on one channel to fill out the sound. As on the Genesis, the extra channels that the 16-bit consoles had over their 8-bit predecessors were commonly used for fattening up the sound with chords, or to create an ADT-style effect. Dynamic sound activity on the SNES was comparable to that of its predecessors, and the musical structures remained very similar to those of the 8-bit era, despite the increased potentials of the chips. Boss music typically had at most three short sections which repeated, gameplay levels had longer cues, and genres still maintained the same influence over the length of sections and songs.[17] There were, of course, a few exceptions, and some interesting approaches to dynamic activity were seen in a handful of cases. The music for *Super Mario World* (Nintendo, 1990), for instance, used a layering technique when the player's character, Mario, would hop on turtle Yoshi's back, which is discussed further in chapter 8. Although there were not many significant advances made in the construction and playback of game music in the 16-bit

FIGURE 3.4
Air Cavalry's take on Wagner's *Ride of the Valkyries* (Cybersoft, 1995).

consoles, there were to be some interesting developments in the music of PC games.

PERSONAL COMPUTERS GET MUSICAL

Recognizing that gamers and musicians wanted better sound from their PCs, add-on third-party FM soundcards began to develop in the mid-1980s. Soundcards were designed with the gamer and composer in mind: they generally had a joy-stick game port that could double as a MIDI port with an adapter. As well, lines in and out for speakers, headphones, home stereos, and microphones were often included, creating advances in not just playback, but also in composition for the home user. Although earlier soundcards had been sold,[18] the first popular PC soundcard was produced by the small Canadian company AdLib Multimedia in 1986. AdLib based their card on the nine-channel Yamaha FM chip, YM3812, which was a later version of the popular YM3526 used in many arcade games. To boost sales, the AdLib card was packaged with a MIDI sequencer program equipped with 145 preset voices (*Visual Composer*), and an FM synthesis program to design sounds or instruments (*Instrument Maker*).

Soon after the development of AdLib soundcards, a Singaporean company called Creative Technology (now Creative Labs) developed their own soundcard, known originally as the Creative Music System, but marketed in North America by Radio Shack as Game Blaster. The name itself suggests the importance of gaming in the development of new technologies for PC audio. Although Game Blaster had twelve channels, it used the more primitive PSG subtractive synthesis chips, and therefore was quickly abandoned in favor of the Sound Blaster. The Sound Blaster was essentially a copy of the AdLib card, using the same FM chip, but with added digital audio capabilities for sampling and a game port. Sound Blaster quickly became the standard for game sound after a drop in price, although the cards were not without problems (see Weske 2000). One of the difficulties with the Sound Blaster cards was the fact that sound channels had to be mixed down into one or two output channels, resulting in a loss of resolution in the sound. If a file wanted to play eight simultaneous channels, this meant that the sound came out sounding muddied.[19] A more advanced card, the Gravis Ultrasound, using a "GF1" Gravis-specific chip, was designed with this problem in mind, and was capable of supporting both MOD and MIDI files (see below), with dedicated digital audio outputs for thirty-two channels. The card worked by loading instrument patches into its RAM, rather than the traditional ROM, which meant that whatever samples the user desired could be uploaded to the card. Unfortunately, however, the chip did not support FM synthesis, and as such was not compatible with all of the games that had been developed for Sound Blaster.[20] With such a variety of soundcards on the market, programming music for games became more problematic. By 1989, at the behest of Microsoft, Yamaha made their FM chips available on the open market, so that a standard sound format for PCs could be created.[21]

Another significant development in soundcards came from synthesizer manufacturer Roland. The MT-32, or "Multi-Timbre Sound Module," released in 1987, was designed as a MIDI soundcard, capable of 32 simultaneous voices, with 128 preset instruments. What made it different from its competitors, however, was that it used the more advanced wavetable synthesis. Roland was given a serious boost when they struck a deal with Sierra On-Line. As well as becoming a reseller of their products, Sierra would adopt both Roland's MT-32 soundcard and the AdLib as standards for their games, beginning with *King's Quest IV* (1988).[22] As they had done in the 8-bit era with the PCjr, Sierra would once again use games to showcase the capabilities of new audio hardware components, this time by bringing on board film and television composer William Goldstein (for *King's Quest IV*), and, later, Jan Hammer (for *Police Quest III*, 1991), among others, to compose for the games. The most significant advance of the 16-bit era sound, however, was the adoption of the Musical Instrument Digital Interface (MIDI) protocol.

MIDI was defined in 1983 to allow musical devices (synthesizers, keyboards, sequencers, mixing desks, computers, etc.) to be compatible in a standardized format. Only code was transmitted, rather than actual sounds, meaning file size was very small—a distinct advantage for games, which taxed the memory of the machines. A MIDI command might, for instance, tell a synthesizer when to start and stop playing a note, at what volume and what pitch, and what voice (instrument) or sound to use. Initially, some of this information would vary greatly depending on the devices used, which complicated programming for soundcards, but in 1991 a General MIDI (GM) standard was agreed upon. This standard laid out a template for 128 instruments and sound effects, so that the same number setting would be the same on any MIDI device. For example, a command to "play number 39" would always result in a slap bass. There were also various MIDI controllers, including volume, tempo, duration, key pressure, and so on, each of which contained a specific number assigned to that control.[23]

The advantages of MIDI for games composers were great. No longer encumbered with the awkward tunings or difficult programming languages, composers could instead write their music on music keyboards. The most important advantage of MIDI, however, was the fact that the audio file consisted of only code, rather than recorded digital audio files (which would come later), and thereby would take up little of a game's limited amount of RAM. There were, however, several complaints about the General MIDI standard. First, the selection was limited to 128 instruments, and some of these were taken up with the seemingly ridiculous sound effects such as "bird tweet" (123) and "helicopter" (125), which may have been useful for some game sound designers, but were rarely usable for musicians. Roland responded to the limitations of the GM standard by creating General Standard (GS) MIDI later that same year (1991), which would allow for 128 variations of each of the 128 available MIDI channels.

Another problem with MIDI, however, was the fact that most MIDI hardware playback devices sounded quite different. A slap bass on one person's soundcard might sound very different from a slap bass on another person's soundcard, and what sounded good on a composer's specialized soundcard might sound very poor on a cheap card. The timbre, volume, or sound quality would vary (even the form of synthesis might be different, as shown above). Although for composers of console games this was not a problem, since the consoles had the same hardware in every unit, for PC users, this meant widely varying music playback quality. A few solutions were tried: many game composers would write songs using Roland's Sound Canvas, and this became a standard by which to compare MIDI cards. Another solution was to revisit the idea of "System Exclusive Data" (SysEx), which had previously been used by some sound devices, and meant that each sound device would have an ID code specific to that device. The playback device could then read this code and know exactly what hardware configuration to use—in other words, what sounds and what effects were on which channel, so that number 39, voice 16 might mean slap bass with reverb on a specific card. To address compatibility issues, the MIDI device would always default to the standard GM instrument. The trouble with this method was, of course, the time involved in programming for the myriad different devices. Despite these difficulties, MIDI was quite flexible, and led to some quite original ideas, such as the developments at LucasArts, discussed below.

MIDI AND THE CREATION OF IMUSE

LucasArts' iMUSE technology for PC adventure games, developed in 1991 and patented in 1994, was a unique approach to game sound that was leagues ahead of its competitors. What was original about iMUSE was the introduction of dynamic audio components into a scripting language to allow for more appropriate music in games. Like many other PC adventure games developers (such as Sierra On-Line), LucasArts (then LucasFilm Games) developed their own software engine for building adventure games. Called SCUMM (Script Creation Utility for Maniac Mansion), the first engine was created initially for *Maniac Mansion*, an 8-bit game released on the PC and later ported to the Nintendo NES. The SCUMM engine became the basic building block of many of LucasArts' popular games of the late 1980s and early 1990s, including *Indiana Jones and the Last Crusade* (1989), *Loom* (1990), *The Secret of Monkey Island* (1991), and *Day of the Tentacle* (1993). SCUMM was a scripting technology that enabled the use of other add-on scripting advances, such as INSANE (Interactive Streaming Animation Engine, for video), and FLEM (object naming). iMUSE, the "Interactive Music Streaming Engine," was developed by composers Michael Land and Peter McConnell to allow them to create more dynamic music.[24] Explained composer Michael Land: "The thing that's hard about music for games is imagining how it's going to work in the game. The iMUSE system was really good at letting the composer constantly test out the various interactive responses of the music: how transitions worked between pieces, how different mixes sounded when they changed based on game parameters, etc. Without a system like that, it's much harder to conceive of the score as a coherent overall work" (cited in Mendez 2005).

The developers of iMUSE identified various difficulties with MIDI that were specific to composers of dynamic audio: "Although music and sound effects are an important part of the game's 'feel,' the technological progress which has been made in this area has been relatively limited. The use of technology from the music industry, such as synthesizers and the Musical Instrument Digital Interface (MIDI), has yielded an increase in the quality of the composition of music in computer entertainment systems, however, there has been little technological advancement in the intelligent control needed to provide automated music composition which changes gracefully and naturally in response to dynamic and unpredictable actions or the 'plot' of the game'' (Land and McConnell 1994, p. 2).

MIDI sequencing had been designed for linear music, or at best very limited looping. Music was intended to be played back sequentially in the order set in the MIDI sequence. There were no "provisions for branching or conditional messages," and nor could "the playback system be re-configured to respond differently to the performance data" (Land and McConnell 1994, p. 2). The music could not, in other words, respond intelligently to game events, and the result was, typically, quite jarring transitions between sequences of music in a game (the hard cuts seen in previous game music):

> For example, suppose that there is a high-energy fight scene occurring in the game which, at any time, may end in either victory or defeat. In existing systems there would likely be three music sequences: fight music (looped), victory music, and defeat music. When the fight ends, the fight music would be stopped, and either victory or defeat music would be started. The switch from the fight music to the victory or defeat music occurs without taking into account what is happening in the fight music leading up to the moment of transition. Any musical momentum and flow which had been established is lost, and the switch sounds abrupt and unnatural. (Ibid., p. 5)

iMUSE sought to solve these problems. The iMUSE patent described several components to the software: at its core was a database containing musical sequences. These musical sequences contained *decision points*, or markers, within the tracks. These decision points marked places where changes or branches in the performance could occur based on a condition in the game in real time. When the sound driver reached a decision point, it evaluated the conditions that had been set, and determined the appropriate action. Actions included the ability to turn on or off (or alter the volume of) one or more musical instrument parts, the transposition of musical parts, the ability to change instrument selection, jumping to new parts, looping one or more sequences, delaying the execution of a sequence, detuning an instrument, panning, changing the speed of a sound, and so on. Actions would not take place unless the sound driver encountered a decision point and the correct condition was met. MIDI messages were thus given new sets of conditional controllers by the composer: specifically, hooks and markers, which were given identification numbers with corresponding values in the musical sequence. In hook messages, an action was specified such as "jump to a new location within the sequence," "transpose this instrument part," "increase the volume," and so on. In marker messages, the action was defined by the use of triggers. When a sound played matched the sound specified by the trigger, and a marker having a corresponding identification was encountered, the commands were executed.

FIGURE 3.5
Day of the Tentacle (Clint Bajakian, Peter McConnell, and Michael Z. Land, LucasArts, 1993): Nurse Edna's room, showing the jump to the end of the sequence.

For example, in *The Day of the Tentacle*, when characters in the game enter or leave locales, there are changes in music cues. The player's character Bernard walks around the hallway of a hotel to the accompaniment of a hotel theme song. While Bernard walks around the hotel, a long, looped sequence is played. When the player chooses to open the door on Bernard's right, Bernard changes locale and enters Nurse Edna's room. Upon entering the room, the cue must change from that of the general hotel hallway music to Nurse Edna's cue. If Bernard then leaves Nurse Edna's room, a transition point is chosen, and now, instead of transitioning immediately back to the hallway theme, the music jumps to the very end of the Nurse Edna loop, playing the ending as a brief transitional sequence before transitioning to the start of the hallway theme (figure 3.5).

This transitioning from room to room, then, represents two different approaches to musical transitions: the first is a marker trigger that waits until an appropriate point before transitioning to the new sequence. The second uses a jump hook in the sequence and plays another part of the sequence before transitioning. A jump hook is used in a different way in *Sam & Max Hit the Road*. While the two characters (private investigators, one a rabbit, one a dog) stand in front of their office building, the "street theme" plays. When the player selected for Sam and Max enter their car, the theme appears to speed up. In actuality, the

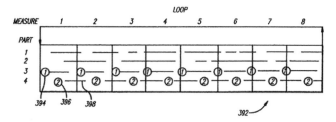

FIGURE 3.6
Loop sequencing in iMUSE, showing an eight-bar loop with conditional responses (Land and McConnell 1994).

MIDI file has two versions of the theme, one at slow speed, and a second cue for the fast speed. The first jumps to the appropriate stage in the second cue when the theme is to speed up.

Loop parameters could also be set within sequences, which defined start and end points, as well as playback parameters (number of repetitions, and so on). The composer, in this case, composed musical sequences, and then conditionalized those sequences, making decisions about which segments should play continuously, change, be enabled or disabled, loop, converge, branch, jump, and so on.

For example, figure 3.6, from the patent document, shows an eight-bar loop sequence (called "392"), which consists of fight music, victory music, and defeat music. The first two channels (parts 1 and 2 listed on the left) contain no messages, and therefore continuously loop. Part 3 is played only when a fighter is winning, and part 4 only when the fighter is losing. Parts 3 and 4 contain hook messages (numbered 394 and 396) at musical phrase changes. Musical phrases are designated as number "398," and are sequences that must be played completely. As the fight sequence begins, parts 1 and 2 play and loop. If the fighter begins to lose, hook message 396 is invoked, causing part 4 to begin playing at the next marker point (between phrases, at the ringed number 2s). If the player begins to recover from the fight, 396 is disabled. If the player now begins to win, 394 is enabled, causing the third channel to begin to play at the next marker point. Thus,

> the fight music, rather than playing along unresponsively, can be made to change [the] mood of the game in response to the specific events of the fight. For example, certain instrument parts can signify doing well (for example, a trumpet fanfare when a punch has been successfully landed), while others can signify doing poorly (for example, staccato strings when the fighter has taken a punch).... Also, it may be desirable to transpose ... the music as the fight reaches its climax. This can also be done either immediately under entertainment system control, or by hook message (if it is necessary that the transposition occur only at an appropriate point in the music

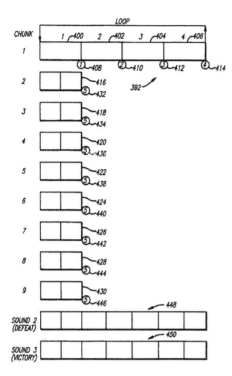

FIGURE 3.7
"Jump to" transition in iMUSE (Land and McConnell 1994).

sequence). The resulting fight music will change mood and character along with the intensity and excitement of the fight, but in a smooth and aesthetically natural way, much like the music would follow the action in a feature length motion picture. (Land and McConnell 1994, p. 5)

When the fight is won or lost, the victory or defeat sequence must be cued from the current looped fight music sequence. This process could be accomplished in two ways with iMUSE. In figure 3.7, the top four measures ("Chunk 1," 400–406) represent one continuous looped sequence, each number representing a two-bar segment of the eight-bar sequence in figure 3.7. There are two jump hook messages (408–414) placed at the end of each of these measures. One message (448) represents a transition to defeat, and the other a transition to the victory cue (450). Chunks (sequences) 2 through 9 represent the various options for transitions, to provide the connection between the end of the measure (400–406) to the beginning of the victory or defeat cues. If the player wins the fight, the command to start the victory cue is queued up, and the engine waits to hit the next marker point (at the end of measure 400 to 406) before beginning the appropriate transition cue, followed by the victory cue.

The theme song for the town of Woodtick on Scabb Island from *Monkey Island 2: LeChuck's Revenge* offers an example of such transitions. Woodtick (a series of docks and ships) has a town theme song that loops whenever the character walks around the docks. When the player enters one of the ships, the music transitions to a "ship theme," of which there are several variants depending on which ship the character enters. The main melody of the ship stays the same, but the instrumentation varies. The last two bars of the sequence offer a transition point: if the player has left the ship, the song returns to the town theme. If the player has not left the ship, the variation loops. The song always plays out its loop when returning to the town theme.

In the swamp scene of *Monkey Island 2*, an example of iMUSE's layering of instruments is heard. In this scene, the player's character must walk from the edge of a swamp, climb into a coffin, and row the coffin across two screens to the "International House of Mojo," a voodoo shop in the middle of the swamp. As the player progresses from the edge of the swamp to the House of Mojo, instruments are added to the theme (figure 3.8). Here I have separated the times at which the different instruments are heard (although they exist at all times in the

FIGURE 3.8
Approaching the "House of Mojo": *Monkey Island 2: LeChuck's Revenge* (Clint Bajakian, Peter McConnell, and Michael Z. Land, LucasArts, 1991) showing layering of instruments in iMUSE.

MIDI file, whether "switched on" or "switched off"). The first channel plays an eerie synth-lead, somewhere between an organ and a choir sound, while the player is standing at the edge of the swamp. This instrument remains constant. When the player climbs into the coffin, the second channel, an open hi-hat, is added. The player then steers the coffin to the edge of the next screen, whereupon a (very quiet) block sound is heard which seems to be at random intervals. Finally, when the player happens upon the House of Mojo, a bass line begins. Unlike other channels of the song, the bass line always begins at the start of its sequence, so there may be a slight delay before it begins.

At this stage, LucasFilm Games had been in competition with Sierra On-Line, a maker of popular graphic adventures. Recalls Mike Ebert, "Everyone just wanted to make something better than *Kings Quest* or *Space Quest* from Sierra ... There was a strong sense of competition against Sierra. I don't know how Sierra felt about us, but in our minds they were the arch enemy" (cited in Wallis 2007). The SCUMM engine that housed iMUSE was created as a response to Sierra's games, notes creator Ron Gilbert: "One day I saw *Kings Quest I*, and it was an 'ah-ha!' moment. After a few minutes of playing it, I was totally frustrated by the silly parser. They made this huge leap from text to graphics, but kept the most frustrating part of text adventures. From that frustration, *Maniac Mansion* was born" (cited in Fish 2005, p. 94). Advances such as iMUSE helped LucasArts to compete in a highly volatile market, but more importantly, drew attention to the possibilities of dynamic audio in games. Many game magazine reviews of the era mentioned the music and the iMUSE engine as selling factors for these games.[25] One reviewer, for instance, notes of *Monkey Island 2*, "It allows the game's music to respond smoothly and spontaneously to unpredictable player choices, creating at the same time a wonderful feeling of continuity in the music" (Linkola 1997). iMUSE helped to set a precedent for music to be more responsive to the player's actions, truly distinguishing the music of games from that of linear media.

AMIGA AND THE MOD FORMAT

Although LucasArts had been advancing game music with MIDI-based developments, there were also interesting developments in another format, on the Commodore Amiga. The Amiga had initially been an offshoot of Atari. It was developed by Jay Miner, who had worked on the Atari VCS and created his own company, Amiga, which was taken over by Commodore in 1984. The Amiga computer went through many different models, but despite the many improvements as the models progressed, the sound hardware remained essentially the same. The sound chip in the Amiga was known as Paula, capable of four-channel 8-bit stereo, which could produce fairly complex waveforms over nine octaves (20 Hz to 29 KHz). Sound could be synthesized on the fly or stored as digital samples and played back through the DAC in stereo. Each channel had its own volume control but no envelope generator, although each channel was capable of modulation, which allowed for tremolo and vibrato effects.

Despite being designed as a games computer, there were initially few utilities available to create sound on the Amiga. Most developers at game companies therefore created in-house programs to sequence music.[26] One such program was created by Karsten Obarski, a programmer and composer at the German reLINE Software game company (see Carlsson 2008 for more on this history). Based loosely on the earlier sequencing techniques of Rob Hubbard's approach on the Commodore 64, Obarski's *Ultimate SoundTracker* sequenced patterns and would export them to assembly language for the composer. The software was released as a commercial product in 1987 and quickly became a standard for games music on the Amiga. It was, however, quite limited, in that it viewed the use of channels in a quite strict fashion, as melody, accompaniment, bass, and lead, and supported only sixteen instruments (samples). Swedish programmers Pex "Mahoney" Tufvesson and Anders "Kaktus" Berkeman released an update to the software in 1989 known as *NoiseTracker*, which allowed for thirty-two instruments and was more open in terms of channel usage.[27] Later versions of *SoundTracker* used what became known as the module format, or MOD, which included both patterns and instruments in the same file.

Most game music on the Amiga was written in the MOD format. Compositions were created using a software program known as a tracker, and resulting music was stored in MOD. A tracker program would store data on the notes, volume setting, effects, and instrument (like MIDI), but could also include digital samples of the instruments in the actual file, limited only by the size of the file (the 880 kB floppy disk). MOD files had an advantage over MIDI, then, in that music or other sound events would sound as the composer/sound designer intended, and in that more possible sounds were opened up for the authors to use. Not only this, but the ease of sampling meant that much more realistic sound effects could be used. Some games, such as *Jill of the Jungle* (Epic MegaGames, 1992, sound by Dan Froelich) included a "Noisemaker," the fun option of allowing the player to hear the sounds in advance of their in-game action by pressing different keys on the keyboard. MOD files were also easier to program for nonmusicians—like many game programmers—and in particular made it easy to sequence repetitive loops.[28] In fact, the tracker format of using blocks to represent music in a linear fashion became a standard that has been incorporated into the design of today's sequencing software. The MOD format was easily adaptable to game sound, in that patterns (sequences) could be arranged to change volume, jump to other sequences, start or stop instruments, and so on. The ease with which MOD files could be constructed no doubt played an important role in their success. iMUSE may have been very progressive, but it was a proprietary tool, and there seemed neither the capabilities nor the desire to construct such software on other systems at the time. However, MOD was not without its difficulties. Although MOD files dominated the Amiga games scene, the MOD format never really caught on for gaming in general because of the required file size and the fact that there was no standard. There were nearly twenty different formats, which would allow for different sampling rates and different numbers of tracks. Although there were a few game companies outside the Amiga scene that used a tracker format (Epic Mega-Games, for instance), the majority used the better-supported MIDI.

By using the Windows program *Modplug Tracker*, MOD files can be opened and explored, so the user can hear the samples individually and view the sequencing data. Using *Modplug* to open one of the files from the *Shadow of the Beast II* game, discussed above on the Genesis, we can see how the tracker format lays out the song (figure 3.9). The white horizontal squares listing the numbers "8," "9," "10," etc. are the patterns (sequences) that make up this particular song. This song plays pattern 8, followed by pattern 9, pattern 10 twice, pattern 11, and pattern 12 twice, before looping. Pattern 10 is open in figure 3.9, showing the 64 notes in the pattern (each pattern in this song has 64 beats). Each row is played in sequential order following the 64 numbers in the leftmost column.

The four channels of available sound are shown in columns. The channel information shows the note to be played based on the sample referred to. Samples were transposed and all set to C5 originally, and these were then transposed to the notes indicated. The second number in each column tells the tracker which sample to use for the note. There are only four sounds in this sequence: Channel one and two both contain sample #07, a thin electric guitar–like sound (called "g1 lead2"), Channel three has sample #08, a fat bass, and Channel four has sample #01, pitched percussion.

Deconstructing MOD files in this fashion shows the many different approaches to song construction in Amiga games. Typically far more complex than the songs of the 8-bit games, songs in Amiga games had a highly varied structure, but usually followed the same basic principles seen in the 8-bit games (shorter loops with fewer distinct sections for battle music, and longer loops with more distinct sections for in-game music). Some tracks, such as the in-game music of *Jurassic Park* (Ocean, 1993), had over forty different patterns.

CONCLUSION

The 16-bit era marked a time when game audio was no longer viewed as an afterthought, but was, rather, the turning point of many interesting developments in the history of games. Many of the technological audio innovations were now coming from within the games studios and were pushed by the game composers, sound designers, and sound programmers, rather than coming from outside sources. The competitive nature of the games industry, however, meant that

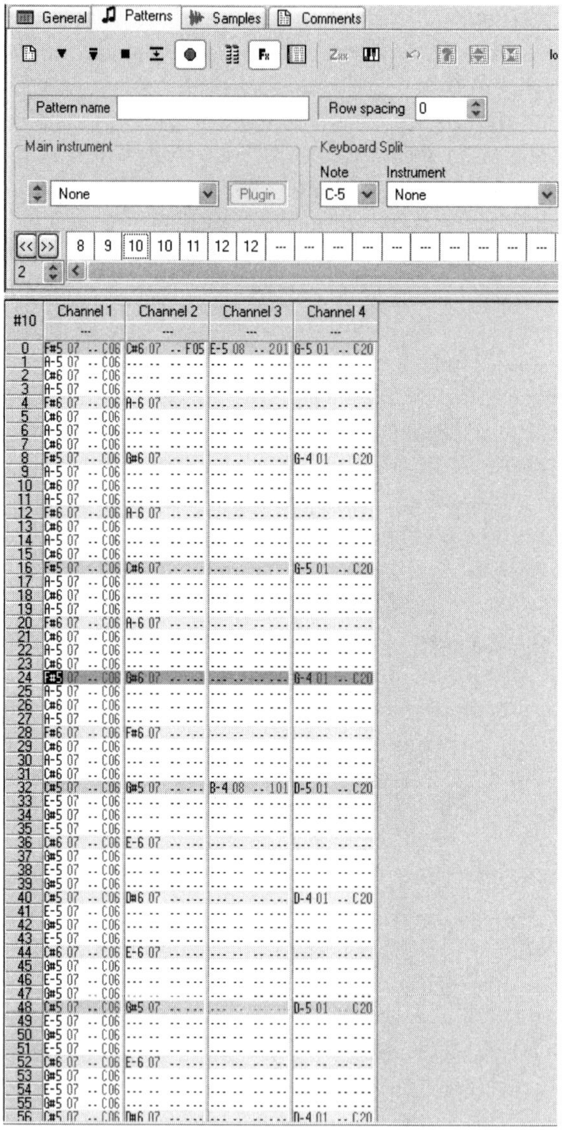

FIGURE 3.9

Shadow of the Beast II (Tim Wright, Psygnosis, 1992) tracker MOD details.

many of the most important advances—such as iMUSE—remained proprietary, in the hands of those who created and patented the ideas. Getting an edge over a competitor was more important than creating standards by which the industry could develop. It is perhaps ironic that iMUSE would work on the back of MIDI, which itself had been a rare example of industry collaboration. As Théberge (1997, p. 85) notes, "the 'innovative' aspect of MIDI was that it was planned as a non-proprietary device (no one owns a patent for either the hardware or the software portions of MIDI)." The proprietary nature of software and hardware developments led to the creation of competing standards, a problem that still exists today. The nature of rapid technological change pushed games toward advancing as hastily as possible, but in a secretive environment. As Denis Dyack, founder of games company Silicon Knights noted recently, "technology would change so rapidly, if you didn't get your game out as soon as possible, within six months, id [software games company] could come out with a new engine and make you look like crap and you'd be dated. So there's this technology curve that people were just completely intimidated by" (cited in Brightman 2007). There were, then, increasing tensions between getting a game out as quickly as possible, and trying to innovate to get an edge.

The development of the General MIDI standard and advancements in sound hardware enabled improvements in sound quality and polyphony, as well as increased memory, allowing for more music and longer songs.[29] Higher-fidelity sampling allowed for more realistic sound effects, and the MOD format brought ease of organization for the countless sequences that were involved in a game, while at the same time it helped to reduce memory requirements for the music, by basing songs on sequencing data. More importantly, it represented a change in game software toward the creation of musician-friendly products. Whereas previously most creators of game music had been programmers (as shown in chapter 2), the creation of MIDI and MOD enabled the influx of more musicians into game development. As a result, sound became a more integral part of games in this era, in such a way that turning off sound was sometimes detrimental to gameplay, as was seen in *Toejam and Earl: Panic on Funkotron*. LucasArts' *Loom* was also such a game, reliant on the player memorizing key sequences of music. Of course, sound effects had always played a useful anticipatory role in game audio, but now music had begun to take on some of this role. Although there were examples of explorations in dynamic audio not discussed (notably Origin Systems' *Wing Commander* [1990], composed by George Sanger, in which music responded to gameplay states), nowhere is this trait as well illustrated in the 16-bit era than in LucasArts' iMUSE games. As shown, the iMUSE design recognized that game music had to be different from standard linear music, and that an adaptable, dynamic score would greatly enhance gameplay. Transitions between spaces in gameplay could now be smoother, with the music matching and responding to what was occurring in the game. The blueprint had now been set for the directions in which game audio was to evolve.

PRESS RESET: VIDEO GAME MUSIC COMES OF AGE

In 1988 Williams's *NARC*, the first 32-bit arcade game was released, but the arcades—which had seen a decline during the 16-bit era—had now almost disappeared. Even though earlier arcade games had typically been far more advanced in sound technology than home games, with the arrival of 32-bit machines and CD-ROM technology, home consoles and computers soon overtook the arcades. At a time of decreasing revenues, many coin-op manufacturers kept to older, more affordable sound chips. Although graphics continued to improve, numerous arcade games released by the smaller companies throughout the 1990s continued to use the same sound technology that had been around for a decade or more.[1]

By the early 1990s, most home computers had FM soundcards supporting MIDI, but many of these soundcards were cheaply produced, and the FM synthesis made MIDI music sound disappointing in the face of CD releases. When CD-ROMs became popular, MIDI in games was for a large part abandoned in favor of more realistic sounds. Popular early CD-ROM titles like *7th Guest* (Trilobite, 1992, music by George Sanger) were released with impressive high-resolution graphics and live recorded music.[2] Since the audio was not reliant on a soundcard's synthesis, CD-ROM technology ensured that composers and sound designers could not only know how the audio would sound on most consumer configurations; they could also now record sound effects, live instruments, vocals, and in-game dialogue. The downside of the CD-ROM technology was that the discs could hold only a maximum of 72 minutes of uncompressed *Redbook* (CD) audio. With a game included on the disc, audio still had to fight for space. As various compression technologies were developed (such as MP3), however, much less data was required to store audio, and game companies began incorporating more compressed audio into their games.

Another important advance in game audio in the 1990s was the ongoing evolution of three-dimensional (3D) or *surround* sound. Surround sound gives the listener the perception that the sounds are emanating from a three-dimensional space. It is likely that, other than in movie cinemas, it was in the arcades that many gamers first experienced surround sound, although it was nearly exclusively used in racing and simulator games. The first PC soundcard to support surround sound was Diamond Monster Sound, in 1997. Parameters such as a room's size and acoustic properties could be programmed into a game, which would initiate filters and effects to simulate the space (see Miller 1999). Surround sound would become an important element in game design in the following decade, as Matthew Lee Johnston of Microsoft explained: "Traditional stereo has been used to localize a sound in the player's forward visual field. What 3D audio adds is the ability to localize the sound behind the player, which is arguably way more important, since the sound is usually the only way to provide the player with feedback about what's going on behind them. Some games use maps and have 'rear view' options, or even let you pan your visual field around to look, but using 3D audio to position an object behind the player is not only more immediate and instinctual, but it allows the player to focus simultaneously on the fore and aft perspective (cited in Miller 1999).

In order to create a three-dimensional atmosphere, the system must position the sound source and the listener in a three-dimensional environment, define the environment in terms of dimensions and acoustic properties, and synchronize the sound to graphics. A dynamic 3D audio system must also process this in real time, based on the location of the player's character. There were many different technologies developed in the 1990s that called themselves "3D" but which varied greatly in quality, such as *spatialized 3D* or *virtual surround* (Warwick 1998). Of particular relevance to games was *positional audio*, which used signal processing to locate a single sound in a specific location in a 3D space. With 3D positional audio, sound objects in a virtual space could maintain their location or path of motion while the gamer's character moved about (ibid.). Volume was then adjusted depending on the distance to the player's character.

To effectively implement surround sound technology into games, new software developments were required. Beginning with *Windows 95*, the Microsoft *Windows* platform was packaged with DirectX, a series of multimedia application programming interfaces (APIs) that improved the speed with which sound and graphics cards could communicate.[3] Quickly becoming the standard, DirectX allowed games programmers to access "specialized hardware features without having to write hardware-specific code" (Warwick 1998). In other words, the DirectX interface bridged software and hardware, allowing for better control of sound mixing and output. One element of DirectX, called DirectMusic, was a particular advance for music in games. DirectMusic overhauled the older MIDI protocols by offering the industry-ratified Downloadable Sounds Level 1 (DLS-1) specifications, providing over one thousand channels, with better timing mechanisms, and real-time control (see Hays 1998).[4] DirectMusic opened up MIDI to the possibility of higher-fidelity wavetable synthesis and sampling, while at the same time it allowed MIDI to have more extensible controls. Now, no matter what soundcard a player had on his or her personal computer, the results could be much more predictable.

Gaming on personal computers had by the 1990s developed into a rapidly evolving industry, with far too many variants to discuss here. I will, therefore, focus on three examples of the most popular games that exemplify different approaches and technologies: a puzzle adventure game (*Myst*), a first-person shooter (*Doom*), and a simulation game (*The Sims*). As others have noted, "in 1993 [the popularity of] two games signalled that something new was happening in computer gaming. They were *Doom* and *Myst*" (Kline, Dyer-Witherford, and de Peuter 2003, p. 113). *The Sims* came later, but it quickly became one of the best-selling computer games of all time.

Surround sound conveniently arose at about the same time as a new genre in games, the first-person 3D shooter (often now referred to as *FPS*).[5] 3D shooters were born with the release of *Wolfenstein 3D* (id software, 1992), composed and with sound designed by Bobby Prince, who went on to write the music and sound effects for one of the most popular PC games of all time, another FPS game, *Doom* (id software, 1993). *Doom* had a science-fiction-based narrative in which a space marine is sent to Mars where he must fight the demons that have come through the gates of Hell, thanks to a military-industrial conglomerate's experiments. Perhaps learning from *Wolfenstein's* difficulties (in which only one digital sample could play at any one time, so sounds had to be prioritized), sound effects were a key part of the sound of *Doom*, alerting the player to not only the location of enemy demons, but also the type of demon. Prince (2006) described the concept for the sound:

> There were several classes of sounds in *Doom*. One was general active sounds that were not attached to any one demon. These were more or less ambient sounds, but they didn't play until demons close to the player "woke up" (usually based upon the player making some noise in the area). Then there were demon active sounds that were attached to individual demons. These sounds let the player know what class of demon was around the corner. Each type of demon had a sight sound that played when the demon "saw" the player. There were also attack, hurt and death sounds particular to each type of demon. Another helpful thing about the sound driver was that the volume of sounds depended upon the distance from the player to the source of the sound. This helped keep the overall volume down during non-combat. It also stood to help scare the pants off the player when a demon in a dark niche woke up and immediately screamed his attack sound.

A similar use of sound effects can be heard in the popular 3D stealth game *Thief: The Dark Project* (Eidos, 1998). Sound cues helped to inform the player of nearby enemies, and also helped to inform nearby enemies of the player. Guards usually alerted the player to their presence through sound by walking heavily, singing, or whistling. If the player, playing as thief Garrett, made too much noise, nonplaying characters would be alerted to his presence. The player had to walk softly, muffle footsteps with moss and stay away from hard pavement, grates, or tiled floors. If a guard or other enemy was alerted, the player had to remain still and hide until the enemy gave up searching for him. Other stealth games have followed with similar ideas, such as *Splinter Cell* (Ubisoft, 2002), in which the music ramps up if the player has been discovered. These types of games rely heavily on surround sound technology, helping the player to locate objects and people in a three-dimensional space. They have also elevated the role of sound design and clearly reinforce the idea that playing a game with the sound left switched on is often critical to success.

Myst (Cyan, 1993), an interactive mystery puzzle game, brought a new audience to gaming.[6] People who had not previously been interested in games began to see the allure of a beautifully invented world with difficult puzzles to be solved as part of a narrative. *Myst* was a first-person puzzle in which the player moved about by clicking on the main display and interacting with various objects. Solving puzzles led to new "Ages," or self-contained worlds with further puzzles. One of the attractions of *Myst* was its unusual soundtrack. Rather than rely on standard melodic music (which would have undoubtedly become repetitive in the many hours it took to solve each puzzle), the game used minimal ambient music and sound effects to fill the silence and create an eerie atmosphere. As composer Robyn Miller described,

> Actually, we were weren't going to put music in *Myst*. Imagine *Myst* without music! Rand and I always wanted to create a world. We wanted to put ... you, the player, in that world, and make you feel as if you were really there. We knew the *Myst* world needed to be as believable as possible and we felt that music was not part of that equation. So, instead of music, we wanted to create an aural mood with sound effects ... the main focus became making the music as atmospheric or "environmental" as possible.... For me, as a composer, it was always about creating a more believable virtual world experience for the player.[7]

Minimal musical motifs were heard with ambient effects as the player entered specific locations, or when specific puzzles were solved or devices activated. For instance, in figure 4.1, the musical melody motif near the start of the game (which is repeated throughout this level on various instruments) is played while the player is on the stairway leading up to the telescope platform. Here the theme is on panpipes with a cello-like synthesizer and brief piano flourishes.

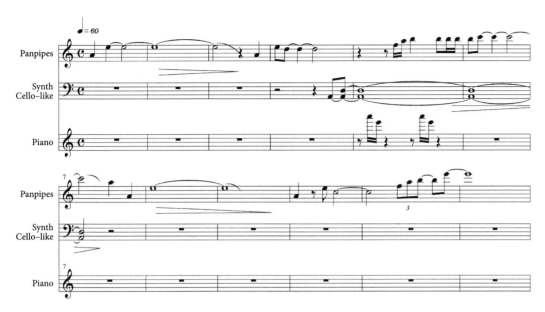

FIGURE 4.1
Myst, "Above Stoneship (Telescope Theme)" (Robyn Miller, Cyan, 1993).

Played at a slow pace, such a minimal approach was beneficial to a game like *Myst*, in which players may be stuck for a significant amount of time at any one stage. Avoiding too "memorable" a theme, or any sense of real "beat," was important to avoiding listener fatigue and to not distract the listener from the activity of puzzle solving. These brief themes would typically loop repetitively until the player changed location, and then would hard cut out to the ambient sounds, illustrating one problem with the rapid jump to Redbook technology: the dynamic MIDI techniques had been abandoned in favor of a return to linear tracks and loops.

With players annoyed by a game's repetitive looping, several methods were explored. One approach to keeping the player interested in and attuned to sound was allowing the player to select the music, such as in *The Sims* (Maxis, 2000; certainly not the first to use this ploy, but by far the most popular). *The Sims* was a spin-off of other popular simulation *God games* ("in which the player oversees the development of an entire city or civilization from a near-deific vantage point," Kline, Dyer-Witherford, and de Peuter 2003, p. 270), including *SimAnt* (Ocean, 1991) and *SimCity* 2000 (Maxis, 1993). *The Sims* was one of the most successful games ever released, with over fifty million games or add-ons sold worldwide.[8] The game was a kind of virtual dollhouse simulation of everyday life of various virtual people, called Sims. The player had to organize their sleep, work, food, and social activities. Kline et al. (2003, pp. 269–293) note how *The Sims* took advantage of the Internet to offer customers the opportunity to add input to the game, through trading items, telling stories, and so on, thus pioneering user-generated content in new ways (beyond modding—that is, modifying using mod packs). In terms of sound, players could select the background music (once a stereo system had been purchased), which allowed for rock, classical, country, or Latin, and included several songs to choose from in each category. The more recent release *The Sims 2* (EA, 2005) even allowed users to include their own MP3s in a subfolder that then allowed the player to play the songs through a radio in the game. In-game music for *Sims 2* was composed by Mark Mothersbaugh of Devo (released on Nettwerk, 2005), with additional songs licensed from popular bands and re-recorded in the original "Simlish" language. Although popular artists had been involved in game soundtracks previously (see chapter 6), *The Sims* series perhaps represents the first time these artists went back to the studio to re-record songs in a new language specifically for a game.

HOME CONSOLE AUDIO MATURES

The first 32-bit home consoles, the Panasonic FZ-1 3DO and the Atari Jaguar, were released in 1993. The CD-ROM-based 3DO system was never really popular with gamers, in part because of its high price, although it had truecolor graphics,[9] full motion video, and 16-bit CD-quality audio. Likewise, the Atari Jaguar also had advanced architecture but saw little significant success. There were, however, a few popular titles, most notably a port of *Doom*, and *Tempest 2000* (Atari, 1994). *Tempest 2000*, a remake of an old Atari classic vector-graphic tube shooter,[10] was so popular, in fact, that it was one of the first games to have a separate, commercially sold soundtrack, composed in MOD format by Ian Howe of Imagitec Design. Nevertheless, two other 32-bit consoles would subsequently be released which would have significant mass appeal: the Sega Saturn and the Sony PlayStation.

Sega released their 32-bit Saturn in 1994, a CD-ROM-based machine with eight processors, two of which were reserved for audio. The Saturn Custom Sound Processor (SCSP), manufactured by Yamaha, consisted of a 16-bit DAC and a 32-channel PCM sound generator, capable of CD-quality sample rates. The main drawback to Saturn's sound system was the limited amount of RAM allotted to sound. Because audio samples had to be downloaded raw (decompressed) into the audio memory buffer, this meant that there was a limited amount of space for simultaneous sounds; so the sample rate was often reduced to conserve memory, thereby reducing the fidelity of the sound. The Saturn saw its highest popularity in Japan, where it sold close to six million units—twice the combined sales of the rest of the world. One of the reasons for the ultimate failure of the Saturn in North

America and Europe was the competition with the Sony PlayStation, a system that was cheaper and easier to program for, and thereby had the support of many more games designers.

The Sony PlayStation had begun its life as a CD-ROM add-on component for Nintendo's SNES system. Nintendo had joined forces with Sony to better compete with Sega in the video games market, but the two companies could not agree on the system, and Nintendo eventually signed a contract with Philips. Sony decided to press ahead with its own 32-bit system, the PlayStation (see Kent 2001). Undercutting Nintendo in price, the PlayStation was enormously successful, selling over 85 million units. The PlayStation's CD-ROM drive could also play audio CDs, and, in fact, there were some games in which it was possible to pause the game, and stick in an audio CD to substitute for the games' audio (such as *Twisted Metal 4*, Sony, 1999). Like the Sega Saturn, the PlayStation also offered MIDI support for ease of programming. The sound chip was capable of twenty-four channels of CD-quality sound, and allowed for real-time effects like ADSR changes, looping, reverb, and pitch modulation.

Despite the advances in sound fidelity, in some ways, the PlayStation was a step backward in terms of the way music was presented in games. As on personal computers, Redbook audio meant that there were compressed audio files with more channels and higher-quality sounding instruments used (as well as the ability to use instruments not included in the GM MIDI specs, such as sound effects and vocals), but this was at the cost of dynamic adaptability and interactivity, and, as on PCs, many games went back to rapid fades and hard cuts between tracks, which typically looped continuously in game levels. Not all PlayStation games depended on Redbook audio, however. One notable exception was Nobuo Uematsu's soundtrack for *Final Fantasy VII* (Squaresoft, 1997, figure 4.2), which relied on MIDI from the on-board synth chip.[11] The use of MIDI in the game meant that there could be more room for very dynamic music without having to loop endlessly (the four hours of music was later released on four CDs), and it also freed up some of the CPU time for the extensive 3D graphics in the game. More important was that it allowed for quicker transitions between tracks and a more dynamic score.

After dropping out of their deal with Sony, Nintendo bypassed the 32-bit machines altogether, going straight to a 64-bit release in 1996, the Nintendo 64 (N64). The product's lack of available games in comparison to the Sony PlayStation eventually meant that the N64 would not see the dramatic kind of sales achieved by Sony, although it did reportedly sell thirty million console units.[12] The N64 also well surpassed the PlayStation in technical capabilities in many ways. The main processor controlled the audio and was capable of producing 16-bit stereo sound at a slightly higher sample rate than CD quality (48 MHz). Some games supported surround sound, and this was enhanced further by the third-party add-on release of RumbleFx 3D Sound Amplifier, a device that could help

FIGURE 4.2
Final Fantasy VII, "Battle music" (Nobuo Uematsu, Squaresoft, 1997).

to mimic surround sound on a stereo system. DSP filters and effects like chorus, panning, and reverb could also be implemented in the internal CPU, or in the software, in real time.

Whereas the PlayStation had been reliant to a large extent on CD audio, Nintendo stuck with a General MIDI-based system. There were several custom sound programs for Nintendo developers to compose music, one of which was known as MusyX. MusyX offered its own programming language, SMaL, which could influence the way a sample was played back. Unlike DSP-based parameters, the waveforms in SMaL could be changed in relation to MIDI controller values. MusyX offered wavetable synthesis with samples the composer could input, in a MOD-like format. Similar to iMUSE, markers could be set in sequences and multiple sequences could be played simultaneously to allow for cross-fading, or layering of sounds with a mapping program. Not all games used the MusyX system, however, and the degrees of dynamic audio in games varied considerably. There were, however, many examples of popular games that were still considerably dynamic. *Banjo and Kazooie* (Rare, 1998, music by Grant Kirkhope), for instance, had a dynamic MIDI-based score, which changed instruments in the track as the player moved about various locales. *The Legend of Zelda: Ocarina of Time* (Nintendo, 1998, music by Koji Kondo) used a variety of dynamic approaches, discussed further in chapter 8. For instance, when the player's character encountered a threatening enemy, a subtle cross-fade occurred between the game-play music and the threat-music. Although critics may have disparaged the MIDI audio, in terms of advancing a dynamic approach to game sound, Nintendo was leagues ahead of its competitors in the console domain.[13]

In the face of Sony's and Nintendo's success, by the late 1990s Sega was in trouble: They had achieved unexpected success with the Genesis, but their systems since that time had floundered. They introduced the first 128-bit console, the Sega Dreamcast, in 1998, with a disappointing consumer response, despite impressive capabilities (see Kent 2001, pp. 563ff). The sound had two processors, and, unlike the Nintendo 64, samples did not have to be decompressed, improving real-time audio fidelity. More important was that the dedicated audio processors had their own memory, so that sound quality was not compromised by other aspects of the game. The Dreamcast reportedly sold only about six million units until it was discontinued in 2002, and with the release of PlayStation 2, many of Sega's top designers jumped ship, dooming Sega in the console realm.[14] The 2000 follow-up to the immensely popular PlayStation had ensured that fans of the original system would be suitably impressed with the new machine. With the ability to play DVD movies and the option of add-ons for modem and hard drive, the PlayStation 2 took an important step toward becoming a "home entertainment center." Its games were stored on DVDs capable of holding 5.7 gigabytes, and it fully supported the multichannel surround sound standards AC-3, DTS, and Dolby Digital, offering up to eight separate speaker channels (see box 4.1, "Dolby Formats"). The sound-processing unit was capable of 16-bit audio with a maximum sample rate of 48 kHz—better than CD audio—and had an additional 48 MIDI channels. However, limitations still meant that sound quality had to be compressed to save space, with the result being that cinematic scenes typically had high-quality full surround sound, but when the player began to use other resources requiring real-time processing, the music and sound would take second place and often drop down to two-channel stereo. This was improved by the PlayStation 3 (PS3), Sony's immensely popular follow-up to its PlayStation consoles, released in 2006. The PS3 is able to run up to 512 channels and apply different layers or DSP filters in real time. It is also capable of streaming audio in 7.1 at 96kBs, though reduced channel formats (5.1, for instance) have higher bit-rate streams, which is particularly important for Sony's online service for multiplayer games. Nevertheless, the processor, known as the Cell, also handles graphics and other game functions, such as AI, meaning that audio must still compete for shared system memory and CPU processing.

Box 4.1
Dolby and Surround Sound Formats

DOLBY DIGITAL (also known as Dolby AC-3) is the current standard for home theater surround sound, and also present in many movie theaters—the 5.1 surround system. Dolby Digital supports up to 5.1 channels, and therefore can also refer to mono (1.0), stereo, or Pro-Logic (2.0), or five channel audio (5.0). Specifically surround formats are referred to as "Dolby Digital 5.1." Dolby Digital 5.1 is the standard for DVD-video and HDTV (high-definition television), used by pay-per-view and digital TV channels. It provides up to five independent channels (left, right, center, surround left, surround right), plus an optional sixth (LFE, or low frequency effects), typically handled by the subwoofer. Since the sixth channel is not full frequency (it only handles deep bass, 3 Hz to 120 Hz), it is referred to as ".1."

DTS DIGITAL SURROUND is a competing format to Dolby Digital, a 5.1 surround system available in movie theaters, and optional on some DVD movies for home theater. DTS is not a standard soundtrack for DVD or HDTV, but offers higher data rates than Dolby Digital (that is, it uses less compression), resulting in more data demands, and hence is not as useful for games as Dolby Digital.

DOLBY SURROUND PRO-LOGIC is the standard for Hi-Fi VHS or analog television. It is encoded in stereo (or stereo analog). Pro Logic II can be found on most new receivers compatible with all stereo and matrix-encoded surround software. Pro Logic II is an update of the original Pro Logic and can be used to freshen up Dolby Surround-encoded videotapes and DVDs. It also works wonders with stereo CDs and radio broadcasts.

DOLBY DIGITAL PLUS provides up to 7.1 channels of audio, comparable to DTS-HD high resolution audio, and is "better than DVD" quality sound (in that it has a higher bit rate and new coding efficiencies).

DOLBY TRUE HD also provides up to 7.1 channels, lossless audio; is equivalent to DTS-HD Master Audio, and was developed for high-definition TV and Blu-Ray disc players.

DOLBY DIGITAL EX is another "extended surround" format for home theater, equivalent to THX Surround EX. To a regular 5.1 configuration, it adds at least one (typically two) back channels, with speaker(s) behind the audience, allowing sound effects behind the audience, resulting in 7.1 surround.

Nintendo had responded to Sony's PS2 with their Game Cube in 2001, but the Game Cube failed to recapture the market that Nintendo was looking for. The competition was fierce, and the game titles for the Nintendo were more family-oriented, typically appealing to a younger market. The Nintendo Wii, released in 2006, however, distinguished itself immensely from competitors through its unique control system, a handheld remote with motion sensors. Designed to bring new gamers into the world of video games, Wii advertising focuses on the populations typically ignored by many games manufacturers—the very young, the elderly, and families. Although the sound capabilities of Wii are less than its competitors,[15] Nintendo instead created a novel idea in the form of a tiny speaker in the controller. Various in-game actions result in sound emanating from the device, creating an even more dynamic, immersive audio experience. The sound effects of the bow and arrow in *The Legend of Zelda: Twilight Princess* (Nintendo, 2006), for instance, give the impression of an arrow being shot from the player toward the screen.

The success of home consoles for a time was viewed as a threat to the PC market; after all, consoles were becoming full multimedia devices, and many people who had used their PCs for little more than playing games and surfing the Internet could do these through a much cheaper console. It was no surprise, then, that rumors of a games console from Microsoft began around 1999, and a system was officially announced in 2000. Microsoft's entry into the console business the following year, the Xbox, was built around a Pentium III processor with an 8 GB hard drive for music, graphics, and saved-game information. Games were supplied on 5.7 GB DVD discs, and the Xbox was also capable of playing DVD movies and audio CDs, making it a full multimedia device. The Xbox featured its own audio processor, known as SoundStorm, which would support Microsoft's DirectX protocol.[16] Xbox Live was an important part of the console's success, an online multiplayer subscription service which allowed for episodic content (downloadable new content for games), and access to Xbox Live Arcade, which included classic arcade games such as old Genesis and PlayStation games. The upgraded Xbox 360 (2006) requires that developers support at least Dolby Digital Live 5.1, as well as allow gamers to use their own playlists (from a port allowing a plug-in of an MP3 player).

OTHER PLATFORMS: RHYTHM-ACTION, HANDHELDS, AND ONLINE GAMES

In addition to the arcades and home market, video games have also been developed for other platforms, including specially controlled rhythm-action games, handheld consoles, mobile telephone games, and games designed for the Internet.

A brief overview of this alternate gaming world will round out the history presented thus far.

RHYTHM-ACTION GAMES

Rhythm-action games are video games in which the player must respond in some way to the rhythm or melody being presented, either through repeating the same melody or rhythm by pressing buttons (with hands or feet), or kinetically responding in some other way to the rhythm, often using specially designed controllers. Rhythm-action games to some extent have been incorporated into some other types of video games—in several of the *Legend of Zelda* games, for instance, the player is required to memorize short melodies and play them back (*Ocarina of Time*), or have their character "dance" to various rhythms (*Oracle of Ages*, Nintendo, 2001). In chapter 3 I discussed one such game, *Toejam and Earl: Panic on Funkotron* for the Sega Genesis, which included a percussion memory game. Although these games integrated elements of rhythm-action games, these elements were just one small component of the game, and so they are not discussed further here.

Atari was one of the first companies to release an electronic rhythm-action game, with their *Touch Me*, designed by Ralph Baer and released as both a coin-op in 1974 and handheld in 1978. *Touch Me*'s original 1974 flyer discussed the use of sound: "'Beep' or 'Bleep'? *Touch Me* challenges the player to remember the sequence of sight and sound, and correctly repeat the pattern ... When the sound occurs, the corresponding button lights to give a visual clue ... Did you correctly repeat those sounds when the button lit?"[17] There were four buttons and four tones on the machine whose patterns would get progressively more difficult. *Touch Me* did not catch on, however, until it was redesigned by Milton Bradley and released as *Simon* in 1977. Similar to *Touch Me*, each button on *Simon* had a corresponding sound and color, and increasingly difficult melodies had to be memorized. A wave of copy-cat games followed, including *Super Simon* (a two-player version by Milton Bradley, in 1980), Parker Brothers' *Merlin* (1978), the Tiger *Copy Cat* (1979), and Castle's *Einstein* (1979). More complex was the *Logix T.E.A.M.M.A.T.E* (Parker Bros., 1980), a tabletop console, which had a speaker and a primitive sequencer that allowed the user to create his or her own melodies, described in a 1980 *Consumer Reports* magazine: "By way of introduction to this musical entertainment, the toy provides a preprogrammed version of 'Oh, Susanna.' It didn't really encourage us to proceed, since it was rhythmically faulty. Persevering, though, we found music-writing rather a challenge—at first. But we became frustrated when our laborious compositions were erased when the toy was turned off" (p. 655).

The popularity of rhythm-action games continued into the home console era. Nintendo introduced a "Power Pad" to the NES in 1988, a floor mat with control buttons built in for the feet, whereupon games like *Dance Aerobics* (Bandai, 1989) would become forerunners to today's popular arcade rhythm-action games. *PaRappa the Rapper* (SCEI, 1996), released on PlayStation, incorporated kinetic elements into a storyline: PaRappa was trying to win the love of a girl, Sunny, and had to practice rapping to the beat of various drummers to improve his skill. A button was to be hit in the correct order with correct timing to keep the beat, significantly relying on memorization, much like *Simon*. Handheld consoles have also spawned their share of rhythm-action hits, including *Elite Beat Agents* (for the Nintendo DS, 2006) and *Electroplankton* (Nintendo, 2006) in which elements must be tapped or spun with the stylus.

There are often add-on user interfaces or controllers for rhythm-action games. *Donkey Konga* (Nintendo, 2003) included "DK Bongo" drums, *Guitar Hero* (RedOctane, 2005) a guitar-shaped controller, and so on. *Beat Mania* (Konami, 1997) included a five-key controller and accompanying turntable that had to be manipulated according to on-screen instructions during a series of increasingly difficult songs. Dancing games, such as Andamiro's *Pump It Up* (1998), Roxor Games' *In The Groove* (2004, which has since been bought out by Konami), *Britney's Dance Beat* (THQ, 2002), and of course *Dance Dance Revolution* (Konami, 1999) are probably the best known of the rhythm-action games, spawning considerable fan communities around the world, and perhaps reviving interest in coin-op consoles (see, e.g., Demers 2006). Other music-based games, including remixing games such as *FreQuency* (Harmonix, 2001) and singing games like *SingStar* (Sony, 2004), have also more recently put the player in a partial role of musician (composer as well as performer; see chapter 6).

HANDHELD CONSOLES

Handheld video games (smaller, battery-powered portable consoles with built-in screens) became popular alongside other games consoles and the arcades. Mattel had manufactured handheld LED-based games such as *Missile Attack*, *Baseball*, and others as early as 1976, and as shown above, Atari had released a handheld version of *Touch Me* in 1978. Milton Bradley released the Microvision in 1979—a more advanced type of console, with interchangeable cartridges of games such as *Bowling* and *Pinball*. Early *tabletop* games—small, one-game arcade ports—were also popular in schoolyards in the early 1980s, though these were generally without sound, or very limited in sound capabilities. It is interesting that a 1980 *Consumer Reports* report on games mentions sound in a few cases, indicating that sound played an important role even this early on, although its effectiveness was questionable. The description of Vanity Fair's *Computer Matician 3010* tabletop model, for instance, which asked a series of math questions, included sound: "The correct answer elicits a high-pitched, repeating beep and the word 'right' flashing at the top of the screen. An incorrect answer is punished by a penetrating low buzz and the word 'wrong' flashing at the bottom of the screen ... most of the children were unnerved and annoyed by the strident beeping and buzzing" (*Consumer Reports*, Nov. 1980, p. 654).

Sound improved as the developers of home consoles released handheld versions of their home games to fans. The Atari Lynx (1989) was the first color handheld game, and had four-channel 8-bit sound. NEC released Turbografx Express a year later, which was basically a portable version of the Turbografx16. Both of these models, however, failed to generate any real consumer excitement. Sega's Game Gear was released in 1991, using the same primitive sound chip that was found in the PCjr. The Game Gear was fairly successful, with about 250 games developed for the system, as was Sega's 1995 Nomad, a handheld version of the Sega Genesis.[18] Other companies had some moderate success with handhelds, such as Neo Geo's Pocket and Pocket Color of 1998–99, a 16-bit handheld version of the Neo Geo home console, with a six-channel PSG chip. Without a doubt, however, the uncontested leader of handhelds was the Nintendo Game Boy. Nintendo had released handhelds previously with its Game and Watch system of 1980, but it was Nintendo's Game Boy which would capture the hearts of players, and through its various guises see over 100 million units sold (Wing n.d.).[19] The original black-and-white Game Boy received its first update in 1996 when Game Boy Pocket was released—essentially a more streamlined version of the original but with no other major changes. The second update came with Game Boy Color two years later. Though this model included improved graphics, the sound remained the same for these three models; a three-plus-one channel stereo sound PSG, the fourth channel offering 4-bit noise, with a simple envelope generator. The Game Boy Advance, released in 2001, was the first to upgrade the sound, by adding two 8-bit DACs to the original configuration.[20] Not only the hardware but the software was improved: the Advance BIOS contained many sound-related functions for converting MIDI to Game Boy data,[21] although it is worth noting that Nintendo did not even bother to release information about sound in their press release specifications, suggesting that sound was not considered as relevant on handheld games as it was on home consoles.[22]

The Game Boy had a very distinct sound, which is perhaps one of the reasons why it has been so popular with chiptune musicians and the instrument on a remix album of Beck songs, *The GameBoy Variations* (*Hell Yes*) (Interscope, 2005). On the Game Boy system, the first two channels were square waves, which were commonly used for chords or melody.[23] Channel 3 was a programmable (variable) wave channel with thirty-two 4-bit programmable samples, though it was commonly used for bass lines. Channel 4 was a white noise generator, most often used for percussion sounds, which typically sounded like a bit of scratchy static rather than drums, as shown in figure 4.3.

More recent developments in handheld technology have led to handheld consoles becoming full multimedia devices, capable of playing movies and MP3

FIGURE 4.3
Aladdin (Seiko Kobuchi and Chihiro Arisaka, Capcom, 2004) for the GameBoy Advance, with fairly typical usage of GameBoy channels.

audio, such as the PlayStation Portable (PSP), with 3D multichannel sound and integrated stereo speakers. The Nintendo DS has even become a musical instrument in its own right, with tracker, MIDI, and sampling software available. It has a built-in microphone, stereo speakers with virtual surround, sixteen hardware sound channels, and two built-in samplers. There are also some interesting musical add-ons for the Nintendo DS, including an X/Y MIDI controller resembling Korg's "Kaoss Pad," MIDI keyboard controller, and wireless DS synthesizer. Overall, however, handheld game audio has lagged behind their console cousins because the games are typically played in a public domain, and as such audio plays a secondary role to graphics (see below).

MOBILE PHONE GAMES

The history of mobile phone games (distinguished from handheld gaming in that games are not the primary intended use of the machines) in many ways echoes the history of consoles and handhelds. The earliest mobile phone game, *Snake*, written by Taneli Armanto on the Nokia 6110 in 1997, was black-and-white and lacked sound. The phone also featured basic *Memory* and *Logic* games. These games were originally installed on phones by the phone companies, but are now commonly purchased through mobile networks or through Internet download. As well, mobile phones are increasingly developing toward small computers, known as smartphones, allowing for more complex games, such as Nokia's N-Gage game deck with changeable cartridges and Bluetooth multiplayer gaming for small groups. One of the most important elements of mobile gaming has been network capabilities. Even many early games had multiplayer modes and simple games like checkers could be played with live competitors.

Mobile gaming is rapidly becoming an important part of the games industry, with publishers like Jamdat joining forces with Electronic Arts. At the time of writing, Jamdat leads the mobile gaming world, but Namco is in second place, having re-released its classic arcade games like *Pac-Man* and *Galaga* to the mobile community. Vivendi Games is also plundering old games for material, releasing a series of Sierra back-catalog games in 2007, including *The Incredible Machine* (1992) and a *Leisure Suit Larry* game. It is likely that the popular games of the early consoles and arcades are all to be re-released in the coming years in mobile form, although those games that used cover songs without licensing will likely see their music change.

Mobile games today are comparable to 16-bit home consoles in terms of graphics quality, but audio remains very difficult to produce for a variety of reasons—not least of which is the lack of standards. Many of the same difficulties and constraints that plagued early computer games are now seen in the mobile game audio world. Audio resources on phones can be as small as 100 kB, and as such, many of the same techniques of the 8-bit era have been reproduced to save space. As composer and self-confessed "annoying ring tone guy" Peter Drescher elaborates, "The most important trick is to be as ruthlessly efficient as possible. You want to squeeze every last drop of variation out of each and every byte of audio data at your disposal. Repetition is the enemy, compression is your ally, and creative use of limited resources is your battle cry. If you're making sound effects, this means low-resolution, highly compressed samples used in multiple ways. If you're writing music, it means MIDI'' (Drescher 2006).

Mobile audio also has different requirements from other games owing to the casual nature of the games—people playing mobile games are, at present, primarily using their phone to play games while they "kill time," and games are secondary to the other functions of these machines. Nokia's guide to sound for phone games, for instance, warns, "The game should be playable without the sounds. Allow silent starting of games. If intro music is implemented, there must be a way to switch it off. Prompt for sound settings at the start of the game.... Do not include loud or high-pitched sounds, have sounds on as the default, [or] use sounds that are similar to ring tones and alert tones" (Nokia Corp. 2005). On the other hand, Nokia reminds developers, "From a cognitive point of view, the auditory channel is an excellent way to relay information and give feedback to the player. While the background music can be used to enhance the emotions and mood of the game, a specific sound effect can be used to communicate meaningful game information" (ibid.).

Real-time network play on mobile phones has become increasingly popular, with the introduction of games like *Bejeweled Multiplayer* (Jamdat, 2006). Some games can also interface with their PC counterparts, such as *Ragnarok Mobile Mage* (Skyzone Mobile, 2006), so that players can continue their game after they have left their house.

ONLINE GAMES

The history of online gaming can be divided into roughly two categories:[24] casual games (easy-to-learn games with mass appeal like *Sudoku*, *Tetris*, and so on), which are usually one-player (although there are competitive casual games, including those packaged with MSN Messenger, for instance); and multiplayer worlds, including those called MUDs (multiuser domains or dungeons), MMORPGs (massively multiplayer online role playing games), MMORTS (massively multiplayer online real-time strategy), and MMOFPS (massively multiplayer online first-person shooters). There are other online games that do not really fit into these categories, such as the online version of *Sims*; however, for the sake of brevity I will refer to all of these multiplayer games as massively multiplayer online games, or MMOs.

Casual games have been around for a long time on the Internet, from HTML-based quiz games to more elaborate Java or Flash-based games.[25] The present preference for developing web-based games is Macromedia Flash, and so I will focus on Flash for the remainder of this discussion. Flash was in fact created by a game developer, Jonathan Gay, who had developed PC games in BASIC but initially enjoyed success with *Airborne* (Silicon Beach Software, 1984), one of the first Macintosh games to use digital music (*Ride of the Valkyries*, during the opening sequence). With this history, Flash was developed with the notion of creating a smooth animation and sound program in one package. Since becoming part of Macromedia, Flash has become far more complex and developed its own scripting language, ActionScript, which allows for more complex programs.[26]

With Flash, developers can create games and animations with synchronized soundtracks, although synchronization between sounds is difficult. Using a timeline-based approach, sounds that begin simultaneously will stay in sync, and so tracks can be kept separate. Synchronization between layers of sounds can be unreliable, however, particularly on slower computers, and synchronizing audio to visuals can also be difficult. Streaming sound over the web can mean that visual frames will sometimes be skipped in order to remain in audio sync.

One of the more interesting uses of sound in contemporary casual games comes from *Warbears: Mission 2* (composer Filipe Ferreira, 2006).[27] The game is basically a Flash based point-and-click puzzle that takes place on a single screen. There are four characters (bears) that the player controls to work together to solve a puzzle. The music is essentially one long loop,[28] but different segments of gameplay elicit different melodic elements and sound effects, which add a layer overtop of this loop. When the player clicks on the bear Ryoh to cut down a tree with his sword, for instance, a panpipe-like melody plays overtop of the main loop (figure 4.4). When the player clicks on the bear Lucas to push switches to control the alarm in the house, a new bass line is added.

The other significant form of online gaming is massively multiplayer online games (MMOs), which have become a tremendous part of the game industry. The history of MMOs goes back to at least 1969, when a two-person version of *Spacewar!* was written for PLATO, an early file-sharing system developed at

FIGURE 4.4

Warbears: Mission 2: showing three variations which are added over the main percussive loop: the panpipe melody, a guitar stutter, and timpani-like sound (Filipe Ferreira, 2006).

the University of Illinois. Over the next decade, many MMOG games would be developed for the system, including a *Star Trek*–based game called *Empire*, a flight simulator called *Airfight*, and several *Dungeons and Dragons* games. Developments that would allow users to kill one another (*Mazewar*) and communicate with one another (*Dungen*) soon followed. PLATO went through a series of advancements, the most relevant to this discussion being the PLATO IV computers from 1972, which had a "Gooch Box," a four-voice synthesis chip. Later, a Gooch Cybernetic Synthesizer, a sixteen-channel chip, was added.

Other universities developed online games, and by the late 1970s the creation of multiuser dungeons, or MUDS, formed, beginning with MUD1, in 1978, a real-time multiplayer game with many of the characteristics of MMOGs today, most notably the idea of character development through experience (see Cox 1994). Commercial response was soon to follow, with games like *MegaWars* (1983) and *Islands of Kesmai* (1984) on CompuServe. LucasArts was quick to join in, with a release of *Habitat* for the Commodore 64 Q-Link (1985). *Habitat* had color graphics and some sound effects, such as dial tones when the player picked up the virtual phone. With the rise of the World Wide Web in the 1990s came a new series of online games that charged subscription fees and had bigger budgets, but music remained relatively poor in quality in comparison to offline games as a result of music's file size and the nature of downloading through modem. Three games sometimes referred to as the "Big Three" dominated the 1990s: *Ultima Online*, trading on the success of the offline *Ultima* games, was released in 1997 (Electronic Arts); *EverQuest*, launched in March 1999 (by Verant Interactive, later acquired by Sony), and Turbine's *Asheron's Call* (1999). More recently, Linden Lab opened up its innovative "3D virtual world" called *Second Life* to the public (2003), a game that quickly became the most popular non-combat-based-MMO. I take up compositional approaches to MMOs in chapter 8.

CONCLUSION

The next generation ("next-gen") games systems (referring to the most recent—at time of writing—generation of consoles, including Xbox 360, PlayStation 3, and Nintendo Wii) are much closer in terms of capabilities to home computers than their predecessors, reducing further the line between home entertainment systems and home computers. Arcade games have tried to lure players with ever more sophisticated playing consoles that include rumble effects and built-in full surround sound.[29]

Says producer and audio supervisor Mike Verrette of Ironlore Entertainment, "The PC used to be capable of so much more than the original Nintendo and the other early consoles, but that gap is smaller now" (Lehrman 2007, p. 22).

Some might even say that next-gen games represent an end to the technological audio constraints of the past, as certainly, many of the technological problems have been solved. However, constraints do remain, and there are still many difficulties to overcome in the production of game audio, including problems of budget, time, and increasing expectations placed on game audio by consumers and developers. Technological problems also remain, particularly in that the development of software has failed to keep up with the upgrades in hardware. Most sequencing software is still loop-based and linear, for instance, and there are few affordable cross-platform *middleware* audio solutions.[30] With hardware companies each competing to introduce their technologies as standards, resulting in many different requirements for each console system, cross-platform middleware software has been slow to develop, or tends to remain proprietary (such as Sony's SCREAM engine). In fact, developing a title for all three consoles can create significant problems since tools and compression technology, for instance, can vary from one system to another, and solutions created for one console often do not work on another (see Lehrman 2007, p. 22).

Another remaining problem in consoles is audio streaming. In streamed audio, music is sampled into long (typically stereo) files stored on the CD/DVD and played directly in real time in the game, through a RAM buffer. Although this often cannot work for downloadable games (since the files are too large), streaming audio off a disc allows for more real-time processing in console games. The problem, however, is that speeds are still relatively slow and demands on the processor means audio must compete with other game aspects, such as graphics, reducing channels or otherwise compressing audio requirements. Typically, sound is allowed to occupy only 5 to 10 percent of system resources. Jason Booth, designer at Harmonix, elaborates:

> On PlayStation 2, you have two megs of RAM for audio. All of the sound for wherever you are in the game has to reside in that memory. Sometimes you have to leave room in there for a streaming buffer, but you also have to worry about the speed of the disc spin. Data on the outside of the disc reads faster than data on the inside, so you have to take that into account—data for loading a new level might be on the inside, while data used during run-time is placed on the outside. A common technique is to load in the sound effects ahead of time and stream the music. But of course, you have to be okay with the rest of the team with that: They can't be loading textures at the same time you're streaming music. (Cited in Lehrman 2007, p. 22)

Streaming technologies can be expected to advance in the coming years, although they are already greatly improved over the previous generation of consoles.

Particularly important to the development of games today is the convergence of the various platforms of media and technology: I can play games and check my email on my phone, connecting it to my computer to continue playing. I can connect to other gamers online through my Xbox, my computer, or my phone. I can watch movies on my PlayStation Portable, compose music on my Nintendo DS and upload it to friends online through my PC or email it to a friend so that they can use it as a ringtone on their phone. As technologies for portable systems continue to develop at a frenzied pace, this collapse of media platforms into multiuse devices will become even more important, and we can expect games to play an increasingly important role for portable devices. In many ways, games have driven and will continue to drive these technologies, particularly in the area of sound.

As discussed in the previous chapter, the rapid development of technologies has depended to some extent on the creation of and agreement on standards. In the case of audio, groups such as the Interactive Audio Special Interest Group (IAsig) have been working toward these means by creating and recommending such standards, although the industries involved still work very much on a proprietary level, which arguably slows progress. One interesting future development for games may in fact be the convergence of different platforms altogether, as Silicon Knights' Denis Dyack suggests, the result of which will mean more time put toward the development of games, and less time wasted porting games between systems:

> I think we're moving towards a homogeneous platform whether people like it or not. At the end of the day, I think it's in everyone's best interest that there be one hardware console, whether it be Sony, Microsoft, Nintendo or whether all three of them got together and said, "Ok we're going to agree upon a standard for everyone to make." In the movie industry it helped tremendously because as a content creator, all we want to do is make games and entertain people. Don't get me wrong, I love the hardware platforms, like the Sony platform and I think the Wii's got some really unique things and Microsoft's platform we obviously love a lot. However, we'd rather spend time making the games than worrying about the hardware. And if everyone had the same hardware and when you made a game you knew you got 100% penetration because anyone who plays this game had to buy this hardware platform just like a DVD or whatever standard media format's going to be. I think that would ultimately be much better for gamers. If the value of that technology continues to diminish, and it's becoming more and more expensive to manufacture and research & develop these, eventually there's going to come a breaking point where everyone goes, "You know what, let's stop spending all this money on R&D into this hardware where no one really cares about it as much as they used to because of the value of it. Everyone's got one, so why don't we just spend our money on making games because all the money is in the software anyway?" So I think it's going to get to the point where the value of the hardware, like a PS3 or an Xbox 360 or a Nintendo Wii or whatever in the future, is going to be very low. (Cited in Brightman 2007)

The many different platforms and forms of video games have all traveled similar trajectories in terms of audio production, from no sound, to basic linear

MIDI in one channel, to multichannel dynamic audio in surround, with complicated approaches to sound playback. But the history of games, as shown, is itself nonlinear, influenced by industry, technology, and social needs, knowledge, and desires. As Jean-Louis Comolli wrote of film, it is a "stratified history, that is, a history characterized by discontinuous temporality" (cited in Belton 1992, p. 159). Technological developments throughout its history have influenced not only the ways in which game audio has been produced, but also the ways in which it has been received by its audience. As in early film sound, "The expectations of audiences—and what they perceived as 'realistic'—were changing year by year" (Belton 1999, pp. 234–235). Moreover, as in film, "each new technological development (sound, panchromatic stock, color) points out to viewers just how 'unrealistic' the previous image was and also reminds them that the present image, even though more realistic, will also be superseded in the future—thus constantly sustaining the state of disavowal" (Manovich 2001, p. 186). The development of game sound has represented an ever-increasing drive toward greater fidelity and higher realism, a subject I take up in chapter 7. However, the drive to realism is not the only determinant in the development of technology, as shown, and it is now necessary to examine in further detail the industrial, commercial aspects of the industry and the processes by which game audio is created.

CHAPTER 5

GAME AUDIO TODAY: TECHNOLOGY, PROCESS, AND AESTHETIC

What goes into making a game? How do the game's music and sound effects get implemented? Who is responsible for ensuring that the dialogue does not conflict with the sound effects? Who makes the decisions regarding how the game should sound? The roles and processes involved in developing a game can vary greatly from game to game, from platform to platform, and from company to company, but a general sense of the process at a large company will help to answer these questions and to explain some of the audio decisions that must be made that impact the game as a whole. Audio production is not merely a series of compromises dictated by technological and industrial constraints. It is also a series of compromises with a team of people who work collaboratively, which has important implications for its production.

At its widest level, the game industry is comparable in structure to the book publishing, film, or music industries. Much the same as publishers in the book industry, game *publishers* are generally the overseers of the entire development process. Publishers provide some of the financial backing for the project, may provide royalty advances, and are largely concerned with producing a marketable project. Publishers, therefore, may make some important decisions regarding the design or development of a game to ensure that they have a viable product that will sell worldwide; they ultimately have creative control over the product. At present the top publishers include (among others) Electronic Arts, Nintendo, Activision, Sony, Ubisoft, THQ, and Microsoft, showing the clear importance of the console manufacturers on the development industry.[1] Publishers typically command the *developers*, the company/studio/team that designs and produces the game. Developers may be specialized toward producing for a specific platform or genre, or may develop for several markets. Developers are generally split into three divisions: third-party developers, in-house developers, and independents. Third-party developers usually work closely with one publisher in developing a project. In-house developers, also known as studios, are the subsidiaries of publishers. Rather than being contracted by the publisher, they are owned by and directed by the publisher. Independent developers, on the other hand, are not owned by or typically contracted by a publisher. They often rely on self-publishing, through the Internet, festivals, conferences, or word-of-mouth.

Within a development company, there are several important overseers to any project. The *producer* is generally in charge of the entire project's development process. These may be internal to the developer, or, in the case of third-party developers, external to the developer, hired by the publisher. The producer oversees all aspects of a game, including creative, legal, marketing, contracting, and so on. A *lead designer* then typically oversees the concept and design of a game, particularly the production of the design document (see below). The other major players include the lead programmer (overseeing the implementation and programming aspects of the game), the audio lead/audio director (see below), and the art director (overseeing the graphics aspects). Underneath these jobs are the support jobs, consisting of writers, programmers, level designers, sound designers, artists, and so on. The number of support jobs, of course, depends on the size of the company and the size of the game. Some jobs are contracted out to third parties, particularly in the case of audio (see box 5.1, "Audio Roles").

THE PROCESS OF TAKING A GAME TO MARKET

As with other aspects described below, the process described here represents an overview of one production model. Production varies greatly from company to company, from platform to platform, and from genre to genre (for more detail on the entire process, see Kerr 2006 and Manninen et al. 2006). Although mock-ups or initial prototypes may be created in the early stages of a game's development, the main pre-production phase involves the creation of a design document. The game design document represents the overall vision of the game, detailing the storyline, dialogue, maps, audio, graphics, animation, and programming. The entire team—including the audio team—works from this document during the production process, although each team may develop a more detailed document for their specific task based on the design document (see below), which describes the game in detail.[2]

Once the publisher has approved the design document, a team will be put together for the production phase of the development, which involves the creation of all of the different elements of the game (graphics, sound, cinematics)

Box 5.1
Roles of the Audio Team

The audio team of a games development company can vary quite significantly, depending on size and budget. Many smaller companies still have one audio person to complete all of the sound effects design, music, voice work, and implementation, while larger companies can have full teams of composers, sound designers, and voice actors all working on one project. Most development companies have in-house sound teams, but music jobs in particular are being increasingly contracted out. Although I have separated the main roles here, it is possible that these roles may be filled by the same person, or even be teams of people.

At the head of the audio team is typically the *sound director*. The sound director is responsible for the overall audio vision and design of a title. He or she oversees the design, defines and drives the creative and technical direction. Sound directors must coordinate schedules, budgets, staff, and technology, and manage outsourced asset creation personnel (casting, dialogue directors, mixers, engineers, and so on). They are responsible for organizing external contract work, as well as creating, editing, and mixing original content. They may also be responsible for the final mix.

SOUND DESIGNERS may also play this same role, creating an audio design document and managing the audio production pipeline. They will work with integrators and audio tool developers to create, integrate, and manage audio assets, and are responsible for sound effects libraries. This effects library may be purchased externally, contracted out, or developed in-house.

DIALOGUE/VOICE-OVER ARTISTS are, of course, responsible for providing the dialogue. They may be in-house, but it is more likely that these artists are cast externally for projects and managed by the audio director. The *dialogue director* oversees the dialogue process, often coaching the dialogue artists.

LICENSING/CONTRACTING DIRECTORS are responsible for obtaining rights to licensed IP, and contracting out work externally.

COMPOSERS are responsible for the music composition of the game. In smaller companies, they are frequently also responsible for the sound design. They may also be in charge of orchestration of their work, although on larger projects there may be teams of orchestrators working together. They are typically responsible for contracting out and overseeing live recordings.

AUDIO PROGRAMMERS or audio engineers are responsible for audio tools development, and integration of all audio assets in a game. In many cases they also play the role of sound designer. They will be responsible for developing in-house audio tools to work in conjunction with the game's AI, graphics, and physics engines.

and their integration into the game engine. At various stages in the development process, the game will undergo several quality assurance phases, which will test and validate the gameplay, user interface, and market needs. Once the game has been developed, it will undergo a debugging process to check for any problems ("bugs") in the programming or playback of the game. Once it passes the debugging, the game's documentation and manuals are produced, localization takes place (see below), and the game may be ported to the various platforms for intended release (for instance, a game developed for PlayStation 3 may then be programmed to work on Xbox360). When the game is released, attention turns to marketing, but there is still necessary upkeep or maintenance that may include releasing patches, or upgrades, to fix uncaught bugs and potentially to provide the user with new content.

Within this entire process, the audio team may become involved at any stage in the development of the game. Most often, the sound team does not join the process until very late in the project, when the game and its parameters have already been defined. At this stage, the audio team simply populates the game with sound (Selfon 2006). Other audio teams work more closely with the design and development of the game, to ensure that audio can play a significant role in a game's development. As with film, the ideal, suggested by famed film sound designers Walter Murch and Randy Thom, is that sound should be considered at the earliest (that is, the script/design) stage (Geuens 2000, pp. 197–198).

THE AUDIO PRODUCTION PROCESS

In some ways, the game audio production process resembles that of the film audio process (for discussions of the film sound production process, see Davis 1999, Rona 2000, or Kompanek 2004). There are similar recording techniques for live sounds and *foley*,[3] similar techniques for spotting, and many of the same tools in terms of recording and software are used. Comparing the music process of film and games, *LAIR* (Factor 5, 2007) composer John Debney elaborates,

> The process is similar. There are definitely scenes that one has to compose specific music for. A lot of the game play, i.e. the battles or the big set pieces, essentially has to be scored in some form or fashion. So that's all similar to a film.... Aesthetically the biggest difference for me in scoring a video game is that you don't have as much finished product. Much of the time I would be writing to a description of a battle ... literally just a one or two line description. I would also be writing to maybe twenty seconds of game play that in reality is going to become ten to twenty minutes of game play. That was the biggest difference for me. It was more about writing to a concept or description rather than writing to anything specific. (Cited in ScoreKeeper 2007)

However, there are also significant differences in the processes. Apart from dialogue and some production sound, film audio is generally a post-production activity that takes place after the film has been edited and the visuals *locked* (the final version set). A significant amount of time is spent balancing and mixing sounds in a film's post-production, which is a great distinguishing trait between film and game sound. In games, since (with the exception of the cinematics) timings are variable and the visual sequence is constantly evolving, "post-production" as the practice exists in film does not generally exist in game audio production, although there are a few notable exceptions, discussed below.

There are also other differences in the processes, and so it is worth spending some time describing the game audio development process in some detail. However, it should be noted that the production process in video games may differ significantly from what is presented here. Different genres have different types of recording needs: a simple puzzle game is not going to require dialogue, for instance. Moreover, different companies have different budgets and can spend more or less money on team size. Sony's *God of War 2* (SCEA, 2007) music team, for instance, consisted of four composers, three orchestrators, three ensembles (brass, string, and choir), a variety of ethnic soloists, and the development/implementation team (Bajakian 2007). Smaller companies may have one or two people who must perform the equivalent of all of these jobs. The platform can also affect the production process: PlayStation 3 games are going to require many months or even years of work, whereas for a mobile game, audio is typically given about a week for the entire process. I have, therefore, described a semilarge production, with separate composer(s), sound designer(s), orchestrator(s), voice actors, and programmer(s). I have broken the production phase into the three main components (music, sound effects, and dialogue) with a more specific discussion of pre-production, production, and post-production in each category. Further details on the production processes themselves can be found in Alexander Brandon's book, *Audio for Games: Planning, Process, and Production* (2005).

THE PRE-PRODUCTION STAGE

The first stage in the audio workflow is the creation of an audio design document. Supplementary to the game design document, an audio design document details the design and implementation of the game's audio. There may be separate music, dialogue, and sound design documents, but I have incorporated these here. An audio design document is also not necessarily a part of every game, and even when the intentions are there, a game's development does not always follow the plan. Damian Kastbauer, a sound designer working for a major developer, commented that "while there is sometimes an overarching concept of how things should sound for a given project, such audio design documents are often a myth and the process becomes more about doing what is right for the game [at the time]" (pers. corr., March 29, 2007). An audio design document is designed to assist the audio team, as well as the programmers who will need the document to implement the sound into the game. Says Keith Zizza, Audio Director for Impressions Games, "Designers will want to absorb it, programmers will demand it, and producers, along with just about anyone else who is involved on the project, will want to at least skim it. Whether it's one page or one hundred, it should be as descriptive as it needs to be for you and your development team. The end result, hopefully, is a harmonious one—working with and enhancing graphics, writing, game design, and the overall gaming experience" (Zizza 2000).

An audio team who joins the production process early on may only have storyboards, concept art, crude gameplay, or character sketches from which to develop a design document. Nevertheless, there are many decisions that can be made at this stage, in order that work can begin on the sound early on in the process, and to ensure that audio plays a significant role in the game. First, it is necessary to determine the general game type, in terms of the theme and genre, to determine the style of sound design needed, and the type of music that would be appropriate. One common way of approaching questions of style in music is to create a *temp track*.[4] A temp track places preexisting music temporarily in place of the final composition, defining basic parameters from which the composer can work. Different composers, of course, have different approaches to their musical scores. Koji Kondo (2007), composer of the *Super Mario* and *Zelda* series, for instance, states that he likes to view the entire game as one composition, with each song within the game as part of a larger complete work. In dealing with franchise games or episodic content, it is also important to consider how the sound will relate to previous games, associated films, and so on.

After determining style and mood, the second most pressing issue is to deal with the functionality, or the game-specific behavior of audio—in other words, how the sound interacts with the gameplay. Will music be merely incidental, or will it be a dynamic score? What role will sound design play in the interface? Here the rules for interactivity are defined, since the game design dictates the sound design. *Spotting* is the next major element in the audio's development. At this stage, it is determined which parts of the game should have ambient sound and music. Specifically, this involves defining cue point entrances, exits, play-ins/play-outs, and game state changes, as well as deciding if game variables (such as player health, surface properties, and so on) will be used to change sound parameters. Kondo (2007) suggests keeping in mind the rhythm of gameplay in determining the structure of sound. For instance, in *Super Mario Bros.*, the rhythm of the hi-hat was used to emphasize the internal rhythm of the game,

Box 5.2
The Music Cue Sheet

Music cue sheets help the composer to organize and design the soundtrack, as well help the programmer to know how to implement the files into the game. Many composers have different approaches to cue sheets: some organize by emotion, some by instrumentation, for instance. Organizing where the game needs music is a great first step to arranging the time needed, orchestration needs, recording sessions, and other important aspects of creating the game's score. The cue sheet below shows a section from Jeff Simmons's music cue sheet from the 3D MMORPG *Earth Eternal* by Iron Realms (2007).

TABLE B5.2
Sample music cue sheet

Area Cues				
File no.	File name	Action	Time	Notes
1	dungeon_01	Nonlooped	2:07	Slightly dramatic or dark mood
2	Caves_01	Looped	1:37	Scarier, more foreboding than dungeon but less somber than King's Grave
3	Desert_01	Nonlooped	1:57	Egyptian/vaguely Arabic
4	Mystical_01	Nonlooped	1:49	Places meant to be very mystical
5	Gothic_01	Nonlooped	2:00	Darkness filled with metallic elements

and melody was used to bring that rhythm to life. It is also important to consider the controls and how these should influence that sound aesthetic: if buttons are rapidly pushed and the gameplay chaotic, the sound should reflect this physical activity of the player.

For the music, a cue list can be created with preplanned and "to-be-determined" cues (see box 5.2, "Music Cue Sheet"), breaking the script into acts or chapters or segments, defining what is happening dramatically, and creating an *emotion map* for the game, as well as for each individual level (see figure 5.1). Does the level end in a boss? Are there mini-bosses? Do we find a key item? Where are the significant points of tension and release?

As composer Charles Deenen has described, there are six basic audio emotions: happiness, sadness, surprise, disgust, anger, and fear, and each of these can be mapped to major scripted events.[5] Composer Scott B. Morton (2005) writes,

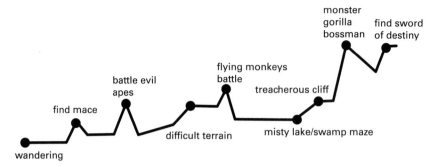

FIGURE 5.1
Emotion map for game's level tension and release patterns.

> This musical arc is often more important than the literal events themselves because it can infer deeper meanings … more than simple actions on the screen can.... Composers should start thinking beyond "What does this level sound like" to "What role does this level and its characters play in the grand scheme of the game and the plot? How do I portray that with the music I write? Where do I place the music within the level to bring this across in the most effective manner?" … Create a musical climax in your game. Don't use your most intense music until you've reached critical points in the game's dramatic arc. Is the final boss battle more important than the miniboss battle? Show it in the music. A player should be able to subconsciously interpret the importance level of events based on the music that accompanies them.

In terms of sound design, style will also be explored during this preproduction phase, taking into consideration genre, sample rate, resolution, prioritization, and other sound considerations. As with music, spotting the game and creating a list of assets needed is the first step in the sound design of a game (see box 5.3). This involves a reading of the script or design document, looking to spot for objects, actions, environments, pace, tension/release, characters/personalities, and so on. Spotting the game in terms of the emotional needs of sound design is also important: generally, there is a rhythm or movement within a level or game in terms of emotional peaks and valleys. As with music, an emotion map of tension and release points can help the sound designer in deciding which sounds need emphasis, which sounds may interfere with one another, and which sounds are secondary in importance. Asset lists are often based on descriptions of levels, and are broken down into sound types (weapon sounds, ambient sounds, menu sounds, foley, and so on). The asset list can then be used to track recording in order to be able to reproduce sounds at a later stage, if necessary. In addition to sound effects and foley, ambient sounds are a key part of a game's overall feel. This may include music, or ambient dialogue, or it may include outdoor environmental sounds. Creating a mood (of safety, of excitement, and so on) can be used

Box 5.3
Dialogue Cue Sheet

Since dialogue lines have increased to several thousand per game, it is becoming increasingly important to track dialogue sessions. The dialogue cue sheet can track as-recorded files, any DSP effects on the voice, format, file size, and so on.

File name	Character	Location	Dialogue	As recd.	DSP FX	Notes
Sh001	Sharon	Level 3 cave	"Help!"		Reverb cavex03	
Kev001	Kevin	Level 3 cave	"Hang on! I'm coming!"	Hang on!	Reverb cavex03	
Mons001	Monster1	Level 3 cave (just outside)	"Grrrauh!"			Still to add DSP
Kev002	Kevin	Level 3 cave	"What was that?"		Reverb cavex03	

to prepare a player for a particular situation, or to trick the player into thinking an area may be safe when it is not (Kutay 2006). Says Steve Kutay (2006), sound designer at Radius360:

> The psychological impact of ambient sounds can add much to the onscreen imagery, though not physically present in the scenery. For instance a distant, sustained cry of an infant suggests vulnerability or insecurity. A broken fence rattling in the wind of an abandoned city, suggests to the player a previous traumatic event. These are subtle examples used to arouse awareness in the player. More obvious sounds should be used to cue the player of his direct proximity to danger. Dark drones or muffled enemy vocalizations will prepare the player for fierce combat ahead. Fear, anticipation and anxiety are easily evoked by the careful placement of ambient sounds.

It is important, however, that ambient sounds not rely on looping. The player will quickly pick up on any distinctive sound that repeats. One solution that was incorporated into the soundtrack for *Halo* (Bungie, 2001) was the idea of permutation weighting, as described by Marty O'Donnell and Jay Weinland (in Fay, Selfon, and Fay 2004, p. 423):

We had multiple tracks playing in many cases (such as an outdoor ambience plus a wind track), each with multiple permutations in the "main" loop tag, as well as detail sounds that could be randomly triggered and were placed randomly in 3D space. One technique to highlight (which was used extensively in the music tags as well) is permutation weighting. Permutation weighting is the ability to assign different probabilities to each permutation to control how often a given permutation is played. For example, there are six permutations of a "main" loop in an outdoor ambience with lengths varying from two to eight seconds and 27 seconds of material. In one of those loops, there is a distinctive owl hoot, which would be repeated every 27 seconds if the material was played back in the same order each time.... Given the randomness of our permutation playback, you actually might hear it on average every 27 seconds but sometimes a little less and sometimes a little more frequently. If that distinctive hoot is still heard too frequently, we can use permutation weighting to assign a high skip fraction to that one permutation that tells the audio engine to skip this permutation x-percentage of the time. We adjust this number until we hear the distinctive hoot at a frequency that seems natural.

With these music and sound design decisions made, a list of required sound assets can be assembled, with separate asset lists for sound design (including, for example, weapon sounds, characters, user interface sounds), music (different modes/levels), dialogue, and additional audio content (for marketing/promotions, cinematics, etc.) (Brandon 2005, p. 21; see box 5. 3, "Sound Design Asset List"). As Zizza (2000) describes, "Reference a separate list of all audio content for the game, including those for demos, marketing, your web site, and so on. If you like having everything in one document, and the content list is on the small side, it's probably fine to include the master list here. In any case, it's good idea to include a general outline of content, well before there is enough detail to have an actual, formal list."

As this stage, it is necessary to determine the technical limitations of the systems being used, including, for instance, how many channels of sound will be used, whether the delivery will be in surround sound format, and what production values the sound will have. Finally, implementation must be considered, including the tools and technology available and required (to be built or bought), such as platform, sound engine, and playback engine. Composer Richard Jacques described that it may be useful to think as the programmer, in creating simple if–then statements, using examples from *Sonic 3D* (Sega, 1996), which used Redbook audio tracks cued dynamically:

Example 1, Level 1, Act 1: Play Green Grove Act 1 music
IF Sonic picks up speed shoes
THEN play "speed shoes music."
IF Sonic picks up invincibility icon
THEN play "invincibility music"

IF Sonic has collected 100 rings
THEN play "100 rings jingle"[6]

In this way, the programmer can see exactly how music or other audio elements are to be implemented, and the composer or sound designer can get a feel for what will work in the game. Finally, a schedule and budget typically follows, including time for design, asset creation and production (including recording sessions, and so on), re-dos, implementation, and testing/quality assessment.

THE PRODUCTION STAGE

If the game was not spotted for music cues during the pre-production phase, the spotting of cues will take place from a solid, playable form of the game, if one exists. If a playable does not exist at this stage, composers may create a series of *scratch tracks*, or rough drafts of cues. Composers typically have their own way of creating music at this stage, and the music's creation also depends on the size of the company: smaller companies are unlikely to use orchestras, and so synthesizer tracks can be created, which are more affordable and more easily reworked when changes need to be made. In a large company, once scratch tracks have been approved, temporary melodic assets, or multitrack splits will be delivered to orchestrators, who will orchestrate the songs. Charts are taken to ensembles and pre-records (of synthesized versions and soloists) are delivered to the orchestra. Recording sessions are undertaken and then mixed, mastered, and *sweetened* (altered with layering, effects, and so on).

The production of game sound can typically take place in a number of venues. In the recording studio, stock sound CDs or sound effects libraries are commonly used. Oftentimes these stock library sounds are manipulated and layered to achieve a desired effect. In the studio it is also possible to record custom sounds with the use of various props. Some companies have dedicated foley studios or foley pits, which are designed for in-studio recording, such as footsteps or clothing noise. In addition to in-studio recording, many companies incorporate some field recording—that is, recording outdoors or in various locations other than the studio. Once all of the sound assets have been gathered, typically sounds are manipulated in the studio, treated with various effects, or sweetened to create a more exciting sound and to distinguish the sound from other games that may be using the same effects libraries. This usually involves layering sounds, adjusting various elements of the sound, equalizing and compressing the sound, or using various digital signal processing (DSP) effects (see box 3.1).

One of the most important advances in sound technology on next-generation consoles is more powerful DSP, including the processing of DSP in real time (that is, while the game is actually being played). Being able to add DSP effects onto sounds in real time in the game saves a lot of recording time. For instance, previously, to get the effect of footsteps to change when walking from, say, a stone path into a cave, the effects would have to be pre-recorded onto the footsteps sound file. Each different location would have to have a pre-recorded sample of the sound. Now, DSP filters can be set for locations, and so selected sounds can be processed in real time in that location. Only one set of recorded footsteps is needed to create potentially unlimited sound effects from that one original recording. In other words, with real-time DSP, audio can respond to physics graphics engines to create more realistic-sounding effects in the game during real time, as Sotaro Tojima, sound director for *Metal Gear Solid 4* (Kojima, 2007) describes:

> For example, in the scenario where a bottle falls off a table, hits a metal shovel, and then rolls onto a carpet, conventional sound processing would have the bottle make the same sounds regardless of the environment, or what it collides with. That same scenario on the PlayStation 3 might have the bottle make a metallic tink when it hits the shovel, and then create a muffled rolling sound as it travels across the carpet. If the room had its own sound variables, the bottle's sound might get take on some echo if in a bathroom, or get slightly quieter if in a bedroom. Then you have to factor in on-the-fly surround encoding, which would make the bottle pan from front to back or side to side in your room, depending upon the way it rolled. (Cited in Shah 2006)

The audio team also typically oversees the production of dialogue (voice-over), since this must be mixed with the other audio in the game. In the early days of game dialogue, friends of the audio developer were often drafted to record voice parts, but today professional voice actors are commonly used and the process is much more in-depth. Dialogue can be an important part of a game's overall sound, as Marty O'Donnell and Jay Weinland elaborate in a discussion of *Halo*:

> The dialog in *Halo* was one of the areas that helped to give *Halo* a unique flavor. There are two types of dialog: cinematic dialog that is a traditional linear script and dynamic dialog. As you play through *Halo*, your Marines will dynamically alert you to what is going on around you, warn each other and you of danger, chastise, apologize for allies getting shot or killed by friendly fire, and generally amuse you. This aspect of *Halo's* audio could not have succeeded without the hard work of AI (artificial intelligence) programmer Chris Butcher who gave us many possible AI states in which a character might say something and controlled how much was said to make it all seem natural.... The cinematic dialog also works well due to both a great storyline by the Bungie team and excellent writing by Joseph Staten. Scripts for the cut scenes and other interior scenes during gameplay were written and storyboarded so that we could clearly deliver the plot to the player. There is about one hour and 15 minutes of cut scenes in *Halo*, and that puts this part of *Halo's* production on par with a short feature film. (Cited in Fay, Selfon, and Fay 2004, p. 428)

Dialogue events can be separated into several distinct types: ambient dialogue (also known as *walla*, background ambience for environments where there are background people, such as crowds at a baseball stadium, shop, or market); scripted events (which are in-game scenes in which the player can typically walk away, but if he does so, he or she will miss some important information); cinematics; AI cues (also known as *barks*, which are nonverbal lines such as screaming); voice-over narration; and the in-game lines (see Chandler 2005). Together, these dialogue events can represent thousands of lines of script. *Halo 2* (Bungie, 2004), for instance, had more than sixteen thousand lines of dialogue.

Much as it is necessary to organize assets for sound or music, dialogue assets must be carefully cataloged. A script can be broken down into a dialogue sheet by character or scene (see box 5.4, "Dialogue Cue Sheet"; see also Chandler 2005). Casting must take place for each localized area (if the dialogue is being localized; at times this is not possible and subtitles are used). Generally, studios will cast one actor for several roles. It is therefore important that a cue sheet is carefully organized, so that actors do not end up in the same scene, "speaking to themselves" in a game. Studios will record by character, rather than sequential order, so recording sheets for each separate actor must be produced. Details regarding the As-Recorded Script (ARS), which are changes made to the script when recorded, must be described. Dialogue is often recorded in an ADR studio,[7] which is designed for film over-dubbing, but is very suitable for games dialogue work. The *dry files* (raw, unaltered) are delivered and checked for quality. These files are then cut into single asset files for integration and treated to various effects or editing as necessary. Once audio editing is complete, audio is set to video clips of the game, particularly in cinematic sequences. Additional recording sessions and retakes are often part of this process.

An increasingly complex component of game audio is localization. Localization is the process by which a game is adapted for a specific territory or target market. Typically this includes the major European languages (French, German, Spanish, and Italian), and may include Asian markets as well. Localized versions are either completed at the same time as the original version (known as *sim-ship*, or simultaneous shipping, for worldwide release), or *post-gold*, which is a remake of the game with localized assets after the original version is complete. Ensuring a wide market in terms of distribution helps to minimize some of the financial risks involved in producing a game. To some extent, localization is genre-specific, as the Game Localization Network (2005), a company specializing in localization elaborates: "Shipping a game with a translated manual (a 'doco' version) might be considered sufficient for a [*sic*] arcade racer but it will not engage and assist players of a story driven RPG. An RPG that is targeting a large language market might benefit from a 'full' localization (user interface, in-game text, spoken audio, manual and support documents), a similar game targeting a smaller market might be better shipping as a 'sub-titled' version (user interface, in-game text, manual,

Box 5.4
The Sound Design Asset List

The sound design asset list tracks the assets needed for the game, and can be adapted to also function as an audio report, which can detail where the sound came from, any DSP effects it was treated with, and so on. These asset lists can be as simple as the one presented below, or incredibly detailed including take number, audio channel information, equipment setup notes, and information regarding equipment used to record, along with SMPTE time codes, track numbers, file names, or other identifying information. The cue sheet below shows a section from the sound effects asset list from Jeff Simmons's cue sheet from the 3D MMORPG *Earth Eternal* by Iron Realms (2007). Used by kind permission of Jeff Simmons and Iron Realms.

Hits and Impacts		
Swords		
File no.	File Name	Time
50	sword_flesh_impact01	0:01
51	sword_flesh_impact02	0:01
52	sword_flesh_impact03	0:01
53	sword_leather_impact01	0:01
54	sword_leather_impact02	0:01
55	sword_leather_impact03	0:01
56	sword_wood_impact01	0:01
57	sword_wood_impact02	0:01
58	sword_wood_impact03	0:01
Staffs		
File no.	File Name	Time
59	staff_flesh_impact01	0:01
60	staff_flesh_impact02	0:01
61	staff_flesh_impact03	0:01
62	staff_leather_impact01	0:01
63	staff_leather_impact02	0:01
64	staff_leather_impact03	0:01
65	staff_wood_impact01	0:01
66	staff_wood_impact02	0:01
67	staff_wood_impact03	0:01

and support documents), thus contributing to the bottom line by saving the cost of audio recording.''

Localization is necessary to create a realistic game environment, no matter what the player's language, but it is more than just straight translation: the user interface must be intuitive to that market, the story must be as polished in the translation, and the audio must be as realistic and engaging as the original (see Game Localization Network 2005). Localization may include changes in controller layouts, animation sequences, or frame-rates that may require adjustments in audio. What's more important, there may be significant cultural differences in the various territories that require changes in gameplay. Different music may need to be selected for different target markets.[8] Legal or cultural issues can arise from the different ratings systems in various territories, owing to censors and public opinion. For instance, Germany has very strict laws regarding violence, which for audio may mean toning down the sound effects to reduce the impact of violent sequences. When the narrative of the game is significantly revised for another culture, this is known as *blending* (Thayer and Kolko 2004, p. 12). Blending can involve writing new narratives to target a specific culture, and therefore might also require new graphics and new sound. Examples of blended games include, for instance, *Crash Bandicoot* (Naughty Dog, 1996), in which the main character underwent an appearance change for the Japanese market, and *Half-Life* (Valve, 1998), which had to replace human characters with robots to satisfy different rating standards in violence (Thayer and Kolko 2004, p. 17). Obviously, changing a character from human to robot involves significant changes in audio.

The final stage in the audio production process is the integration of the music, sound effects, and dialogue. Integration of audio into the game involves much more than writing a few lines of code. Describes Marty O'Donnell, ''The implementation side of it is really huge ... it's not just about, 'We need a sound.' It's all about 'Here is this vehicle or here is this weapon, which has many different components and many different ways it needs to act in a 3-D audio environment''' (cited in Hanson 2007, p. 49). O'Donnell even goes so far as to suggest that implementation is responsible for at least 50 percent of the final audio result. It is, after all, the ways in which audio is integrated into a game that will have an impact on the effectiveness of that audio. Integration typically determines how audio will be cued or triggered in a game, as well as what aspects of the audio may be changed by the game state or game parameters (see Whitmore 2003). For instance, music or ambient tracks may be triggered by location, by game state (such as player health, or enemy health), by time-ins or time-outs, by players, or by various game events.

The music files the composer writes must be able to be integrated into the game in a variety of ways. Integrating the music, for instance, may involve cutting the music into *splits*, *loops*, or *chunks* in order to create a more dynamic score. As John Debney, composer for *LAIR* described (in ScoreKeeper 2007), ''There was almost two hours of music which in the scheme of games is not a lot. They'll take that two hours and cut it up and turn it into hours and hours of music.... the mechanics of writing music that they could cut really easily was important. A lot of the action oriented pieces are, by design, pretty rhythmic so that they could cut it very easily.''

In addition to the actual cues being cut for integration, various musical elements may be altered in real time in the game engine, such as DSP effects, tempo, or instrumentation. Middleware tools, such as *ISACT*, *Wwise*, *FMOD*, and others are increasingly being used to decrease production time and costs, and to integrate a more dynamic score into the game. Canadian company Audiokinetic's middleware solution *Wwise*, for instance, allows audio developers to prototype the integration of audio in a game simulation before the game is even finished. Environmental effects can be rendered in real time, and occlusion and obstruction effects can be managed within the software, mixing up to four simultaneous environments per object. Sound prioritization for real-time mixing is also included, as is randomization of various elements for effects such as pitch or volume, to enhance realism. Real-time game parameter controls can also be set, to adjust sound properties based on parameter value changes in a game. So, for instance, if a player's health is running out, music could be sped up, or could increase in volume. Also important, the software allows the user to validate audio profiles for each platform, to manage the performance in terms of CPU and memory usage, in order to adapt and adjust performance before the final integration.

An equally important part of production is the placement of sounds in the three-dimensional space. Use of high-definition (HD) format in television and the adoption of 5.1 have led to a growing consumer demand for surround sound in games. All next-gen consoles are compatible with Dolby Digital's discreet surround 5.1 (see box 4.1). With capabilities of 7.1 in some games systems, surround sound is rapidly becoming the norm, and indeed is expected, particularly as consumers upgrade their home-theater equipment. Spatial positioning of sound is increasingly becoming an integral part of gameplay. Surround sound is used to help create a more realistic and immersive environment in games, as Richard Dekkard of HammerJaw Audio describes in the use of surround in *Auto Assault* (Net Devil, 2006):

> Anything that moves in the game is panned dynamically in the surround field. This includes all vehicles, enemies, explosions, etcetera. There are also stationary sound-emitting objects that are panned dynamically. There are many ''George Orwellian'' propaganda towers all around that you will hear panned interactively. In addition to these interactive elements, we have six levels of ''prebaked'' surround sounds. These include weapon sounds, music, weather, environmental audio, interface sounds, and your own vehicle explosion is in surround sound. We have taken it to every extreme we could. (Dolby.com n.d.)

Surround can be useful for more than just its immersive quality, however; it can be used as an audio cue. A basic example is the use of surround in the gameplay of the Shadow Mario character in *Super Mario Sunshine* for the Nintendo Game Cube (Nintendo, 2002), in which the positioning of audio indicates to the player where the translucent Shadow Mario would pop up. Similar use of surround sound to position enemies was seen in the stealth and first-person shooter games discussed in chapter 4. Another interesting use of surround sound can be heard in *Onimusha 3: Demon Siege* (Capcom, 2004), in which the player is given the option of adjusting his or her "listening position," setting the perspective of the audio as either that of the player or camera. Surround sound, therefore, can play a variety of important roles in games, as Marty O'Donnell and Jay Weinland elaborate for *Halo*:

> Knowing that a Marine "had your back" just over your right shoulder brought a sense of security, just as hearing a Hunter's metal armor behind you would bring a sense of impending doom. There were many audio elements in the game that received 3D positioning, such as weapon sound effects, bullet impacts, speech, mechanical objects, particles such as flying dirt or sparks, and outdoor detail ambiences, such as wildlife, rivers, and waterfalls, to name a few. In essence, everything you hear in *Halo* that is not music or an ambient bed is 3D positioned ... All 3D audio is subject to occlusion, obstruction, Doppler, and HRTF. Anytime a solid piece of geometry gets between the player and a sound source, it is occluded and obstructed. A good example of this is in the hangar bay of the alien ship where there is a dropship with the engine running. As the Master Chief steps behind a column, the sound of the engine is occluded, rolling off both the gain and the high end of the sound ... HRTF (Head-Related Transfer Function) also adds to the audio experience by filtering sounds, depending on which direction the character's head is facing. You can hear it affect the dialog in the cinematics as well as in the sounds that play during combat. Probably the best way to hear this effect, however, is listening to your own footsteps. As you move the Master Chief around in *Halo*, listen to the sound of his footsteps on various surfaces. Then run through the same areas looking down toward his feet rather than straight ahead and listen to those same footsteps; the difference is stunning. (Cited in Fay, Selfon, and Fay 2004, pp. 424–425)

Sounds are mastered individually. Mastering of separate sound elements (dialogue, effects, etc.) helps to adjust the sounds' dynamic ranges. At present, there is still too little dynamic range within games (see Bridgett 2008). With real-time mastering, unwanted audio information can be removed in favor of a much more realistic, cinematic dynamic range. As Alexander Brandon elaborates, "another delusion held by all audio folk who gleefully cling to their BBE Sonic Maximizers is that all sound needs not be normalized to überhigh levels, in some cases creating a WAV file that in *Sound Forge* looks like a solid brick ... proper balance of dynamic and frequency range is vital to avoid butchering the ears of the average listener" (Brandon 2005, p. 46). Bridgett (2008, p. 129) argues that one reason for this loss of dynamic range was perhaps the fact that "video games were born in arcades where they had to compete with the sounds of other nearby games consoles" and as such, as noted earlier, sounds had to be loud to attract attention. He goes on to argue that the cinematization of games is changing their "cultural positioning" and thus leading to an aesthetic that is closer to film or classical music, in which sounds demand a certain "listening etiquette," in which they are "expected to be listened to in isolation and given the audience's undivided attention, they are not expected to compete simultaneously with other [environmental] sounds."

THE POST-PRODUCTION STAGE

"Post-production" in games typically involves some degree of mixing. Mixing adjusts the interplay of all audio components in a game to ensure that there is no overlap between frequencies, including deciding which elements should be emphasized and which should be deemphasized in the mix. The mixer must listen for what Charles Deenen calls *believability gaps* in the audio: awkward silences, too much repetition, an unnatural imbalance (in EQ, dynamic range, and so on), or unrealistic dialogue.[9] Integration may also involve dynamically mixing a score, such as in *Grim Fandango* (LucasArts, 1998), which adds or drops instruments at certain key moments or environments. Mixing is, therefore, ideally something that should be considered throughout the whole audio design process, although this differs from developer to developer. As Ed Lima, audio director at Gearbox Software, elaborates: "I think about the mix throughout the entire design process. I generally try to bake some slight equalization curves or tendencies into families of sounds. For instance, explosions might be bottom-heavy, voice-over might occupy a higher band or the music might be designed with specific instruments and frequency bands in mind" (in Henein 2007, p. 56).

At present, sounds in games are, in a sense, competing with each other—dialogue, sound effects, ambience, and music all inhabit the same aural space. Particularly since dialogue and the sound effects of, for instance, combat, are often in the mid-range, there is a constant risk of creating what film sound designer Walter Murch calls a "logjam" (in Oldenbourg 2005). For instance, if a player's character is in an open field, talking to a nonplaying character, and is supposed to hear a gunshot in the distance, if the composer has chosen to include a lot of mid-range activity in that cue (e.g., snare drums and guitar), the gunshot, the conversation, and/or the music is going to be obscured. Whereas this has always been problematic in film sound and other linear media, in games the added unpredictability of where these events may occur makes the mixing far more difficult a task.

Real-time mixing in games now allows for sounds to be prioritized. As such, if the player must hear the dialogue to know what the next stage in the game is, the music or that explosive sound can drop down in the mix, as Rob Bridgett, sound director for Radical Games, describes:

> Ducking music and FX when dialogue occurs is a very basic way of achieving a more cinematic effect in games, and also of ensuring that essential information is conveyed and is clearly audible. The interactive mixing process can identify a whole slew of prioritised sound effects that need to be heard at designated moments in game play and sometimes dropping a sound entirely is the best option. Ducking importantly allows subtraction of sounds so that you don't just have to make everything louder in order to hear it.... Dynamically carving out frequencies from a music track when dialogue is playing for example is a great way of generatively allowing space in the music to exist when a dialogue event occurs. (Bridgett 2006)

As Bridgett (2008, p. 127) argues, previous attempts at mixing in games meant that a group of sounds had to be "limited and compressed to extremes in order to compete with other sounds and music," or, in cases where simple mixing existed, implementation (via text file) was awkward and not "artistically useful." In some ways, Bridgett (2008, p. 131) argues, it was almost beneficial that these older systems could not handle a significant amount of audio information at any one time, which limited the amount of simultaneous sounds:

> With the increased memory and available voices of next generation consoles and more sophisticated audio compression codecs, such as Microsoft's *XNA* and Sony's *ATRAC* allowing for a reasonable quality sample rate at roughly 10:1 compression, the amount of sounds that can now be played simultaneously has increased roughly ten-fold. This means a heavily increased role for in-game run-time mixing in order to prevent a cacophony of sound effects from playing back during run-time. Assigning a finite amount of available voices is one particularly crude way around this, but there emerge problems of really important sounds not being played back because other important sounds are also playing. Mixing in video games, as in cinema, is concerned with sound removal and subtraction rather than pushing volumes up. In mixing, it is often very subtle fader ducking that is required to allow a more important group of sounds to be made prominent above others.

There are still several necessary procedural stages and technical aspects to be explored by game audio designers. In particular, the psychological aspects of mixing can be a challenge, because the most effective mix may not be the most realistic: "For example, consider any number of movies where the protagonist walks down a busy city street, and the audience hears primarily the interior monologue of the character's thoughts, not the traffic sounds" (Grigg et al. 2006). It has been proposed that what is required is a "smart audio engine" that could

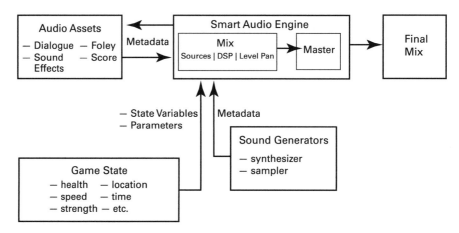

FIGURE 5.2
High-Level Smart Audio Mix Engine, adapted from Project Bar-B-Q (Bajakian et al. 2006).

take various sound assets, filter them with DSP according to various in-game parameters (game states, for example), perhaps synthesizing the sounds themselves in some cases, mix and pan within the engine in real time, master in real time and then send the sounds out to the player, as in figure 5.2.

There are different models for audio mixing in a game, including a post-production model as outlined by Bridgett (2007). Typically, post-production mixing has occurred in games only in cinematic sequences, in which the visuals can be locked down. Bridgett, however, working with Randy Thom on *Scarface*, created a model of "snapshot mixing" to mix sound, music, and dialogue by breaking the game down into several types of mix, including generic gameplay actions, locations, and specific events. Different mixes were developed for different areas of gameplay.

It is also possible dynamically to reduce or eliminate various frequencies from a music track in order to avoid a logjam with the dialogue. Describes Jay Weinland of the game *Halo* (in Hanson 2007, p. 51):

> One of the things that's pretty cool about our code engine is that we actually have real-time ducking in our game.... So that we can control any individual sound, we can control how we duck it under cinematic or other types of dialog, which is our biggest challenge. If the character is giving you some very important information, and all of a sudden three grenades land at your feet and blow up, you don't want that line to get stepped on. We have real-time parameters where we can say, "we'll duck this sound nine dB over two seconds and let it ramp back up after the dialog is done, over the course of another second and a half." So it allows us real-time control over the volumes in the games, and it helps us to make sure that we can always hear the important dialog and other things that are important.

Such prioritization of sounds, though necessary, can mean that the mixer is making decisions that affect the ways in which the player hears and interprets sound. The composer may believe that the music at a particularly dramatic point in a game should have priority, in order to draw the player emotionally into the scene, while the dialogue may feature a *reveal* (a plot point that will guide the player); while the sound designer might have also spent much time unnecessarily prioritizing the sound of a key dropping off a desk on the right-hand side of the soundscape, for instance. Each of the sound assets may be thought by its creators (or indeed, the player of the game) to require priority. The mixer, then, must make difficult decisions regarding which sounds the listener should hear, potentially altering the intended impact of the audio, and the ways in which the audio information is received by the player.

CONCLUSION

It is important to note that there are specific differences in the production processes between film and games that impact the final sound of the game. For instance, in film sound, ambience is often recorded in the production space: if not at the time of filming, then typically on the same day, in order to "corroborate, for the spectator, the original inscription of the character's speech" (Geuens 2000, p. 219). Argues Jean-Pierre Geuens in his book *Film Production Theory*, "ambiance is the cement which holds the entire aural construction together" (ibid.). But of course, as with animation and some CGI-heavy live action films, there is no production space in games. There is no ambient background in which actors perform. As such, the sounds are all dubbed in. Dubbing used to be viewed as a last resort by filmmakers, since a good recordist working with a good mixer could get up to 70 percent of the production track into the finished film (ibid., p. 212). Geuens (ibid., p. 216) argues that in dubbing, we "falsify the space" since the original context of place is lost, resulting in an unnatural sound. It is "a procedure to be avoided because newly recorded tracks invariably sound flat and dead in contrast with the location recordings" (Michael Rabiger, in Geuens 2000, p. 212). In games, however, all sounds must be created in the studio or in field recordings, and then built up to sound real. Without a real reference point for the space that is being created on-screen, these sounds are inevitably in some ways "less than real," and as such, in many ways sound designers compensate by creating a "more than real" sound in the studio (a topic I take up in chapter 7).

At the same time, the issue of mixing is much more complicated in games, which must take into account not only real-time changes in gameplay, but changes in the player's positioning of the character. Mixing in film is based on the assumption that the audience is static, an unmoving, passive receiver of the sound. Mixing in games must be based on the assumption that—though the player's actual position may not change—the player's character (and, by extension, therefore, the player) is constantly changing position. Planning to mix a surround-sound game, therefore, requires a set of skills that are becoming increasingly specialized.

As game audio develops, the roles involved are becoming more and more specific and dedicated. Whereas one person used to be responsible for all aspects of audio production and implementation, there are now teams of people with a variety of levels of artistic and technical skills. What needs to be stressed is that game audio is a collaborative process; the programmer cannot implement without the music, and the music, as was shown, depends to a significant extent on how it is implemented. Sound design must take into account the dialogue, and so on. The teamwork involved in creating game audio suggests an important reconstruction (or reduction) of the notion of "author." As shown, sound design, dialogue, and music are as much about integration as they are about composition, and the ways in which the sound is implemented greatly affect the ways in which these sounds are received. To some extent such a relationship exists in film, but it is taken to an extreme in games. Music must adjust to the player's actions, in real time, to other audio in the same scene, and so on.

Moreover, when musical splits or "chunks" do not exist as a single linear track, there is no single "musical text," and the author is to some extent the player/listener, whose moves affect the playback of these audio chunks, as is the composer, who is responsible for composing them, and the programmer, who chops them up and places them in a game. Cultural theory has for several decades been dealing with the notion that audiences themselves may construct meaning from texts, and the notion of text itself has become increasingly blurred. In games, these concepts become even more indistinct, as the player becomes an active agent of change, and the text is malleable and impermanent. This is taken even further in online games, for which there is no scripting, and no final version. Localization also further disintegrates the notion of games as a "text" or complete "work." Not only is every game different owing to the participatory interactive nature of games, but games may be altered significantly for different markets, raising the question of what is the "authentic" version. This reduction of text and authorial power may even have an impact on the future development of popular music in general, as popular songs increasingly are licensed for games, a topic discussed in the next chapter.

CHAPTER 6

SYNERGY IN GAME AUDIO: FILM, POPULAR MUSIC, AND INTELLECTUAL PROPERTY

The global video games business represents an enormous cultural industry. The leading industry organization, the Entertainment Software Association, claims that over 75 percent of heads of households in the United States now play computer or video games.[1] Sales statistics fluctuate with the release of new consoles (approximately every five years), although overall statistics since the birth of the industry indicate an ever increasing incline in sales. Worldwide hardware and software sales are forecast at 46.5 billion dollars (based on retail sales) for 2010,[2] and are increasing at an average 11.4 percent compound annual rate (Kolodny 2006).[3] Despite these impressive numbers, the actual number of games that sell over one million units in a given year is only a handful.[4] Indeed, only a small percentage of games released ever make a profit, meaning that games software sales, much as in the music industry, depend on a few stars covering some of the costs for the many unsuccessful releases. Moreover, whereas the music industry today is being "democratized" by the exceptional quality available to the home "bedroom musician" and the distribution by Internet sites, independent game developers face increasing challenges.[5] Publishing a game on the Xbox360 or PlayStation 3 represents a development cost of 50 percent more than previous platforms. Because of the advances in capabilities, production and marketing costs are now averaging about twenty million dollars per title.[6] While independent developers can still enjoy some success—particularly in the casual, downloadable and portable games markets—their chances of success with a major title are slim. Profit margins are diminishing, forcing games publishers to reduce risks in several ways. The major companies—such as Microsoft and Sony—are increasingly developing their own games in order to ensure themselves exclusive releases, thereby guaranteeing sales for their own hardware (Sony, for instance, employs over 2000 developers in fourteen studios).[7]

Relying on well-known intellectual property (sequels/episodic content, film or other market *synergy* or crossovers, and so on) is an important way to offset some of the risk. Music licensing in particular is becoming an increasingly essential element of a game's marketing strategy, as it helps to reduce some of the costs and risks of bringing a game to market (see Kerr 2006, p. 70). Synergy with mass media entertainment markets is so important that, as Aphra Kerr points out, some publishers have gone so far as to purchase other studios in order to gain access to intellectual property.[8] Anything that can be done to reduce the marketing costs— such as presenting already-known stars or intellectual property—is viewed as a surefire way to ensure a game's success. After all, the most expensive element of marketing (that of building awareness) has already been achieved when using preexisting IP (cited in Kerr 2006, p. 70). Of course, tying games to other intellectual property is nothing new, as can be seen in 1975's *Man Eater*, whose flyer advertised, "take advantage of the *Jaws* rage" (figure 6.1), and a similarly styled *Shark Jaws* (Atari, 1975), which was obviously capitalizing on the film, but could not get away with titling itself just *Jaws*, and so nearly hid the word "Shark" (figure 6.2).[9] Games based on film, as Jeff Smith (1998, p. 192) notes of the relationship between music and the movie industry, are important because "they not only presell the film project and thereby serve to minimize financial risk, they also provide a ready-made set of images and narrative elements that can be regenerated in any number of distribution channels." Smith writes, "By creating multiple profit centers for a single property, synergy spreads risk among several different commodities. A successful soundtrack album can help defray the production costs of an unsuccessful film, and vice versa" (ibid., p. 188).

In terms of game audio, the associations with known intellectual property sometimes come in the form of the use of star talent in voice recording. Having a star associated with a game assists in marketing, creates awareness, and generates buzz. For instance, well-known cult Hollywood actors, such as Mark Hammill and Malcolm McDowell, contributed voice acting to 1994's *Wing Commander III* (Origin). More recently, Rockstar Games had Ray Liota, Burt Reynolds, and Dennis Hopper record voice for *Grand Theft Auto: Vice City* (2007). Most major game releases, known as AAA or *triple-A* titles, will likely soon feature well-known voice actors. Writing about the increasing role of star talent dialogue in animated films, Joe Bevilacqua (1999) notes that the competitive nature and need to draw a wide audience is driving the increased use of celebrities, at the expense of experienced specialized voice actors. More important, there are aesthetic implications of such a choice, since unlike screen actors, specialized voice actors are specially trained in microphone techniques.

Like dialogue, sound design is also experiencing increased crossover with Hollywood, as franchise games are developed after the release of films (such as

FIGURE 6.1
Man Eater (Project Support Engineering 1975) arcade flyer.

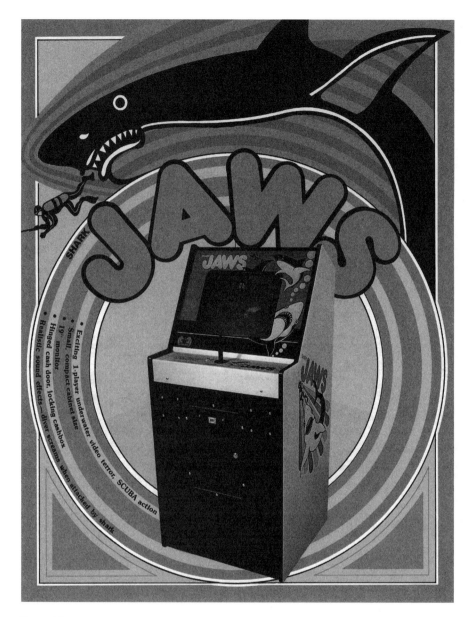

FIGURE 6.2
Shark Jaws (Atari, 1975) arcade flyer.

Scarface), or simultaneously (as in *The Chronicles of Riddick*). In the case of *Riddick*, sounds were often borrowed from the production/post-production film recording (Droney 2004). The film's sound designers at Soundelux were brought in to work with Swedish Starbreeze Studios on the game "to sonically tie together the opening and closing flashback scenes that reference *The Chronicles of Riddick*, as well as create a long list of sound design effects for use in game play" (ibid.). Sound effects, such as weapons, were shared between game and film. Supervising sound editor Scott Gershin describes:

> Part of what's intriguing about this franchise ... is that it's different stories in the same universe. For the game, David Twohy, Vin Diesel's Tigon Studios and Vivendi Universal wanted to preserve a sonic landscape with as much *Riddick* flair as possible. But stylistically, it's different. There's also a culture, of course, to video games. Sometimes, gaming people consider film sound designers to be too "Hollywood." ... With Riddick ... we connected the lines between mediums. We tried to develop a symbiotic thread, while stylistically going with the different media as their own entities. (Ibid.)

In addition to differing aesthetics, Hollywood sound designers and voice talent are relatively new to the games industry, unlike popular music, which has a longer history of synergy, or collaboration. I have broken down music's association with games into three major categories: popular music or musicians as the subject or narrative component of a game, popular musicians as composers for games, and the use of licensed popular music in games.[10]

POPULAR MUSIC AND VIDEO GAMES

There is a growing symbiotic relationship between the music industry and the games industry. Commonly, games are being used to promote and sell music, and recording artists are being used to market and sell games. Games with a musical subject or narrative, or rhythm-action games, have generally enjoyed great success, from the electronic *Simon* game of 1978 (Milton Bradley), to *PaRappa the Rapper* (SCEI, 1996) on the PlayStation, and more recently, music-based games like *Guitar Hero* (Red Octane, 2005), which won five Academy of Interactive Arts and Sciences Awards in 2005, and was nominated for seven D.I.C.E. awards,[11] as well as several Game Audio Network Guild awards. Games where music is the primary driving motive or narrative element can be roughly divided into three categories: musician-themed games, creative games, and rhythm-action games. It is possible for these categories to overlap; however, there are often distinct goals or intents behind these types of games.

In terms of musician-themed games, bands or artists can appear as characters in the games. The first band to appear in a video game was Journey, in the

1982 Atari classic by Data Age, *Journey's Escape*.[12] Engineered by the band's manager Herbie Herbert, the game contained just the song "Don't Stop Believin'" when it was originally released for the Atari VCS home console in 1982. The manual describes the game's objectives: "You're on the road with Journey, one of the world's hottest rock groups. A spectacular performance has just ended. Now it's up to you to guide each Journey Band Member past hordes of Love-Crazed Groupies, Sneaky Photographers, and Shifty-eyed Promoters to the safety of the Journey Escape Vehicle in time to make the next concert." The arcade version came out just a few months later with digital-camera photos spliced onto raster graphic bodies, and which played various Journey tracks, including "Stone in Love," and "Still They Ride" from their *Escape* album (1981), as well as a track from what was then their new album, *Frontiers*, called "Chain Reaction," which the game was intended to help promote. These tracks all relied on built-in sound chips, but during a special bonus concert scene, a hidden cassette player inside the arcade machine would play their hit "Separate Ways."

Since *Journey's Escape*, there have been countless musician-themed games, including Aerosmith in a side-scrolling shooter called *Revolution X* (Midway/Acclaim, 1994) and *Michael Jackson's Moonwalker*, released by Sega for the Genesis and the arcades in 1990. Unlike many musician-based games, *Moonwalker* was not released to coincide with an album—in fact, it relied on two older songs from *Thriller* ("Beat it" and "Billie Jean") and three from 1987's *Bad* ("Smooth Criminal," "Another Part of Me," and "Bad"), both put out by Epic. The game, then, as with that of Aerosmith, became less about the songs and more about Jackson's public persona. Some games, such as *Motown Games' Rap Jam* (Mandingo, 1995) for the SNES did not even feature music from the label, but did include several rap artists as characters, including LL Cool J, House of Pain, Public Enemy, Queen Latifa, and Coolio. More recently, various pop idols have been promoted in a kind of in-game advertising. Pink, Kylie Minogue, and Sum 41, for instance, have video clips spliced into Acclaim's *Summer Heat Beach Volleyball* (2003) at key segments of play after accumulating a certain amount of points. Rapper 50 Cent is featured in *50 Cent: Bulletproof* (Vivendi, 2005), which goes one step further with marketing, containing exclusive tracks and more than a dozen videos—making the game a "must have" for fans of the artist. These games have been primarily aimed at fans of the specific artists or genres of music, and the artistic personas are used as the key marketing element of the games. In a sense, the music is a peripheral or secondary aspect of these types of games, with the attention instead on the marketing power of celebrities.

There are also popular music-based games in which music plays a central role in the game's narrative and is a primary aspect of gameplay, including creative music games and rhythm-action games. Remixing, production, and composition of original songs are an important part of creative music games. *MTV's Music Generator* series (Codemasters, 2000), for example, began as what was essentially sequencing software with sequences provided and became a remixing project of various popular music songs. Users are given an editing bay of riffs, beats, samples, bass lines, and vocal sequences, and can assemble music from a variety of genres. In this case, players are given the opportunity to interact with and participate in various popular songs. *FreQuency* (Harmonix, 2001), and its sequel, *Amplitude* (Harmonix, 2003), also used sequences of popular music, but in more of a playful game environment than that of MTV's game. In *Amplitude*, for instance, there are several different modes—a "remix mode" of solo song construction, in which the player can create an avatar called a "FreQ" that will play along with the parts written, or a "duel mode" in which one player chooses a sequence and another player must duplicate it. In solo mode, the player must tap buttons along with the beat of the music, blasting musical elements (guitar, drums, bass, vocals, synth, and effects) from a science-fiction styled racetrack. The game therefore takes the elements of a composition game and crosses over with rhythm-action games, which require the player to coordinate actions to a beat or melody in a game. (See Juha Arrasvuori 2006 for more discussion on rhythm-action games.) Some rhythm-action games have involved original music, but more recently they have used licensed songs. *Guitar Hero* (Harmonix, 2005) featured thirty tracks of licensed music, including hits such as Deep Purple's "Smoke on the Water," Megadeth's "Symphony of Destruction" and White Zombie's "Thunderkiss '65." Many of these games have also included special controllers—Nintendo's *Donkey Konga* (2003) and Namco's *Taiko Drum Master* (1999), for instance. included a set of bongo drums or taiko drum, respectively, or ARC's *BeatMania* (1997), which included a DJ-style turntable controller. Similarly, dancing games, where the player must dance to the beat of a song, began with Nintendo's *Dance Aerobics* (Bandai, 1987), which included a special mat called a Power Pad. It was *Dance Dance Revolution* (Konami, 1998), however, that took dancing games to the masses.

In addition to starring in games and being part of creative or rhythm-action music games, there have been many popular artists involved in creating original soundtracks for games. After the development of Redbook (CD) audio for games machines in the mid-1990s, it became much easier to hire popular musicians to compose for games, although a handful of game soundtracks were created by popular musicians prior to the use of Redbook audio in games. The most well known of these was probably Brian May's involvement with *Rise of the Robots* (Time Warner Interactive, 1994), an adventure-fighting game released for the SNES, Sega Genesis, and PC. The soundtrack combined electronics with a few repeated guitar chords from "The Dark," originally off May's *Back to the Light* album (Hollywood Records, 1993).[13]

With the arrival of CD audio, games manufacturers were quick to bring popular bands on board: Alien Sex Fiend's 1994 score for Ocean Software's *Inferno* was one of the first complete musical scores for a Redbook audio–based game by a popular band, followed by Pop Will Eat Itself's soundtrack for *Loaded* (Interplay, 1996).[14] More famous, however, was Nine Inch Nails frontman Trent Reznor's involvement with *Quake*'s music and sound effects in 1996 (id Software). Excluding the first track, the disc was even playable in a standard CD player. Inside the game, ammunition boxes were branded with the Nine Inch Nails logo, just in case fans missed the connection between the soundtrack and the best-selling artist. More recently, Reznor has been involved with a new alternate reality game, *Year Zero* (42 Entertainment, 2007). It is difficult to separate the game from the music—as both are part of one large viral multimedia marketing campaign. The game (which, unlike a video game, takes place in real time in the "real world" and the players must uncover clues in tour merchandise, websites, and so on) is tightly integrated with the concept album, whose songs are written from the game characters' perspectives. The *Los Angeles Times* suggests, "*Year Zero* is a total marriage of the pop and gamer aesthetics that unlocks the rusty cages of the music industry and solves some key problems facing rock music as its cultural dominance dissolves into dust" (Powers 2007).

Artists are also re-recording some songs for integration into games—for instance, singing hits in the imaginary "Simlish" language for the *Sims* games series, as noted earlier. It is also increasingly common for various "exclusive" tracks to be released in games, or at least, to have an exclusive release several weeks or months ahead of an album release. One of the first games to exploit this idea was the soundtrack to *Wipeout Pure* (SCEE, 2005). As Sergio Pimentel (2006b), the music licensing manager for the game, describes: "The final soundtrack was made of exclusively composed tracks for the game or unreleased tracks that were completed with a *Wipeout* mix of the track." Such exclusivity ensures that the "completist" collector fans of the musician will purchase the game, while fans of the game may go on to purchase music by that artist. This process is helping to create a form of mutual dependence between the music and games industries.[15] With this increase in star talent infused into the composition area of games, however, come bigger risks in terms of production costs, and some games developers are still slow to warm to the idea of larger audio budgets.

Soundtrack underscores composed by game composers are increasingly turning up in iTunes and in retail stores and are being marketed alongside games. *Halo 2* (Sumthing Else Music, 2004), scored by Martin O'Donnell and Michael Salvatori, for instance, had a separate selling soundtrack with remixes by popular artists (Incubus, Breaking Benjamin, and others) along with in-game tracks.

More popular than having well-known artists compose original music for games, licensing existing music or exclusive remixes has become a mainstay of the gaming industry today. In the early days of video games, most composers of the music were in fact programmers working on other aspects of the game (graphics, storyline, etc.). Games were typically written in assembly language, making it difficult for many musicians to become involved in songwriting. In some cases, songs would be written by a music composer and then translated by a programmer for the game, but in most cases budgets were tight and music was not viewed as an important aspect of the game (it was rare to even be credited for the composition). Since music then consisted of code, rather than sampled sounds, and there was therefore little understanding of copyright law in such cases, there was significant borrowing of music without copyright clearance. As composer Mark Cooksey explains, "At the time the copyright law was a bit of a grey area as far as computer music was concerned and we got away with doing cover versions" (in Carr 2002b). As such, many early video games used precomposed music, including classical and copyright-free traditional popular or folk songs, a few borrowings of popular artists, and in a small minority of cases, licensed music.

When the 16-bit machines became popular in the late 1980s and early 1990s, cover songs had largely disappeared from games music. By this time, "borrowing" popular songs also meant dealing with copyright and licensing issues, an idea that seemed to have been ignored in earlier games without consequence, but which would surely draw the attention of the music industry as improvements in technology continued, certainly with the rise of Redbook audio. A few examples exist of public domain use from this era—Beethoven's *Moonlight Sonata* as the title theme to *Adventures of Dr. Franken* (DTMC, 1993) on the Super Nintendo, for instance, as well as a few unlicensed but not public domain examples, such as Orff's *Carmina Burana* (*O Fortuna*) as title theme for *Dracula Unleashed* (Sega, 1993) on the Genesis. Although licensed music was rare on the 16-bit machines, there were a few exceptions, including *Rock 'n' Roll Racing* (Blizzard, 1994), which used George Thorogood's "Bad to the Bone," Deep Purple's "Highway Star," Steppenwolf's "Born to be Wild," and Black Sabbath's "Paranoid," in which a guitar sound takes on the part of the vocals. In most cases, vocal melodies were replaced by another instrument, and the original song construction had to be altered considerably to fit the constraints of the technology.

After the introduction of Redbook audio in the mid-1990s, it became far more popular to license precomposed music, even releasing the games soundtracks as separate CDs. One popular earlier example of this was *Wipeout XL* (Psygnosis, 1996), which featured many popular electronic acts, including the Chemical Brothers, Future Sound of London, Underworld, Fluke, Prodigy, and Daft Punk. The game was even cross-promoted by Sony, who delivered the soundtrack along with the game and PlayStations to popular dance club DJs in London and New York (see Kline, Dyer-Witherford, and de Peuter 2003, p. 234). Using games to sell soundtracks and music accelerated in the late 1990s and has continued ever since. The involvement of popular artists in game soundtracks has now become far too frequent to mention—in fact, it is almost at the point where it would be unusual for a hit game to be released by a major developer that does not have a popular artist involved in its soundtrack. Soundtracks to games sold separately as music CDs have also become increasingly popular, even reaching platinum status, such as *NBA Live 2003* (Electronic Arts, 2002).

Today, "music is an essential part of the gaming experience and gaming is an essential vehicle today for music discovery," notes David Dorn (in Berardini 2004), Senior Vice President of New Media Strategy for Rhino Records, who have partnered with Electronic Arts. Video games have become a valid outlet for breaking new bands, and for gaining exposure for bands who are looking for a wider market, just as Jeff Smith (1998, p. 1) notes of the film *Wayne's World* (Paramount, 1992) as reviving interest in Queen. Some have even suggested that games are "the new MTV," although such optimism may be better tempered by saying that games are "*a* new MTV," notes music industry scholar Holly Tessler (2008, p. 25). Electric Artists (not to be confused with Electronic Arts), a music marketing agency, published a white paper on the relationship of video games to music after surveying "hard-core gamers," releasing such impressive statistics as: "40% of hard-core gamers bought the CD after hearing a song they liked in a video game"; "73% of gamers said soundtracks within games help sell more CDs"; and "40% of respondents said a game introduced them to a new band or song, then 27% of them went out and bought what they heard" (Electric Artists n.d.).

Games have indeed helped to bring publicity to new artists, such as Good Charlotte, whose song "The Anthem" brought them attention after being included in *Madden NFL 2003* (EA Sports, 2002). Chicago's Fall Out Boy sold 70,000 copies of their album the week after the music was released, after appearing in *Tony Hawk's American Wasteland* (Neversoft 2005), without ever having received any radio airplay (Charne 2006). Ghanaian reggae artist Selasee likewise saw great success after Electronic Arts bought a single, "Run," for *FIFA 2006*. According to the artist's public relations manager, Louis Rodrigue, "His career is rocketing because of the FIFA game."[16] Those in the games industry even see the use of their games as a way to promote bands that they enjoy; as Marc Canham, director of Nimrod Productions describes:

> I really do not care much about furthering the career of big bands. They already have the privilege of steering their own destiny so long as they keep hard at it. My aim for *Driv3r* was to create a soundtrack that was a collection of new acts from around the world that I liked, plus a selection of original material that I wanted other people to like too.... We had managed to obtain several exclusives on the soundtrack, meaning that we had new or unreleased tracks from the bands involved such as Phantom Planet and Hope of the States which was amazing marketing fodder for the music press. (Canham 2004)

What is particularly notable about these games is that, in part, the game becomes about the music; the soundtrack is the key selling and marketing aspect of the game. *Driver: Parallel Lines* (Reflective, 2006), for instance, used popular artists in its advertising and on its soundtrack. On the opening page of the game's website, a picture of Professor Griff from Public Enemy is featured. Video clips feature the various bands talking about the music for viewers of the website (such as Grand Master Flash, Suicide, Yeah Yeah Yeahs, Audiobullys, Paul Oakenfold), reinforcing the idea that the music is a key part of this game's experience. Moreover, some games companies are becoming full multimedia conglomerates and are aligning themselves with particular social groups and taste cultures, which are themselves often developed around genres of music. Rockstar Games, for instance, sponsors various club nights and owns a line of skateboarder clothing (see Kline, Dyer-Witherford, and de Peuter 2003, p. 235).

THE IMPACT OF POPULAR MUSIC ON GAMES, AND OF GAMES ON POPULAR MUSIC

In addition to marketing and industry issues, the use of well-known music in games raises many questions in terms of music's production and consumption. There are, for instance, semiotic considerations that come into play when popular music is used in games. Music in games is heard in highly repetitive atmospheres: to point to another statistic noted by Electric Artists (n.d.), "92% [of players] remember the music from a game even after they've stopped playing it." It has yet to be determined how this repetitive aspect of gameplay affects the reception of the music. As well, the intertextual references in the music (or game) likely help to connect the game or music connotatively to specific types of films, books, or social groups. Indeed, certain types of games have become associated with specific genres of music—the *Madden NFL* football series (EA Sports), for instance, features mainly hard rock and hip-hop. Driving games require "driving music" and are more likely to include dance music. Sergio Pimentel (2006a), music supervisor for *Driver: Parallel Lines*, for instance, commented that he drove his car around listening to many types of music until he found the right "feel." Expectations are being set for fans of these games, which can sometimes be limited by the availability of the tracks, as Toby Schadt, the composer for *Downhill Jam* found:

> In further efforts to differentiate *Downhill Jam* From the Neversoft line of *Tony Hawk* games we created colourful, fictional characters for *Downhill Jam*. Whereas previous titles featured an intimidating cadre of real-world skating talent, *Downhill Jam* instead pushes the humor envelope with stylized personalities that sock it to Tony Hawk during interview segments.... To further differentiate the characters from each other, we created unique music playlists for each skater. Our gothic skater, Jynx, was to have all the songs you would expect from the '80s goth catalogue: Bauhaus, the Sisters of Mercy, and their ilk. Gunnar, the Norwegian muscle-bound import, has a taste for cheesy hip-hop that matches his in-game lingo. Budd, the

mellow hippie soul-searcher, loves reggae. Ammon, the revolutionary, was to have tracks from Rage Against the Machine and the Clash. In the end, we failed to get the music we requested from our licensing department. The music in the final version of the game is good, but it's just what you would expect from a Tony Hawk game, and we had hoped to do something more creative. (Schadt 2007, p. 37)

It is possible that such use of well-known songs or styles may be a deterrent to some players, and indeed may be a distraction for any player, distancing them from the attempted immersive aspects of the game. In a discussion of the use of precomposed music in film, Royal S. Brown (1994, p. 52) claims that the use of precomposed music can evoke Barthes's concept of the myth-sign, and that "the device of incorporating a song such as 'Dixie' or an anthem such as 'The Star Spangled Banner' into the fabric of ongoing music to accompany a film, as Breil did for *The Birth of a Nation*, is one of the strongest trump cards a film composer and/or arranger can play. For even the briefest recognizable snippet of such a piece . . . can evoke in the listener an entire political mythology."

Rick Altman (2001, pp. 24–26) expands on this idea, suggesting that the use of licensed music in film has a particular affect, and can serve a specific narratorial purpose through the establishment of mood: "Popular song depends on language, and is predictable, singable, rememberable, and physically involving in ways that 'classical' [orchestral] music usually is not." There are, therefore, significant semiotic implications of using precomposed music. Not only may the song alter the meaning of the game, but the game may alter the meaning of the song for the player.

The participatory nature of games, particularly in creative remixing and rhythm-action games, can also alter the reception of the music. For instance, in *SingStar*, a PlayStation 2 game published by Sony in 2004, players sing along with a selection of popular songs in a way rather similar to karaoke, although the game component comes in to play when the game scores the player based on the accuracy of their vocals compared with the original recording. A player may choose to have fun by not attempting a high score, by intentionally singing off-key or in an unusual way, potentially changing the meaning of the original song. Remixing tracks and fan compilations are becoming increasingly popular, with internet distribution and mini-stardom within remixing communities also altering the relationship to and the meaning of songs for players and listeners. In fact, the competitive aspects and the rhetoric of superstardom in the fantasy atmospheres of games are perhaps enough to change the meanings of the songs for the audience. Toru Mitsui has raised a similar question in regard to the "participatory consumption" of karaoke, which, he argues, "should be regarded as significantly different from older patterns of consumption" (cited in Théberge 1997, p. 252). It could also be argued, as Paul Théberge (1997, p. 253) indicates, that it is not merely issues of consumption that are at stake, but "the integrity of the musical work and claims of authorship and originality,'' since players become an active agent of change in the music. If players are remixing sequences (whether individual samples, audio chunks, layered *stems* or *splits*) of an artist's music, does the remix artist have the right to distribute or sell their remixes?

One of the most significant ramifications of choosing licensed music in games is that there is limited adaptability inherent in most popular music, whereas games require songs that may need to adapt to gameplay states or player interaction. Licensed songs are (for the most part) designed as linear music, and therefore the placement of this music in a game is generally limited (to cinematics such cut-scenes, title themes, credits, and so on), as is the genre of game where such music may be appropriate (such as racing games, which have a more linear playback).

Explains Keith D'Arcy (2004), the director of music resources for EMI Music Publishing: "If you're working with a specific record label on licensed audio for a game, you may be able to obtain splits of tracks for developing adaptive audio, but the actual process may prove quite difficult.'' Artists generally do not want to provide splits (individual sequences or samples of their songs), since this opens them up to the possibility of piracy and reduces their creative control over the ways in which their music is played back. The songs are likely not going to be heard in the ways in which the artist had originally intended, and must be significantly altered to fit the available technology and the nonlinear aspects of gaming: they may be looped, cut, or have elements like vocals removed. This raises further questions about notions of authorship in such cases. Who is the author, and what is the "authentic" mix? Moreover, when dynamic splits designed for in-game playback are released to CD, the playback devices are not designed to handle the capabilities of adaptability and interactivity. For example, there is no "randomizer" for music splits built into the hardware (yet): what, then is the "right" playback version, and who makes this decision? And what happens to the reception of music when the well-known and well-used structural forms based on verse–chorus variations disintegrate in the face of games, where structures may be altered significantly in real time by choices made by the player?

Perhaps most important, in light of the popularity of games and the recent integration of games with popular music, it is conceivable that artists may develop new approaches to songwriting, keeping in mind the required adaptability of a song for games: how might this affect the ways in which popular music is composed? Film music scholar Charlotte Greenspan (2004) has noted that popular songwriters like Irving Berlin adapted their songwriting style for use in Hollywood film by creating longer, more complex, and more sophisticated music. Certainly, there are other examples of popular songs being adapted to the playback media throughout history, such as the length of a record, and later the 45 RPM single, and then LPs. Might the song structure of popular music soon adjust to the needs of the gaming industry?

In terms of playback, it may be that we will see games where users can in-sert and tag their own playlists. Users can already insert their own music into many games—all games on the Microsoft Xbox360—but as yet they cannot spec-ify where they wish the songs to play back. Mood tagging, for instance, may allow players to choose what battle music they want to hear. Sound director Rob Bridgett of Radical Games in Vancouver has discussed the issue of user-generated playlists, concluding that a game soundtrack could in fact become totally user-defined and controlled, with separate playlists for combat, stealth, stunts, and so on:

> Further to this, one can imagine a situation whereby the content of a piece of music can be scanned and "beat mapped" by the console. It would be able to put the tracks into categories based on tempo, key or on "genre" fields for certain categories of gameplay. It could even transition seamlessly from track to track in much the same way the DJ software (such as Native Instruments' *Traktor DJ*) currently allows the user to overlay tracks of similar tempos. The sound implementers can be clever about how they set up the structures for any customizable content to fit into the game. They could automate the breaking up of any track. . . . Identifying intros, outros, high inten-sity looping sections, as well as calmer sections or sections from different songs in the same key, musically educate the console to transition in a "musical" way from a track in the same key to a related key. Programmatic stripping of audio data into useable chunks and re-appropriating of that data is ripe for exploitation in online consoles that allow for user defined musical content to be used in any game. The old notion that licensed music wasn't adaptive will become a long forgotten adage. (Bridgett 2005)

Could future popular artists even insert their own suggested emotional tags into their songs and provide transitional sequences? Bridgett also elaborates on the downside of such an approach to game sound, including the fact that the use of precomposed music in games has placed a new pressure on games companies to use big-name composers and exclusive content just to get players to listen to the intended music. Moreover, having user-defined playlists means that "the notion that a game is a complete cultural artifact, a *gesamtkunstwerk* (or 'totally inte-grated work of art'), in that its music, sound, performances, and visual style are all part of the experience" may be lost (ibid.). Unlike specially composed music, licensed music "remains a substitutable quantity: If the copyright holders want too much money, if the master recordings are lost, if there is an unavoidable de-lay in completing the track, game publishers will often either find an alternative song for the soundtrack, or simply do without it" (Tessler 2008, p. 22).

There are also economic consequences of the increasing crossover between licensed intellectual property and games. A reliance on a blockbuster model in the games industry has resulted in driving out independent developers and reducing creativity, since the purpose is no longer to create a great game, "but to generate a short-lived but omnipresent brand name whose contents can be exploited in as many venues as possible" (Geuens 2000, p. 7). Game developers are under increasing pressure to create a "mass market" product that can enjoy synergistic relationships with other media forms (Kline, Dyer-Witherford, and de Peuter 2003, p. 227). Moreover, the games must adapt to the demands of not just the market, but also the marketing. For instance, being associated with niche groups and subcultures may narrow a game's potential market, but it eases the pressures of deciding how to market the game. Moreover, "the incorporation of current musical styles potentially accelerates the speed at which a game's value is exhausted—if the music is outdated, the gamer gets bored—and this increases the turnover rate of game purchases" (Kline, Dyer-Witherford, and de Peuter 2003, p. 234). As Tessler (2008, p. 22) notes, the use of licensed music can place other constraints on a game's development: "Will a video game's market release be postponed if a given act is dropped from its label? If the band breaks up? If the album's release is pushed back by the label?" Indeed, working with licensed tracks may lead to legal quagmires whereby the game gets tied up waiting for the release of a song.

CONCLUSION

Although statistics appear to support the notion that games help to sell popular music, it remains to be seen if licensed music on games' soundtracks helps to drive those games' sales. Says composer Garry Schyman,

> Licensed music makes sense in games when it is appropriate. In sports games and racing games it's an obvious choice—it works and sounds right. In any game that needs source music, it would make sense to license the songs rather than have the composer write new ones. What I think is a big mistake is thinking that "kids" will buy a game because this or that band has contributed tracks to it. If a game is good they will come and if the songs actually are wrong creatively for the game then putting them in will make the game less appealing. Kids are smart and know intuitively when they are being condescended to. Songs do not entice people to buy a game and filmmakers have learned that lesson over and over again. When you look at the top 100 box office films over the last twenty years the list is nearly entirely populated with films with lush orchestral scores that droves of kids paid money to see. (Cited in Bridgett 2005)

Moreover, as Jeff Smith (1998, p. 196) discusses in regard to film, there are many competing interests at stake that may bring about conflict: soundtracks may be primarily promotional tools for games, whereas music publishers "derive their revenues from licensing fees and thus are more interested in pushing their back catalog than in promoting work by new artists." But the record companies, who realize most of their profits from album sales, are more interested in breaking new talent than promoting a game. As such, inappropriate song selection may be made in order to strike deals with the music publishers. Although game composers may have a wary view of the use of licensed music in games, it is clear that, as long as it brings consumers to purchase games or music and eases marketing costs, licensing will remain an important part of the industry. The majority of games still, however, use specially composed music, which is dealt with now in the final chapters of the book.

CHAPTER 7

GAMEPLAY, GENRE, AND THE FUNCTIONS OF GAME AUDIO

As shown in the first chapters of this book, game audio has been significantly affected by the nature of the technology (in terms of hardware, software, production, and distribution technology) and by the nature of the industry (in terms of design, production, distribution, and marketing). Audio in games is also, of course, affected by the nature of games themselves, in terms of genre, narrative, the participatory aspects of games, and the functions that audio must fulfill. As shown in the previous chapter, one of the ways to reduce the risks connected with the highly competitive nature of the games industry is through an association with star talent and licensed intellectual property.

As Martin Campbell-Kelly (2004, p. 45) notes in his history of the software industry, before becoming associated with movie tie-ins and celebrities, the first conscious risk-management strategy for the games industry was genre publishing. He argues that the point of genre publishing was that certain categories of games appealed to specific user-groups and therefore "had less need to overcome market inertia," noting that "From their earliest days, videogames had been classified as racin', fightin' or shootin'" (ibid., p. 281). Genre in games is particularly important in that it helps to set the audience's expectations by providing a framework for understanding the rules of gameplay, thereby not only appealing to specific target markets, but also reducing the learning curve of the game. Within the context of genre, many games function similarly in terms of their user interfaces, their button functions, and their rules of gameplay. These similarities were particularly important in the arcades, when players would walk away from a game before investing their money in a game that was too complicated to learn. Genres are also constrictive in many ways, however, and consumers may lament formulaic game designs. It has even been argued that it was such a formulaic approach to games construction that contributed to the brief collapse of the games industry in the mid-1980s (see Kline, Dyer-Witherford, and de Peuter 2003, pp. 104–108).

Some recent genre-defying games have seen remarkable sales, suggesting that genre is not central to the success of a game. *Electroplankton* (Nintendo, 2005), for instance, for Nintendo DS, in many ways is not even a "game" as traditionally defined. Nintendo president Satoru Iwata has described it as "a means for people to see sound" (in Totilo 2006). In the game, there are ten gameplay modes containing various types of plankton. Through making sounds by blowing into the DS microphone or by using the DS touch-screen stylus, the player makes the plankton move about and make musical sounds. In other words, by manipulating the plankton, the user can essentially make music, integrating notions of games with music production technology. Questions arise, then, as to whether or not such a program constitutes a "game" in the traditional sense. Similar questions have arisen out of recent virtual worlds like *Second Life* (Linden Lab, 2003): "It has no objectives, and the content is entirely user-created. But if *Second Life* isn't a game, what exactly is it?" asks one journalist (Kalning 2007). The success of such games suggests that users are open to new forms and new genres, although it is not yet apparent if their popularity relies strictly on their novelty, or if knock-offs will enjoy similar success.

As with the amorphous nature of popular music or film genres, there does not seem to be any real consensus on game genres; their boundaries shift with each new release. Stephen Poole (2000, p. 44) distinguishes between nine genres, while Mark J. P. Wolf (2002) describes some forty-two different genres (see also Kerr 2006, pp. 38–40). As my intent is to highlight the differences that genre may sometimes place on games in terms of the audio, I will focus on the most popular genres, as defined by the current industry categorizations outlined by the Entertainment Software Association (ESA).[1] The ESA now refers to what it calls "supergenres," presumably since there are too many games that cross over between smaller subgenres or defy genre definition altogether. They list these supergenres as fighting, role-playing, children and family entertainment, action, adventure, strategy, role-playing, shooter, racing, and sports. Game genres such as these are distinguished through several main characteristics, such as narrative, representational rules (the "realism" of games varies by genre, for instance), rules of gameplay, and types of interactivity or interface with the player. Each of these characteristics has a distinct impact on the ways in which audio functions in terms of its relationship to the player, and to the game's narrative or diegesis.

DEGREES OF PLAYER INTERACTIVITY IN DYNAMIC AUDIO

The notion of diegesis, borrowed from film and drama studies, is perhaps ill suited to games. Nevertheless, it provides a useful notion with which we can discuss the different degrees of interaction between player/viewer and the on-screen content, and highlight some of the distinctions between the linear qualities of film audio and the nonlinear qualities of games.[2]

Dynamic audio complicates the traditional diegetic–nondiegetic division of film sound. The unique relationship in games posed by the fact that the audience is engaging directly in the sound playback process on-screen (discussed further below) requires a new type of categorization of the sound–image relationship. Game sound can be categorized broadly as diegetic or nondiegetic,[3] but within these broad categories it can be separated further into nondynamic and dynamic sound, and then divided further still into the types of dynamic activity as they relate to the diegesis and to the player.

Apart from cinematics, which are fixed in a linear fashion, the degree of dynamic activity in a game is sometimes fluid, posing further difficulty in the classification of the sounds. For instance, in adventure game *The Legend of Zelda: Ocarina of Time's* Kokiri Forest, during the first portion of the game, we are continuously in daytime mode as we get trained in gameplay, and the Kokiri theme that plays throughout does not change, except at those points when a player enters a building or encounters an enemy. Though interactive, it is not adaptive at this point. After we complete our first major task and arrive at the next portion of the game (there are no distinct "levels" in this game), we then experience the passing of time, and can return to the forest. Now, if we return at night, the music has faded out to silence. At dawn, it will return to the main theme: the theme has now become adaptive. In other words, a cue that is interactive or adaptive at one point in the game does not necessarily remain so throughout the entire game. Similarly, in online RPG *Asheron's Call 2: The Fallen Kings* (Turbine Software, 2003), the nondiegetic music that plays in the background of scenes as underscore becomes diegetic when players decide to have their character play an instrument or sing along with the music. Not only has the music changed from nondynamic to interactive, but it has also gone from nondiegetic to diegetic. As such, then, although I have distinguished the levels of sound here, they must be viewed as fluid, rather than fixed, for many types of audio cues.

The most basic level of nondiegetic audio for games is the nondynamic linear sounds and music found most frequently in the introductory movies or cinematics. In these cases, the player has no control over the possibility of interrupting the music (short of resetting or turning off the game).[4] In the introduction to *The Legend of Zelda: Ocarina of Time* (hereafter just *Ocarina*), for instance, a short dream sequence movie is played, explaining the plot. If the player does not start the game (leading to further cinematics), the entire introduction sequence loops. At key points in the game, a preset cinematic loads, leading us to the next stage in the plot. In the LucasArts adventure game *Grim Fandango* (1998), the player's character Manny meets with Salvador, the revolutionary, in his underground hideout to conspire to expose the inequities of the corporation for which they work. When Manny gives Salvador the molded impression of his teeth (necessary for access to the building), a cinematic ends that stage of the game (El Marrow) and leads us to the next location (the Petrified Forest). The music during this intermission cinematic begins with the theme for the hideout, and then changes to that of the new location without the player's input: It is, in other words, linear, *nondynamic, nondiegetic music.*

Nondiegetic audio can also contain various levels of dynamic activity. *Adaptive nondiegetic* sounds are sound events occurring in reaction to gameplay, but which are unaffected by the player's direct movements, and are outside the diegesis. As discussed above, the music in *Ocarina* fades out at dusk and stops altogether during the night. At dawn, a quick "dawn theme" is played, followed by a return to the area's main theme music. The player cannot retrigger these events (except by waiting for another day to pass); the sounds are triggered by a timer set in the game engine. *Interactive* nondiegetic sounds, in contrast, are sound events occurring in reaction to gameplay, which can react to the player directly, but which are also outside of the diegesis. In *Ocarina*, the music changes in reaction to the player approaching an enemy. If the player backs off, the music returns to the original cue. If the player manages to find the trigger point in the game, it is possible to hear both cues at the same time in the midst of a cross-fade. The player, then, controls the event cue, and can repeatedly trigger the cue, by, in this case, running back and forth over the trigger area.

There are also diegetic sounds (*source music* or "real sounds") in games, which can be nondynamic, adaptive, or interactive. In *nondynamic diegetic audio*, the sound event occurs in the character's space, but the character has no direct participation with it. These sounds of course occur in cut-scenes, but they also take place in gameplay. For instance, in the underground hideout in *Grim Fandango*, Eva (a member of the resistance) is fiddling with a radio trying to tune in a particular station. Manny (the player's character) has no contact with the radio: Its sound is diegetic, but nondynamic. Diegetic sounds can also be adaptive and interactive. To return to the night–day division of time in *Ocarina*, at dawn we hear a rooster crow, and in the "day" sequences of Hyrule Field, we hear pleasant bird sounds. When the game's timer changes to nighttime, we hear a wolf howl, crickets chirp, and various crows cawing. These sounds are diegetic and adaptive. On the other hand, *interactive diegetic sounds* occur in the character's space, and the player's character can directly interact with them. The player instigates the audio cue, but does not necessarily affect the sound of the event once the cue is triggered. In *Grim Fandango*, there is a scene in the Calavera Café in which grease-monkey Glottis is playing a piano in the bar. If the player gives Glottis a VIP pass to the local racetracks, Glottis leaves the piano open. If the player then chooses, the main character Manny can sit down on the piano and play, triggering a preselected cue. More commonly, interactive diegetic sounds are sound effects, for instance, the sound Link's sword makes when cutting, or the sound of characters' footsteps.

Finally, a level of even more direct audio interaction is that of *kinetic gestural interaction* in both diegetic and nondiegetic sound, in which the *player* (as well as the character, typically) bodily participates with the sound on screen. At its simplest level, a joystick or controller could be argued to be kinetically interactive in the sense that a player can, for instance, play an ocarina by selecting notes through pushing buttons on a controller; but more significantly, here I refer to those times when a player may physically, gesturally mimic the action of a character, dancer, musician, etc. in order to trigger the sound event, most commonly seen in rhythm-action games. In other words, the player must physically play a drum in *Donkey Konga* (Namco, 2003), or play a guitar in *Guitar Hero* (Red Octane, 2005), for instance. These types of games have typically required the purchase of additional equipment to play (outside of the traditional joystick/controller that is included with the game's platform), although this has changed since the release of Nintendo's Wii controller in 2006, which has made kinetic gestural interaction with sound much more common. With the Wii controller, in the latest Zelda game, *The Legend of Zelda: The Twilight Princess* (Nintendo, 2006), the player must literally swing the controller to elicit a sword movement in the game, resulting in the sword swooshing sound.

THE FUNCTIONS OF GAME AUDIO

The varying degree with which the player can interact with the sound suggests that audio can serve a wide variety of functions. Depending on genre, platform, and on the player's familiarity with a game, some games can function without sound altogether, or with altered or substituted sound or music selected by the player. Games for portable players are often designed with the knowledge that these games tend to be played in the presence of other people and may require silence, as shown in the Nokia quote on page 78, which reminded programmers that "The game should be playable without the sounds" (Nokia 2005). More significantly, Microsoft has insisted that music in every Xbox360 game should be replaceable with the user's own music files (Harlin 2007, p. 53). In some ways, the reaction of the game audio community has been that in order to combat the implied "uselessness" or substitutability of games music by these requirements is to make the audio a more integral part of the games experience to ensure that the user does not switch off the sound.

Recent statistics suggest that game audio plays a significant role in consumer preference in product selection, and that audio is viewed as an important component of games (Bush et al. 2007). I have also shown some examples of games in which audio plays a specific role in the narrative or interface, such as stealth games and rhythm-action games. Indeed, it is quite evident that in many cases turning off audio would lead the player into peril. In the *New Super Mario Bros.* for the Nintendo DS (Nintendo, 2006), for example, enemies jump and fly in time to music, so listening to the sound signals to the player when to make his or her moves. Such use of audio indicates that game sound can be a significant element of gameplay in at least some cases, and that it can function in many ways (see also Jørgenson 2008).

Although game audio typically maintains all of the functions found in film or television sound (see Berg 1973; Chion 1994; Cohen 1999; Gorbman 1987; Kozloff 1988; Lissa 1965; Manvell and Huntley 1975; Smith 1998), there are also some distinct differences in the ways in which audio functions in games. There are some functions of film sound, for instance, that are not present to any significant degree in games (with the exception of cinematics). Consider for instance a chase scene in a horror film. There may be many close-up shots, pans, slow-motion shots of feet running, and so on—in other words, the editing of the cue may be quite slow when watched without sound. Here, the music and sound add the energy and pacing to make these edits flow together in a fast-moving sequence. In other words, the sound and music in film is often closely tied to the *edit*. That is, either the film is cut (edited) to the music, or the music is edited to fit the cut. With games, however, most action takes place in real time. Although scripted slow-motion shots do exist, image and music cannot synchronize as closely in games as they can in film, because of the unpredictable temporal aspects of games. Nevertheless, most other functions of film sound are similar to those found in games, and there are some cases where there are significant functions found in games that are not found in film sound.

External to the games themselves is the economic impact that gaming has on various industries (and vice versa), including those of film and popular music, discussed in the previous chapter. As shown, games are increasingly used as marketing tools and have become part of media franchises that may include film or television spin-offs. The interplay between audience and audio has other affects on the ways in which popular music is consumed. In the case of *Guitar Hero* or *SingStar*, there is a direct participatory and performance aspect to listening to the songs, as discussed in the previous chapter.

The direct participation between a player and the audio takes on a new role in rhythm-action or other kinetically based games. These games are designed to have players directly physically participate and respond to the sound. Of course, such games are enjoyable—as is evidenced by their popularity—but the music is also sometimes intended as part of the "edutainment" role of some of these games (training basic motor skills in toddlers, for instance), or designed for aiding in physical fitness, such as *EyeToy Kinetic* (Sony, 2005), which is clearly implicated in the marketing of these games. The sound in the case of kinetic games serves as a main motivating factor, arousing the player physically, and is also the part of the game on which the player must focus attention and to which the player must respond.

As discussed in chapter 6, aside from rhythm-action games, licensed popular songs are most often found in sports games or racing games. These games are so popular that Electronic Arts created the brand name EA Sports to produce sports games, beginning in 1993, and is now the leader in the genre. EA Sports maintains some exclusive licenses with sports associations (Nascar, NFL, NCAA). The games aspire to high realism, as the motto for EA Sports would suggest: "If it's in the game, it's in the game" (later abbreviated to just "It's in the game"). Racing games have also been very heavily reliant on popular songs, particularly dance and hip-hop games. *Need for Speed: Carbon* (EA Black Box, 2006), for instance, features Tiga, Goldfrapp, Lady Sovereign, and Roots Manuva, among others. To a certain degree, an interference or intertextual referencing between the games and the paramusical phenomena associated with these artists (videos, concerts, album covers, and so on) may occur, and indeed, may be intended in some cases (particularly connected are the urban, illicit aspects of certain games to hip-hop music, for instance). Genres such as racing games are much better suited to linear music than many other genres, since the player may be tied to a specific length of track or a particular length of time, and therefore, the timings are more predictable than in other genres. A racing track may last a minimum of three minutes, or a soccer half will last forty-five minutes, for instance, whereas a battle scene is far more temporally unpredictable. In addition, there is a well-established association of cars and motorcycles with popular music—particularly through hit films aimed at a younger audience, such as *Days of Thunder* (Paramount, 1990), *The Fast and the Furious* (Universal, 2001), or even older films such as *Easy Rider* (Columbia, 1969), which have set precedents for the use of popular songs in similarly themed games. Likewise, most popular sports teams have theme songs, and sporting games now are often multimedia "events." In fact, one popular song used by many NHL arenas, Zombie Nation's "Kernkraft 400," was based on a video game song (David Whittaker's music for *Lazy Jones* on the Commodore 64). The use of popular songs in sports-themed games seems fairly "natural," then, in that it is a re-creation of these events.

One of the difficulties with using linear music in games, as noted in the previous chapter, is that it usually lacks the ability to adapt to the on-screen action, and therefore often fails to fulfill many of the other functions of games music. A crucial role of music and sound effects in games is the preparatory function that the audio serves, for instance, to alert the player to an upcoming event, or to forewarn the player of approaching enemies. Anticipating action is a critical part of being successful in many games, particularly adventure and action games. Notably, *acousmatic* sound—sound with no clear origin visually—may inspire us to look to the direction of a sound, to "incite the look to go there and find out" (Chion 1994, pp. 71, 85). This function, though present in films (even if we cannot force the camera to go in that direction, we mentally look there, argues theorist Michel Chion), is far more pronounced in games, as sound gives the player cues to head in a particular direction or to run the other way, therefore affecting player decision making.[5] For instance, in *Ocarina*, a giant rolling boulder is heard and grows in volume as it approaches—giving the player fair warning of an impending danger. The player is aware of the sound and will listen out for the boulder when traversing that particular area in order to decide the appropriate time to move. Stealth games make particular use of this function, as the player is alerted to enemy presence. Although it is possible to play games with audio turned off, this can considerably lengthen the learning curve of a game, and can make gameplay frustrating. Author Aaron Marks (2002, p. 190) explains, "Without [the audio], the player doesn't have any foreshadowing and won't know to take out their weapon or to get out of the room until it is too late. While this can lead to a learning experience for a player, repeatedly dying and having to start a level over can be frustrating enough to stop playing the game" (see also Jørgensen 2008).

Particularly important to games is the use of sound symbols to help identify goals and focus the player's perception on certain objects. Music may focus one's attention, as when a "soundtrack featuring a lullaby might direct attention to a cradle rather than to a fishbowl when both objects are simultaneously depicted in a scene" (Cohen 2001, p. 258). However, sound effects, such as footsteps or gunshots, more commonly serve this purpose. Symbols and *leitmotifs* are often used to assist the player in identifying other characters, moods, environments, and objects, to help the game become more comprehensible and to decrease the learning curve for new players. In *Ocarina*, for instance, the lesser enemies all have the same or similar music, and beneficial items like gems or pieces of heart likewise all have the same or similar-sounding cues. The use of recurrent musical themes can also help to situate the player in the game matrix, in the sense that various locales or levels are usually given different themes. By listening to the music, the player is able to identify his or her whereabouts in the narrative and in the game. In *Ocarina*, musical themes play a key role, such as "Saria's Song," the theme taught to the main character by his friend, Saria. The recurrence of the theme in several places helps otherwise seemingly disparate scenes hold together and provides a degree of continuity across a game that takes weeks to finish, while reminding the player of previous scenes. It also serves to reinforce the theme in the player's mind, so that when he learns to play the theme on the ocarina, it sounds familiar, and when he must recall the theme at specific points in the game, it will be more easily recalled (Whalen 2004). Gerard Marino (2006) discussed his use of *leitmotif* in the game *God of War* (SCEA, 2005), as a way of matching the pace and emotion of the game:

> My initial task was to nail down the main theme of the game. I first focused on the main character, Kratos. The notes I had to go on were "the darkest, most brutal, most evil character ever," and I was given artwork and shown some gameplay. They wanted the music to reflect his soul-consuming quest for revenge on Ares, the Greek God of War, to help the player feel that Kratos will only be redeemed when he exacts his revenge. I rang up my Greek buddy Kostas and got him to translate some words and phrases for me, and settled on writing a theme that contained a rhythmic motive based on the Greek words "Ekthikisi" and "Litrosi" which translate to "Revenge" and "Redemption," so every time Kratos' theme plays his motivation is reinforced.... I initially multitrack recorded myself chanting/shouting/whispering the words 32 times to get a "choir-of-me" effect going at the opening and closing of the theme, which I later turned into an Intakt patch so I could drop the words/whispers into any piece I was writing and have it conform to the tempo in question, so this motive shows up often, especially in the cut scenes.

Music can also be used to enhance the overall structure of the game. This includes direct structural cues, such as links or bridges between two scenes, or which indicate the opening or ending of a particular part of gameplay. A drop to silence (the "boredom switch") can also tell the player that they should have completed that segment of the game, and that the game is waiting for the player to overcome a particular challenge or exit the area. A pause or break in music can indicate a change in narrative, or, continuous music across disparate scenes can help to signal the continuation of a particular theme (Cohen 1999, p. 41). For games like *Vib Ribbon* (SCEI, 1999), the music can literally *create* the structure of the gameplay. Released in Japan for the PlayStation, the game allows the user to input his or her own music CDs, which then influence the game's generation of level mapping. The game scans the user's CD and makes two obstacle courses for each song (one easy and one difficult), so that the game is as varied as the music the player chooses. Although this case is fairly unique, the potential certainly exists for using music to influence structures or to personalize games, as has been explored in audio games designed specifically for the visually impaired.

Equally important in reinforcing elements of gameplay is the dialogue, which can, for instance, disclose clues or assign goals (Kozloff 2000, p. 5). For example, there are often hints and goals given in the dialogue in *Grim Fandango*. When Eva tells us she needs our teeth, for instance, we have to go and find an object that will suffice before we can progress in the game. Listening to dialogue, then, becomes a key element in solving the game. Sound and dialogue can likewise reveal details about places or characters—whether they are a friend or a foe, for instance, either by their musical accompaniment or by the accent, language, or timbre of their voice, while voice-over narrations can let us access a character's thoughts and feelings (ibid.). In *Grim Fandango*, the stereotyped accents and dialects play a key role in quickly understanding characters. South American Salvador is the revolutionary; the men criticizing capitalism in the jazz bar speak with a beat poet lingo, while the corporate boss, Don Copal, has a generic American accent. Changes in voice or accent are also used to indicate other changes in gameplay: If the player chooses to have Manny take a drink of gold leaf liquor, his words slur for a while, providing a little added humor. Although much of the verbal interplay between player and game has traditionally been text based, with lines selected or typed in by the player, games are becoming more vocal, with players literally speaking to a game's characters.

Part of the role of dialogue—and audio in general—is the suspension of disbelief, adding realism and creating illusion. The illusion of being immersed in a three-dimensional atmosphere is greatly enhanced by the audio, particularly for newer games that may be developed in full surround sound, although even more simple stereo effects still have a considerable impact. In *Grim Fandango*, for example, the sound changes in the Calavera Café based on the character's location, and follows the character's proximity to the piano using stereo location and occlusion effects. In addition to spatial acoustics helping to create an environment, the music, dialogue, and sound effects help to represent and reinforce a sense of location in terms of cultural, physical, social, or historical environments. This function of game audio does not differ significantly from that of film; but it must be recalled that a game may take thirty to forty hours to complete even when the "correct sequence" of events are known, and audio plays a crucial role in helping the player to recall places and characters, and to situate him- or herself in such a massive setting, reducing confusion and frustration.

Another important immersive element Gorbman (1987) and Berg (1973) both discuss in relation to film is the historical function of covering the distracting noises of the projector in the era of silent movies. A similar function may be attributed to game sounds created for an arcade environment. Arcade games have tended to have less polyphony and more sound effects and percussion as part of the necessity of the environment, which meant that the games must be heard over the din to attract players. In consoles designed for home gameplay, music may mask the distractions of the computer fan, or other sounds made by the surrounding environment (Cohen 1999, p. 41). Although perhaps to a lesser extent than that of the arcade games, merely having a constant soundscape in a game can help the player to focus on the task at hand in a distracting environment. Argues Oliver Grau (2003, p. 348) in his discussion of cinematic use of immersive techniques, such attempts at immersion are "part of endeavors to extend or overcome the constraints of the film screen." Surround sound technology is one way that audio is employed to conceal or reduce the "actual illusion medium by keeping it beneath the perceptive threshold of the observer" (ibid., p. 340). Audio helps to overcome the two-dimensionality of the image, to help the player feel immersed in a three-dimensional space, particularly in 3D games, as discussed in chapter 4.

Adding to the immersive effects of gameplay is the communication of emotional meaning, which occurs in game audio in much the same way as in linear media. Here, a distinction must be made between communication of meaning through music, and *mood induction*: "Mood induction changes how one is feeling, while communication of meaning simply conveys information. One may receive information depicting sadness without him or herself feeling sad" (Rosar, cited in Cohen 2001, p. 42). Mood induction and physiological responses are typically experienced most obviously when the player's character is at significant risk of peril, as in the chaotic and fast boss music. In this way, sound works to control or manipulate the player's emotions, guiding responses to the game. Where games differ from linear media in terms of this relationship is that the player is actively involved in making decisions for his or her character: there are consequences for actions that the player takes. If the character dies, it is the player's "fault," as this is not necessarily a pre-scripted event out of the player's control. I would argue that this creates a different (and in some cases perhaps more immersive) relationship between the player and the character(s).[6]

IMMERSION AND THE CONSTRUCTION OF THE "REAL"

Immersion, "characterized by diminishing critical distance to what is shown and increasing emotional involvement in what is happening" (Grau 2003, p. 13), is a subject of much debate within the industry and within academia. Salen and Zimmerman (2003, p. 450) argue that the immersive quality of a game comes not from the game itself, but through play, referring to what they term the "immersive fallacy," which they define as "the idea that the pleasure of a media experience lies in its ability to sensually transport the participant into an illusory, simulated reality. According to the immersive fallacy, this reality is so complete that ideally the frame falls away so that the player truly believes that he or she is part of an imaginary world." On the other hand, writer Andrew Glassner (2004) goes so far as to describe various levels or degrees of immersion within a game.[7] He begins with curiosity, or the casual desire to know. The next stage is sympathy, in which the player starts to see the world through the eyes of the protagonist. Once the player sees through the protagonist's eyes, the player can identify with the protagonist: seeing elements of the character in him- or herself, and elements of him- or herself in the character. From there it is possible to reach a state of empathy, or emotional bonding with the character. Finally comes a state of transportation, where the player can temporarily lose the boundary between him- or herself and the character (Glassner 2004, pp. 81–82). Ermi and Mäyrä (2005, pp. 7–8) argue for a three-part division of immersion: the first dimension is sensory immersion, in which "large screens close to the player's face and powerful sounds easily over-power the sensory information coming from the real world, and the player be-comes entirely focused on the game world and its stimuli." The second form is challenge-based interaction, in which "one is able to achieve a satisfying balance of challenges and abilities." Third is imaginative immersion—what others dis-cussed have meant when referring to immersion—in which "the game offers the player a chance to use her imagination, empathise with the characters, or just enjoy the fantasy of the game." My focus here is on this imaginative immersive quality, which is strongly enhanced by audio.

The degrees of immersion experienced by a gamer are probably closest to what Oliver Grau (2003, p. 13) argues: "obviously, there is not a simple relation-ship of 'either–or' between critical distance and immersion; the relations are multifaceted, closely intertwined, dialectical, in part contradictory, and certainly highly dependent on the disposition of the observer." Moreover, immersion may be a quality that comes and goes, depending on the mindset of the player. Regard-less of whether or not immersion exists to any significant extent, it is a state to which most game developers aspire.[8] The construction of a believable, realistic space is a significant part of this drive toward immersion. John Belton describes the similar aspirations of realism in film: "The direction of technological change and the development of sound practice answer, in part, the demand of classical Hollywood cinema for a means of illusionistic production that remains, for the most part, invisible—that is, it will not disturb the willing suspension of disbelief that permits audiences to become absorbed in a film's narrative or diegetic world" (Belton 1999, p. 233).

Audio plays a significant role in the immersive quality of a game. Any kind of interruption in gameplay—from drops in frame rate playback or sluggish inter-face reactions—distracts the player and detracts from the immersion and from audio's playback—particularly interruptions in music such as hard cut transi-tions between cues (see Kline, Dyer-Witherford, and de Peuter 2004, p. 20). Many game audio devices are sold describing the more "realistic" experience the gamer will have upon purchasing these devices, such as the Nintendo DS headphones, Sound Blaster Live! soundcard, or Creative speakers, all of which promise to make games "come alive."[9]

Games are rarely set in realistic worlds, however, in the sense that they do not try to re-create present-day life on Earth. In many ways the realism aspired to in games is not a naturalistic realism in the sense of being a simulation of reality, but a *cinematic* realism that relies on established motion-picture convention. The "cine-real" is a sense of immersion and believability, or verisimilitude, within a fantasy world. It is the imagined real of the sound of explosions in space (which should technically be silent), or of the clarity of sounds underwater (which should technically be muddled). A realistic immersive space is developed with a "naturalness ... mediated by different understandings of perception" (Lastra 2000, p. 191). As James Lastra (2000, p. 207) discusses with regards to film sound, real sounds are not always the most appropriate sounds for film. Moreover, techniques of recording, as in film sound, have gravitated toward a specific aesthetic that is not necessarily the most "natural" sounding.[10] Sounds can be metaphoric and meaningful on levels other than just as an attempt to approximate reality, as sound designer Walter Murch (2000) argues: "This metaphoric use of sound is one of the most flexible and productive means of opening up a conceptual gap into which the fertile imagination of the audience will reflexively rush, eager (even if unconsciously so) to complete circles that are only suggested, to answer questions that are only half-posed." Sound is as much an aesthetic choice as it is a reproduction of the imagined space, Murch argues:

> This reassociation of image and sound is the fundamental pillar upon which the creative use of sound rests, and without which it would collapse. Sometimes it is done simply for convenience (walking on cornstarch, for instance, happens to record as a better footstep-in-snow than snow itself); or for necessity (the window that Gary Cooper broke in *High Noon* was made not of real glass but of crystallized sheeted sugar, the boulder that chased Indiana Jones was made not of real stone but of plastic foam); or for reasons of morality (crushing a watermelon is ethically preferable to crushing a human head). In each case, our multi-million-year reflex of thinking of sound as a submissive causal shadow now works in the filmmaker's favor, and the audience is disposed to accept, within certain limits, these new juxtapositions as the truth. (Ibid.)

In games, as in film, the sounds themselves are largely constructed and assembled. But in games, reality in sound design is never an "original" recorded production-space sound, and rarely a raw recording of a "real object," but usually a make-believe construction of sounds and synthesizer patches—a simulacrum of the real. For instance, if I need a monster roar for my game, I cannot use a production "monster" recording. I may take a gorilla's scream and a human recording of a yell, put them together, add some bass, add some overdrive, perhaps a little high-end scrape to sweeten it further. Even "realistic" recorded sounds such as gunshots are often treated with various effects to make them "more real than real." It is not just sound effects that are simulated in games: the music may also be an unreal construction of multilayered simulacra. Troels Folmann has described his approach to creating realistic orchestral sounds in his music for *Tomb Raider: Legend* (Eidos, 2006), in which all instruments began as high-quality samples (in this case, primarily by the East West company, who advertise the ability to "breathe life into the virtual world, creating a real space").[11] From there, Folmann added "random chaos"; the sound of the turning of pages of the orchestra, a quiet cough, the soft scrape of a chair, and the construction of a multitude of reverberation patterns to simulate the presence of a real orchestra. They may be too quietly placed in the mix for the conscious mind to detect, but, argues Folmann (2006), they help to trick our mind into believing we are hearing a real orchestra.

Sound director Rob Bridgett likens two growing aesthetic parallels with Hollywood and games in the mixing of IMAX and *ride films*, in which surround sound plays a vital role. The simulation ride film, or motion simulator, typically take place in custom-built rooms, and were developed in the mid-1980s but have continued to grow at an exponential rate. The main purpose of ride and IMAX films is a kind of sensory overload, an emotional assault, a complete immersion in the environment. Audio tends to be mixed very loudly and with a very physical effect due to significant use of subwoofers. In such films, audio is "magnified and physically experienced way beyond reality ... [they are] about entertainment, short, sharp and shocking. It is this where the subwoofer becomes the weapon of choice in the armory of the sound designer, to provide the necessary shock and awe for the audience, who generally are there to be 'wowed'" (Bridgett 2005). Sound effects are placed very high in the mix and are designed to make full use of at least six channels, particularly the subwoofer. In this sense, the immersion can come as much from the physical *effects* of sound, as from their *affects*. This use of sound is somewhat determined by genre, as action shooters place more emphasis on the use of the subwoofer than, for example, a role-playing game: "Shoot-em ups may play on either a tension and release narrative structure, one subtle build-up and other part all out kill-death frenzy, or they may opt for the full out continual derangement of a ride film, in which case prolonged immersion may become a problem for the player" (ibid.). Similarly, immersion may be more of a goal in a first-person point of view game than in a "god's view" (overhead) simulation game, for instance.

CONCLUSION

Audio in games functions in a wide variety of ways, and, as shown, removing audio from games (turning the sound effects off, substituting the music, and so on) can significantly affect gameplay. This aspect, however, is dependent to some extent on genre and platform. For instance, Galloway discusses the nature of arcade games in relation to home games as follows: "Arcade games are generally installed in public spaces and require payment to play: computer and console games, on the other hand, exist primarily in the home and are typically free to play once purchased. This material difference has tended to structure the narrative flow of games in two very different ways. Arcade games are often designed around the concept of lives, while console games are designed around health. . . . Arcade games are characterized by a more quantized set of penalties and limitations in play: one quarter equals a certain number of lives'' (Galloway 2006, p. 33). As such, the platform can set the length of games, which, as shown in the first three chapters, directly influences the length of music within a game. Mobile games need the ability to function without sound, as these are often carried into public spaces, whereas home games may need audio to distract from the environmental sounds in order to help immerse the player in the game.

Platform also directly affects genre. Arcade games today are nearly exclusively racing, first-person shooters, rhythm-action, or sports games. Such games are often predisposed toward more linear music, and therefore toward licensed music, and they also have very specific identifiable target markets who venture out to public spaces such as movie theaters where arcade games are commonly now housed.

Genre also affects the style and rules of gameplay. Many role-playing adventure or *Sims*-style games, as well as online games, have extended lifetimes, where players typically save and come back to the same game over several days, weeks, or even months. The use of sonic symbols is particularly necessary in these games to provide a sense of cohesiveness, and to help guide the player along in terms of the narrative and his or her location in the game matrix. For the composer, these lengthy games require much more variation in the soundtrack, since the player will be engaged with the sound for a much more significant amount of time—a difficult problem that can be overcome in a variety of ways, taken up in chapter 8.

COMPOSITIONAL APPROACHES TO DYNAMIC GAME MUSIC

Earlier, I defined dynamic audio as audio that is changeable, a broad concept that encompasses both interactive and adaptive audio. It is audio that reacts both to changes in the gameplay environment and/or in response to the player. It is worth briefly reiterating these definitions before we proceed into a discussion of what dynamic audio really means for *music* producers. Interactive audio I defined as those sound events that react to the player's direct input. As an example, the sound a character makes when pushing the "A" button on the controller to jump is an interactive sound. Adaptive audio, on the other hand, is sound that reacts to the game states, responding to various in-game parameters such as time-ins, time-outs, and so on. The example I used was from *Super Mario Bros.*, in which the music's tempo increases when the timer in the game begins to run out. Koji Kondo (2007), the composer of the *Super Mario* series, has described four components of dynamic music:

1. the ability to create music that changes with each play-through;

2. the ability to create a multicolored production by transforming themes in the same composition;

3. the ability to add new surprises and increase gameplay enjoyment; and

4. the ability to add musical elements as gameplay features.

Dynamic music is becoming more of a requirement for games as production values increase and players tire of the typical looping playback model of older games music. Looping is generally frowned upon as an ineffective way of using music in games, as composer Scott B. Morton (2005) writes in an article about enhancing the impact of game music in drama-oriented games: "Not only have you eliminated the emotional effectiveness of the music by generalizing it and not applying it to a context, but by looping it over and over, you've completely detached the player from even registering it altogether. And what's worse, it usually becomes annoying after a time. Now we've moved down from 'why should we even have music playing here' to 'why shouldn't we turn off the music altogether and listen to MP3s?' Let's be honest. Why even hire a composer in the first place if the music isn't going to play a functional part in the gaming experience?"

According to Koji Kondo (2007), dynamic music should showcase the participatory nature of a game, which might include changing the tempo, adding instrument layers, changing the position of music with character movements, or adding variability to the playback of phrases. Dynamic music, as shown in the previous chapter, has different levels in which it must react to or interact with both the narrative of the game and with the player. As a result, there are many difficulties that dynamic music attempts to deal with which are quite complicated, including the length of gameplay, listener fatigue, multiplayer interactivity, and the individual player's interactivity and participation with the game. In this final chapter, I explore these difficulties and how they influence the musical compositional decisions, before going on to detail some of the more complex solutions that have been explored that attempt to overcome the need for more variable, dynamic music.

The length of gameplay is a critical aspect that distinguishes games from linear media, and as such introduces new difficulties for composers. The nonlinear nature of games means that gameplay length is indeterminate: A player may get stuck and never complete a game, or may start and stop a game repeatedly over a period of days, weeks, or months. Compounding this indeterminacy is artificial intelligence software such as LucasArts' new Euphoria technology, in which what were previously preprogrammed game events are now ever more unscripted and randomized. "You'll never be able to predict exactly what will happen, no matter how many times you've experienced a certain scenario," they promise.[1] The composer, of course, cannot compose an infinite number of cues for a game with variable timings. Well aware that games have a reputation for repetitive, looping music—but trapped by the many hours of music required in a game—composers now commonly reuse cues in several areas within a game, to reduce the amount of unique cues needed, but at the same time without creating a repetitive sounding score. This requires careful compositional planning, and often a reduction in dramatic melody lines, so that the cue is less memorable.

Related to this temporal predicament is the concept of "listener fatigue": games are designed to be played multiple times, and repeated listening can be tiring, especially if a player spends a long time on one particularly difficult area of the game. Some games have begun to incorporate timings into the cues, so that if the player does get stuck on a level, the music will not loop endlessly, but will instead fade out. Composer Marty O'Donnell elaborates in his discussion of the *Halo: Combat Evolved* score (Bungie Software, 2001), "there is this 'bored now' switch, which is, 'If you haven't reached the part where you're supposed to go into the alternative piece, and five minutes have gone by, just have a nice fade-out'" (in Battino and Richards 2005, p. 195).

Multiplayer games pose another challenge to composers. Whereas parameter-based cues may work well for single-player games, if a game is designed to change cues when a player's health score reaches a certain critical level, what happens when there are two players, and one has full health while the other is critical (Selfon 2006)? Or, if a particular sonic trigger is supposed to occur at a specific point in the game, a decision must be made as to whether it occurs when both players have entered the target area, or when just one player has entered. At the same time, there are also some interesting musical opportunities opened up by multiplayer games, such as spontaneous "jam sessions" between characters/players, as in a game like *Asheron's Call 2: Fallen Kings* (Turbine, 2002), in which different species of characters play different types of instruments, and the interaction between players causes changes to the music (see Fay, Selfon, and Fay 2004, pp. 473–499). In this way, players are encouraged to interact with each other, and to play music together.

Multiplayer games are also significantly longer than their offline counterparts, and in some cases may be played regularly for several months or even years. There are typically considerably more locations than in a single-player game, and most critically, there is no control over in-game situations, since there is no scripting. Music cannot be tied to specific events or locations, since "an area that is supposed to be a hotbed of excitement might be completely swarmed with players who cleared out all the monsters, thus making it seem more like a safe haven than a battleground" (Booth 2004, p. 474). As Bjørn Ave Lagim (2002), one of the composers of *Anarchy Online* (Funcom, 2001), a science-fiction based MMO featuring a futuristic world, recalls, "Initially, the composers ... thought that writing music for this game was going to be like our previous game, *The Longest Journey* ... a single player adventure game, and fairly linear in form, and with pre-defined situations and animated sequences.... We soon realized that we were going to have a different approach to the music in [*Anarchy Online*]."[2]

Despite the difficulties in composing music for online games, there are various approaches that can accommodate some of these problems. As Lagim (2002) describes, one approach to the problem of listener fatigue was to have music fade out and back in at regular intervals, so that the music would not get too repetitive or predictable: "Finding a good balance between how long the music would play and how long it would stay silent was the key. Short pauses would make the music annoying and too long pauses would make the music ineffective in maintaining the feel." Fading in slowly was important, since an abrupt jump into music would likely signal that "something is about to happen" to the player.

NONLINEARITY IN GAMES

The most significant problem facing game composers is the nonlinear basis of games in general. Put simply, games are largely unpredictable in terms of the directions the player may take, and the timings involved. Many game narratives progress in a "branching" manner, similar in shape to the branches of a tree, in which there are many possible paths and endings (see figure 8.1).

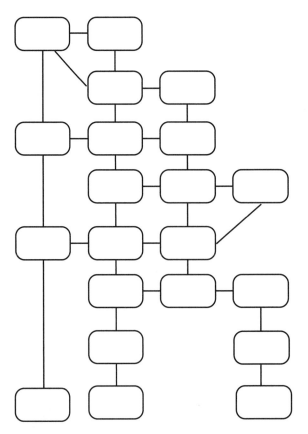

FIGURE 8.1
Branching tree approach to narrative structure.

Branching narratives, which were popular in *Choose Your Own Adventure*–style children's books of the 1980s, provide some story and then ask the reader to make a decision, typically presented in terms of a multiple choice dialogue. Nintendo released a series of similarly styled books in the 1980s in which decisions were similarly left up to the reader:

> "I'm coming, Princess!" shouts Mario. He runs down the hallway and starts to unlock the supply room door. At that moment, the alarm goes off again, louder than ever.
>
> Should Mario look for supplies? Maybe he should find Luigi first. Or maybe he should just head to the Mushroom Kingdom immediately. He'd better decide—quickly!
>
> If you think Mario should search for Luigi, turn to page 100.
>
> If you think Mario should get supplies, turn to page 34.
>
> If you think Mario should head straight to the Mushroom Kingdom, turn to 68. (Bosco 1991, p. 5)

That one scenario allows for three different branches: going to the supply room, searching for Luigi, or heading to Mushroom Kingdom (figure 8.2).

Providing the user with such choices in a game is critical to gameplay, but it also creates incredible complications for narrative. As Andrew Glassner (2004, p. 244) explains, if there are only "ten branching points over the course of the story, and three choices at each branch, that means the author must write a few more than 59000 stories." One solution is to create a "bulging tree" model (figure 8.3), in which branches return to the central core idea, and there is only one ultimate solution.

Needless to say, the impact of the overall branching narrative structure on audio planning is significant. Such structures "limit the author's control over rhythm and pace, repetition, theme and variation, and even causality" (Glassner 2004, p. 244), making emotion maps such as those suggested in chapter 5 difficult, if not impossible. Critically for planning music, "most branching narratives quite reasonably ask the audience to make decisions at points in the story where those choices matter ... an audience's choices are solicited at moments where

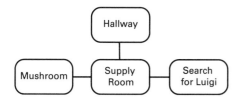

FIGURE 8.2
Branching tree structure in passage from Nintendo book.

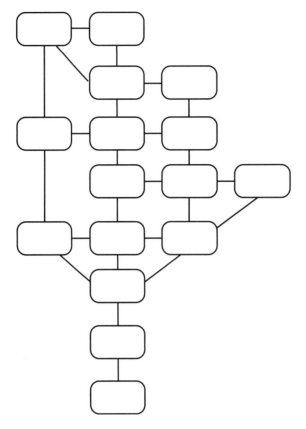

FIGURE 8.3
Bulging tree approach to narrative structure (see Glassner 2004, p. 244).

they make a difference" (ibid., p. 241), which is to say, these transitional points generally occur at times of tension or stress in the narrative, when audio is particularly crucial. Planning to respond emotionally to the visuals or narrative in terms of audio at these junctures, then, is incredibly difficult, and yet incredibly important.

When dealing with musical composition, there are even further breakdowns in the branching structure described. The music may be required to change at many more junctures than the narrative: music must be able to respond to the player's or nonplaying character's actions, and/or to in-game parameters (health, timings, and so on), as well as location-based parameters. Consider, for instance, a three-dimensional room, say, in an industrial warehouse (figure 8.4). From this room (A), the player may have several options in terms of direction, each of which may require a new musical cue: forward to multiple enemy gunfire (B),

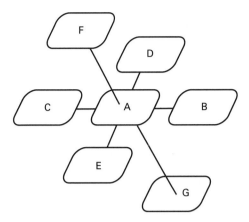

FIGURE 8.4
From one room, A, a player may take at least six direction choices affecting the musical transitions.

back to a blazing fire (C), up to the roof (F), down a trapdoor to the underground (G), left to single enemy gunfire (D), or right to the communications room (E). This single location-based music cue, "room A," must now be able to branch to at least six other cues. Not only this, however, but this must be able to occur *at any point in time*. The player may wait in room A for two minutes or for ten seconds. He or she may even run forward to the enemy gunfire and quickly run back, restarting the original room cue. And this only accounts for location-based cues: other parameters influencing cues may still come into play.

Taking into account the multitude of directions or branches in which a player may progress, the composer must try to create music that can quickly adapt to the decisions made by the player as well as accommodate other dynamic in-game parameters. Although scoring cues for specific gameplay events or even locations may be reasonably straightforward, predicting how these cues may have to connect with other cues at any point in time can be very difficult. Moving smoothly from one music cue to another assists in the continuity of a game and the illusions of gameplay, since a disjointed score generally leads to a disjointed playing experience, and the game may lose some of its immersive quality. Prendergast (1977, p. 11) notes of film transitions, "If not properly handled, transitions can be *very* interruptive in nature, however. It was a difficult and sometimes impossible task to achieve any kind of smoothness between stylistically different pieces." In silent film music, this issue was dealt with somewhat by writing music in short segments that could repeat, with variations, or quickly transition to a cadence (Altman 2004, pp. 261–263).[3]

Transitions in games are in some ways more complicated than those of early film—particularly since, in many cases, film was often accompanied by just a single piano, and the best-selling games are now often fully orchestrated. Paul Hoffert (2007, p. 33) discusses seven elements that must be taken into consideration in composing a transition: volume, tempo, rhythm, key, harmony, texture, and style. Not only this, but since the music may have to transition at any point in time, a potentially infinite number of cues may be needed. There have been a variety of approaches to this problem—some successful, others not so successful—though most scores use several different transition types.

Early games tended toward direct hard cutting between cues, though this can feel very jarring for the player. This was especially common in 8- and 16-bit games. The most common transition today is to fade out quickly, and then begin the new cue, or to cross-fade the two cues, which is to say, fade one out as the other cue fades in. Nevertheless, the transition can still feel abrupt, depending on the cues or the speed of the cross-fade. *The Legend of Zelda: Ocarina of Time* makes frequent use of this type of segue: In places where Link enters a building, the Kokiri theme music fades out completely, and then the "house" or "shop" music cue will begin. However, when Link encounters a threatening enemy, a more subtle cross-fade will occur, and it is possible to situate the character halfway between both cues at the trigger point, in order to hear both cues simultaneously. To further assist in the smoothness of the cross-fades, the *Zelda* cues drop elements as the cue fades in or out. Another common type of transition is to use a quick stinger, also known as a stab (a quick *sforzando* shock chord). Particularly as one of the most abrupt transitions is to that of violent combat, the stinger—combined with the sound effects of violence (gunfire, sword clashes, and so on)—will help to obscure any disjointed musical effects that may occur. A stinger transition is used, for instance, on the roof in *Grim Fandango* when Manny scares away the last of the pigeons. We hear a squawking trumpet blast and then the music cue changes.

Despite the multitude of difficulties inherent in dynamic music, some composers, sound designers, and programmers have been very inventive in creating solutions to some of these problems. We have already seen some approaches discussed, but it is worth going into considerable detail into the techniques involved in creating musical variability and approaching the problem of branching structures. Some of these techniques have not yet been used to any significant degree, but it is worth including them as potential avenues of future exploration. First, it must be noted that many of these techniques depend to some extent on MIDI. Although premixed Redbook music (wave or compressed MP3) files offer higher production values than MIDI, they are not as adaptable to dynamic techniques. At the same time there is also an increasing trend toward more orchestration in order to create a "cinematic" sound, requiring large music budgets. Although orchestras could technically create a dynamic score by recording in small "chunks" of sound, the re-records necessary for a dynamic score make the large-scale use of orchestras less feasible for most games companies. Although it is possible to use small chunks or "wavelets" (see, e.g., *Tron 2.0* [Monolith, 2003] or *No One Lives Forever 2* [Monolith, 2002]), the potential for adaptability is far more inherent in the MIDI format, and there are some functions of MIDI that are not possible with wave files (such as varying the tempo without affecting the pitch). As MIDI expands capabilities with advanced downloadable sounds (essentially "wavelets" themselves), MIDI may return as a force to be reckoned with in game music. Although this generation of games systems will surely see the end of *chip-set* MIDI (based on the synthesis chip provided with the console), there are many signs that MIDI using soundbanks will make a comeback in the world of games, in part owing to the very problem discussed above. At the Game Developer's Conference in 2007, Sony representatives Jason Page and Michael Kelly claimed MIDI was the wave of the future for games (Huang 2007). Now that wavetable samples have reached a high fidelity, MIDI has the advantage over standard Redbook music in its adaptability and smaller size (resulting in faster loading).

TEN APPROACHES TO VARIABILITY IN GAME MUSIC

There are various approaches to musical variation, which ensure that a composition gets a longer "shelf life" and can be more responsive to the player and to the narrative/image. A composer could compose hundreds of variations to the cues, or he or she could introduce some variability by using the same music with, for instance, any of the ten following potential approaches:

1. Variable tempo

2. Variable pitch

3. Variable rhythm/meter

4. Variable volume/dynamics

5. Variable DSP/timbres

6. Variable melodies (algorithmic generation)

7. Variable harmony (chordal arrangements, key or mode)

8. Variable mixing

9. Variable form (open form)

10. Variable form (branching parameter-based music)

It is worth discussing each of these in some detail, as these are developments that distinguish games from linear media composition. The functionality for many of these ideas is already built into some middleware software solutions such as DirectX and *Wwise*, and will likely play an increasing role in sequencing software in the future.

1   VARIABLE TEMPO

Tempo adjustments are fairly common in games, going back to some of the very earliest examples from the late 1970s, such as *Space Invaders* or *Asteroids*, both of which had sounds that sped up as the game progressed. Generally, this concept has been used in relation to temporal issues in gameplay: time is running out on the player to complete the level in *Super Mario Bros.*, for instance, or the tempo is set to increase as the levels in *Tetris* increase. But the tempo of a piece could also adjust in real time to respond to a number of other parameters, for instance, the number of laps on a racetrack, the number of enemies left alive, or the number of units of health the player has remaining. One danger the composer risks, of course, is that if the tempo is too closely synchronized to an action—say, how quickly the player is running—the music may "mickey mouse" the image, so named because it is a common trope in cartoons, which results in a more comical flavor. This was seen, for instance, in the *RoadRunner* game discussed in chapter 3.

2   VARIABLE PITCH

There were several examples of simple variations of pitch discussed in chapters 1 through 3. For example, at its most basic level, the transposition of entire sequences was one way of coping with memory constraints on earlier machines. By transposing a sequence (such as in *Rally X* or *Sonic the Hedgehog*), it was possible to reduce the amount of space required to store the data. A simple transposition cue could be included in the code, along with a reference to the same section of data that held the original musical sequence. Transposition or variable pitch is also a common response to storage difficulties of sample files on older devices and mobile phones. By using a single sample and transposing it up or down, a sample can be used in several places without sounding repetitive. It is also common in mobile phone games to use what Peter Drescher calls the "pitch it up, play it down" technique. A high-resolution original sample can be transposed up an octave, halving the length (and therefore file size). It can be converted to a low-resolution compressed format, and then replayed in the game at an octave lower. Drescher (2006) notes, "Although the game sound might be a little crunchy, you've just cut the size of your file in half without losing too much audio fidelity." These techniques are common in mobile phone games, but are no longer necessary in console games. Another recent interesting approach to variable pitch is found in the *Legend of Zelda: Twilight Princess* on the Nintendo Wii, for instance, in the final battle scene. As Link fights the final boss, with each successful strike of his sword, the musical phrasing rises in pitch. Such use suggests that variable pitch (as with variable tempo) can be used for its affective value, with the increase in pitch matching the increase in tension.

3   VARIABLE RHYTHM/METER

One method of varying early film sound was (along with modulations, transposition, and so on) to adjust the rhythm of leitmotifs or themes. Altman (2004, pp. 373–374) notes: "Rhythmic changes may be used for anxious anticipation, in a major key for pleasant anticipation, or in a minor key for apprehension or fear.... In order to express a lighter or airier mood, the theme may be rewritten with three beats to a measure. Conversely, a theme originally presented in three-four time ... can be given 'weight' by stretching the measure to 4/4. Still greater emotional intensity may be suggested by the use of a nine-eight meter." Similar adjustments could quite easily be made to MIDI scores for games, although I could not find any examples of this possibility.

4   VARIABLE VOLUME/DYNAMICS

Simple variations in volume are quite common in games, notably in "menu screens," where the volume drops down while the player makes selections on the screen, before returning to full volume in gameplay. Cutting the volume altogether (the "bored button" discussed previously) is also an option when the player has spent a long time on a level. When the player makes a breakthrough, the music's volume can ramp back up. Other parameters such as tension or enemy lifespan can also be tied to volume, increasing its affective qualities. In calm periods, sounds could be played *pianissimo*, but as tension increases, they could increase in volume, for instance.

5   VARIABLE DSP

In chapter 4 I discussed the use of real-time DSP and mixing, which is most commonly used on sound effects and ambience. These methods can also be used on a musical track. DSP effects can, for instance, change the mood or feel of a piece. Adding overdrive to the drums in a first-person shooter, for instance, can make a song suddenly feel more aggressive. Adding delay after the player has been popped on the head in a boxing game could create a dazed effect, while reverb can be used to create a softer, dreamier feeling. In terms of simply assisting transitions, as composer Guy Whitmore (2003) describes, "Even if run-time effects are not used adaptively, they can help blur the seams between musical cues." DSP offers significant opportunities to expand the "life span" of a segment of music.

6   VARIABLE MELODY

Algorithmic generation—using the computer itself to improvise musically—is still very much in its infancy, but as we have seen, algorithms have been used in games to determine a variety of sonic choices. Notably, LucasArts' *Ballblazer* employed what composer Peter Langston termed the "riffology" algorithm, in which "dynamically weighted" choices for parameters are decided by the computer,

> such as which riff from a repertoire of 32 eight-note melody fragments to play next, how fast to play it, how loud to play it, when to omit or elide notes, when to insert a rhythmic break, and other such choices. To choose the next riff to play, the program selects a few possibilities randomly (the ones that "come to mind" in the model). From these it selects the riff that is "easiest" to play, i.e. the riff whose starting note is closest to one scale step away from the previous riff's ending note. To decide whether to skip a note in a riff (by replacing it with a rest or lengthening the previous note's duration) a dynamic probability is generated. That probability starts at a low value, rises to a peak near the middle of the solo, and drops back to a low value at the end. The effect is that solos start with a blur of notes, get a little lazy toward the middle and then pick up energy again for the ending. The solo is accompanied by a bass line, rhythm pattern, and chords which vary less randomly but with similar choices. The result is an infinite, non-repeating improvisation over a non-repeating, but soon familiar, accompaniment. (Langston 1986)

One of the beginnings of the results of Langston's approach, "Song of the Grid," is presented as figure 8.5. Langston (1986) claims that although the song passes the "is it music test," it fails to pass the "is it interesting music" test, "because the rhythmic structure and the large scale melodic structure are boring. It appears that for music to remain *interesting* it must have appropriate structure on many levels." As algorithms get more realistically similar to human-generated composition, it may be possible to tie generated music to mood cues tagged to certain in-game events. The entire clip does not have to be algorithmically gener-

FIGURE 8.5
Algorithmically generated song in *Ballblazer* (LucasArts, 1984) (Langston 1986).

ated, but rather, algorithms could control various instruments or sections of the piece. For instance, there could be a drum and bass rhythm that is improvised upon (the riffology method), a change in drum pattern that is randomly developed as time progresses, or a basic melody that is harmonically orchestrated by the computer based on key mood tagging (Langston 1989).

Similarly, granular synthesis also offers some hope for new variability ideas, in which tiny "grains" of samples could be combined (or recombined) algorithmically to create a sound (see box 1.1). In this sense, an intelligent engine could use grains of sound to adapt algorithmically in real time to what is occurring in the gameplay. For example, a segment of play where the player is in stealth mode, sneaking through a tunnel, could use grains of sound altered in pitch to adjust the ambience slowly to the depth of the tunnel. Granular synthesis also offers interesting possibilities for sound effects, in which reconfigurations of sounds could mean that the player never has to hear exactly the same footsteps, gunshots, and so on more than once in an entire game.

7   VARIABLE HARMONIC CONTENT (KEYS AND CHORDS)

It is possible to change the mood of a piece considerably by altering harmonic or chordal characteristics in real time. Changing the key, or changing chords from major to minor, and so on can all have a significant impact on the mood or feel of the music. Such a technique has been used in a few cases, as in *Asheron's Call 2*, as Jason Booth (2004, p. 480) reveals: "We wanted to keep things relatively simple and ambient and avoid ear-catching resolutions and stabs. We also knew there would potentially be a very large number of melodic parts playing over a given background score and that those melodies would be the primary force adding tension and resolution to the composition."

Keeping a lack of harmonic resolution in the game is one way of making the music more adaptable, as Booth describes (2004 p. 480): their solution was "Similar to the concept used in Indian music, [in which] we stated the given scale as a raga (the tonic droned and then played upon for an entire afternoon), creating a meditative space without the repetition and destination of a cycling chord progression." Changes in mode would indicate changes in gameplay; various modes were used for their affective responses and gave the player a sense of awareness of their predicament at that point in time: "A player standing alone in an area would hear the background score in the Lydian mode, but as creatures fill the area, the music transitioned to Phrygian, giving a darker tonality. If monsters continue to outnumber the player, the music might transition to a diminished mode while a quickening drum groove begins to pulse" (ibid.).

Variable harmony may also involve different chordal arrangements. Microsoft's DirectX allows for variations of chords, for example, which can adapt depending on parameters set by the programmer. As Scott Selfon (2004, pp. 52–53) describes in a book on DirectX: "you might have a melodic line in a variation that sounds great played over a IV chord (e.g., an F major chord in the key of C), but you have another variation that provides a stronger option to play on a ii chord (e.g., a D minor chord in the key of C). By selecting and unselecting the various buttons in the Variation Choices window, you can add these kinds of very specific restrictions. An unselected button means that given a matching set of chord conditions, this variation will not be chosen.''

8   VARIABLE MIX

Changes in instrumentation or orchestration can also offer interesting solutions to dynamic music. This has been explored by composers, but not yet exploited to its full capabilities. By adjusting various elements in a mix—bringing up the percussion, for instance, to add tension—a preexisting cue can be altered quite rapidly and cleanly. It would be possible, for instance, to have a piece in which the "sad" saxophone is quite low in the mix until the player's character encounters the "sad" event whereupon it suddenly becomes more apparent. It is possible to hide elements in the mix (mute them completely), and just bring them into the mix at important times, in layers. The music is composed in instrument layers with the understanding that at any time various instruments may be dropped from the mix and others may be added. This works well with some transitions, but it can be difficult to move quickly from cue to cue in a dramatic change.

As was shown in chapter 3, instrument layers were included as part of the iMUSE patent, originally intended for MIDI, although layers function in Lucas-Arts' *Grim Fandango* game using pre-recorded sequences of wave files. In one example, Manny stands on the docks and the underscore plays the "Limbo" cue. If the player has Manny look at the moon, he will recite a poem, and high sustained strings are added to the original cue. Another basic example was used by Koji Kondo in *Super Mario World* (Nintendo, 1990) for the Super Nintendo, in which percussion is added whenever the player's character, Mario, rides Yoshi. This was elaborated upon in *Mario 64* (Nintendo, 1996), where changes in location result in changes in instrumentation. The music piece stays the same, but the arrangement changes: an electric piano is used while the character is on shore, strings are added in an underwater cavern, and bass and drums kick in at various places.

Layering can also get more complex, based on gameplay parameters such as the number of players in an online MMO. In *Asheron's Call 2*, characters are given different motifs or instruments that add a layer to the music. Tumeroks, for instance, a kind of tribal culture, play drums, and other races play different instruments, such as lutes. The location in the game determines the ambient score, and sets the tempo, the key signature, and the music in a "master segment" (see Booth 2005, p. 478). Each character in a scene adds a musical element to the score, localized in 3D. "Much like a subtler version of Sergey Prokofiev's 'Peter and the Wolf,' each of these parts can have many variations" (ibid.). Each character also adds or subtracts from the intensity level of the music. An aggressive monster, for instance, increases the intensity by, for instance, a level of two, with an overall default level of thirty: "This allows us to define a relative intensity for the music based on the rough state of the area. If the area contains mostly avatars, it is unlikely that anyone is in any danger, and the music becomes calmer. Conversely, if the area has a reasonable number of monsters in it, the groove level will rise, and the music will become more intense" (ibid.).

This technique is also used very effectively in the simple puzzle game *Russian Squares* (Microsoft, 2002), in which the goal is to clear rows of blocks by matching colors. As each row is cleared, the music responds by adding or subtracting various layers of instrument sounds. The composer, Guy Whitmore, described his approach as follows: "*Russian Squares* uses instrument level variation to keep the individual cells from getting monotonous. Each music cell is anywhere from two to eight measures in length, and repeats as the player works on a given row ... When combined with other instruments, these variations increase the amount of variation logarithmically. Most often, one to three instruments per cell use variation, and that gives the music an organic spontaneous feel, and prevents that all too familiar loopy feeling. Too much variation, however, can unglue the music's cohesion" (Fay, Selfon, and Fay 2004, p. 373).[4]

I have transcribed ten cues (what Whitmore refers to as cells) to show how the layering approach functions in *Russian Squares* (see figure 8.6).[5] Each block represents one bar of music. The dotted lines indicate a change to a new cue sequence, which occurs with every row of blocks eliminated in the game. Cues have up to six instrument layers occurring at any time, although which layers occur in any cue is not necessarily relative to the one that comes before or after: the only constant is the steady synthesized electric bass line (instrument layer 1), though one percussion pattern is fairly consistent throughout (instrument layer 2). I have not included the addition of sound effects in the game, which occur with row clearances, time warnings, and unmoveable blocks.

Describes Whitmore (2004, p. 375):

Russian Squares uses an additive-subtractive approach to the music, in which the music engine can add or peel away instrument layers. Given that the time it takes to clear a row can be anywhere from a few seconds to a few minutes, this is a very practical solution. It allows for musical development while maintaining direction and momentum. Implementing this technique has some complications, however. In terms of aesthetics, simply moving along a linear curve from low intensity to high intensity does not work, as adding layer after layer and increasing the tempo is not very musical. The music requires larger sections, instrumentation changes, rhythmic shifts, and tonal changes to stay interesting. In this way, the music progresses in a multidimensional manner.

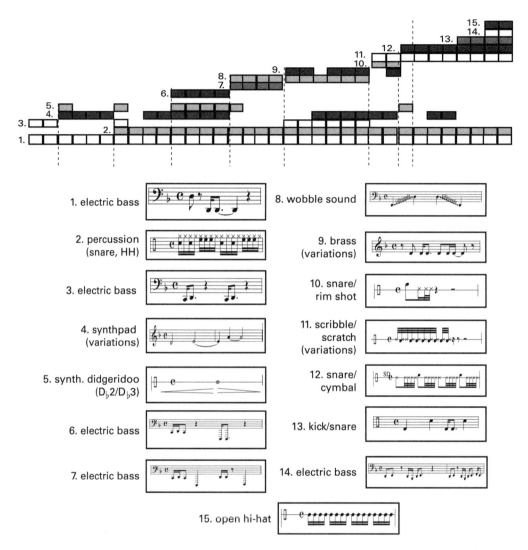

FIGURE 8.6
Russian Squares (Guy Whitmore, Microsoft, 2004), "Gravity Ride" ten cues (two minutes of gameplay).

Such an approach to song construction is already somewhat present in some types of popular music (such as trance, for instance), and could easily be adapted to the needs of games.[6]

9   VARIABLE (OPEN) FORM

Many approaches in music history that have tackled random sequencing of musical segments or sequences are worth exploring as possibilities for game music, including musical dice games and aleatoric music. There are several types of variable sequencing, or "open form"[7] within music. The openness of the structure can vary at any level, including the larger segments of the song, sequences or phrases within sections, or even smaller units within phrases. The idea goes back to at least the eighteenth century, when there was a fashion for musical dice games in Europe. The games were constructed for those who were new to musical composition, so that by selecting the order of sequences, they could create their own minuet, march, polonaise, waltz, and so on.

The first known musical dice game was that of Johann Philip Kirnberger (1721–83), *Der allezeit fertige Polonoisen- und Menuetten componist* (Berlin, 1757). The "Minuet Composer," as it was known in English, allowed for the composition of either a polonaise (through the rearrangement of one six-bar sequence and one eight-bar sequence), or a minuet and trio (both eight bars). There were two tables of numbers provided: one for the polonaises, one for the minuets. Then, twenty-nine pages of music were to be cut and placed onto a deck of cards, with one bar of music (consisting of one soprano line and one bass line for the polonaise and minuet, or two soprano lines and one bass for the trio). The "composer" then threw two dice, consulting the table to determine which card to use next. Notes Stephen Hedges (1978, p. 181), "Obviously, Kirnberger had written a polonaise and a minuet and trio, composed ten variants, segmented the pieces into individual bars and camouflaged the whole thing with a table of numbers. The minuet would always be in D major with a fixed harmonic progression and the trio would always be in D minor. The melody was the real variable. There were 11^6 possible melodies for the first period of the polonaise, 11^8 possibilities for the second period, and 11^{32} possibilities for the minuet and trio." Thus, through sheer mathematics, the composer was ensured an "original" work.

Another such game was the *Ludus melothedicus* (anonymous, Paris, ca. 1758), which separated the bars of music into separate individual notes. The user could then compose an eight-bar minuet and an eight-bar trio, in either D major or A minor. Notes Hedges (1978, p. 182), "What the anonymous author had done was to compose a little minuet with eight variants and then distribute the notes of each bar on a table with nine notes from other variants placed between each not of melody. This guaranteed that one of the nine versions would result no matter where one started among the first nine numbers on the table." The most famous of the musical dice games was constructed by Mozart. The

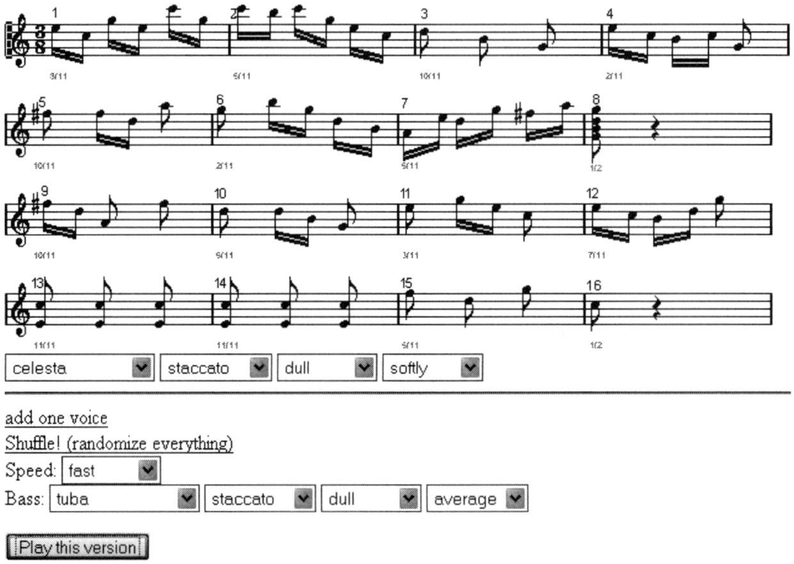

FIGURE 8.7

A modern adaptation of Mozart's musical dice game, by Bram Boskamp, allows the user to select options and have the computer randomize the sequences.

Musikalisches Würfelspiel (Musical dice game), was first published in 1792 in Berlin (figure 8.7). As in Kirnberger's example, the user could form a sixteen-bar waltz by rolling the dice to decide which bar to select next: "the measures are numbered from 1 to 176, and the numbers are arranged in two charts, each consisting of 11 rows and eight columns. To select the first measure, a player would roll two dice, subtract 1 from the total, and look up the corresponding row in the first column of the first chart to determine the appropriate measure number. Subsequent rolls of the dice decide which measure to select from each successive column to complete the melody" (Peterson 2001).

More recently, the technique has been used by the avant-garde in what has been termed "aleatoric" (literally translated as "according to the dice"), "open form," "mobile form," or "moment form." Henry Cowell's *String Quartet no. 3* (1935) consisted of five movements that could be played in any order and with any desired number of repetitions. Cage's *Winter Music* (1957) allowed for even more randomization. It could be played in whole or in part, by up to twenty pianos, and contained a series of fragments, whose order was left up to the player to determine.

Stockhausen's *Klavierstück XI* (1956) provided nineteen sections of which the performer determines the order. *Momente* (1962–1969) took the idea further. Each section, or "moment," was individually constructed to stand on its own, or work together in the larger whole. There were three larger moment-groups (D, or *Dauer*, K, or *Klang*, and M, or *Melodie*) and four informal, or indeterminate "I" moments, as well as a series of smaller moments. The larger moment-groups consisted of a central moment, K, which expressed the characteristics of the group. Each of the three main moment groups were divided by the four I moments. The score also had a series of inserts (*Einschübe*), consisting of characteristic sections from the moment that could be inserted into vertical slots in the score. Instructions were presented as to whether the insert should be from the previous moment inserted into the present moment (to function as "memory"), or from the present moment into the previous moment (to function as "premonition"), from the present moment into the next one (as memory), or from the following moment into the present one (to function as premonition).[8]

Pierre Boulez also explored the possibilities of open form in his *Third Piano Sonata* (1956–57), written partially as a response to the previously discussed earlier work by Stockhausen. The *Sonata* was composed in five movements, or "formants." There were eight potential arrangements of the five formants, according to some quite specific rules, and each formant had a varying degree of aleatoricism. The *Constellation* (or its retrograde, *Constellation-Miroir*) always arose in the middle of the construction. The first and second formants (*Antiphone* and *Trope*) could arise first as a pair, or last as a pair, before or after the *Constellation*, as with the fourth and fifth, the *Strophe/Sequence* pair. *Trope* and *Strophe* were to always be the same distance from the Constellation, thus leaving the performance with eight variations of order. Within the formants, however, there were also smaller divisions. For instance, Trope was circular in form and consisted of four sections or developments (*Texte*, *Parenthèse*, *Commentaire*, and *Glose*). Trope could then begin with any one of the four sections, followed by the remaining three. The stipulation was that *Commentaire* was to be played only once, and the parenthetical material could be performed or omitted (Harbinson 1989, p. 20).

From a programmer's perspective, the *Sonata* is interesting in that it included a series of "if . . . then" statements and tempo markings, similar to a computer program. If the composition was to proceed from segment X to segment Y, for instance, then segment Y must be played at x tempo; Else, if the composition was to proceed from segment Q to segment Y, then segment Y must be played at y tempo (Trenkamp 1976, p. 6). The tempo markings helped to control the transition between segments and the rate of musical events (ibid., pp. 7–8). Musically, some of the difficulties with open form (see below) had been solved by Boulez by the use of symmetry in the form of retrograde inversion palindromes, and more emphasis on texture, tempo, and dynamics (see Harbinson 1989), although there is a "lack of definitive, hierarchical pitch organization [that] results in a bland uniformity of horizontal and vertical pitch structures. This uniformity allows basic sonorities to be easily grasped by the listener, unless the texture becomes too dense. At the same time it offers an ideal background for textural manipulation"

(Trenkamp 1976, p. 9). Textures are reinforced through dynamics, range, and pitch density, alternating between segments to provide subtle juxtaposed textural differences.

Open form as shown by these examples clearly offers some benefits to the games composer. It can provide variation and thus maintain interest, and pre-arranged transition points can make transitioning smoother. Argues composer Henri Pousseur, "Complete performances could be had in many different ways, for the beginning and end of each separate sequence could serve as the beginning or end of the whole, with suitable dynamic modulation. I saw that two sequences could be joined if their respective end and beginning were of like quality (e.g. both high, fast and homogeneous); complete continuity was thus possible with not the slightest sign of the join" (cited in Dack 2004).

Open form has been used successfully in a number of games. *The Legend of Zelda: Ocarina of Time*, for instance, used a variable sequencing structure in the Hyrule section of the gameplay. Since the player must spend a considerable amount of time running across Hyrule field to gain access to other important gameplay areas, the sequences were played randomly to maintain interest and diversity. Every time the game was played, the song would play differently. Even quite early games such as *Lazy Jones* (1984) were created in this manner. The game had twenty-one songs, one of which was selected when the character entered or left one of the gameplay rooms. There were eighteen rooms in total, and each room had its own four-bar song, which played like a segment of one greater song, the title music. Even if the character left the room at, say, bar twenty-one, the rest of the loop would play before it would transition back into the theme song. Most of the loops worked well together, in part because of the ragtime-like bass lines, the same timbres used, and the fact that the game only used two channels (figures 8.8, 8.9, and 8.10).

There are, however, several difficulties that open form presents for the composer. The first difficulty is the goal-oriented, directed nature of linear music that Western listeners are used to. Writes Kramer (1981, p. 542): "Linear music exists in a time world that admits, and even depends on, continuity of motion." Most music we listen to has a clear beginning, middle, and end, and the music is designed to progress toward a final cadence. In open form, "At its close we have the impression of having heard a series of minimally connected sections—called moments—that are a segment of an eternal continuum. The moments may be related—motivically, for example—but not connected by transition. The crucial attribute of moments is their self containment" (ibid., p. 547). Kramer argues, therefore, that if a moment is defined by a process, then each moment must contain its own process: the goal must be reached within the single moment. This makes tying music to in-game action incredibly difficult.

The lack of directedness is related to a secondary problem in open form—the elimination of the dramatic curve. If there is no climax in the music, it can

FIGURE 8.8

Lazy Jones eight-bar track one (main gameplay) (David Whittaker, Terminal Software, 1984), showing the main eight-bar loop that plays during the hallway sequences of the game.

FIGURE 8.9

Lazy Jones four-bar track, which loops if the player stays in one room, or transitions back to the main loop (figure 8.8) if the player exits the room. (David Whittaker, Terminal Software, 1984.)

FIGURE 8.10

Lazy Jones four-bar track, which loops if the player stays in one room, or transitions back to the main loop (figure 8.8), if the player exits the room. (David Whittaker, Terminal Software, 1984.)

very easily become aural wallpaper, or musical ambience. As such, the piece loses its functions, as described in the previous chapter. In particular, any semiotic or communicative functions are lost. After all, "If pieces of this sort are to be as communicative as possible, and if their interior liberty is not to lead to a lack of signification or necessity, their variable elements (which must, of course, be indeterminate to a certain extent) must also display a definition, a characterization, a *sense* of sufficient development" (Behrman 1966, p. 104). Recalling that the important transitions in a narrative occur at moments of tension—moments when the music is most needed to dramatically underscore the action—open form is ill suited to such times. Composer Elliott Carter argues, "What contemporary music needs is not just raw materials of every kind but a way of relating these—of having them evolve during the course of a work in a sharply meaningful way; that is, what is needed is never just a string of 'interesting passages,' but works whose central interest is constituted by the way everything that happens in them happens *as* and *when* it does in relation to everything else" (Kramer 1988, p. 205).

The difficulty in composing a meaningful piece in open form is evident. Argues Kramer (1981, p. 548), contrast between sections must be distinct enough to prevent comparison, but they must feel as though they belong to part of one longer piece. Nevertheless, there are many places in games where open form can be effective, particularly when combined with preordered, precomposed cues.

10   BRANCHING STATE-BASED MUSIC AND THE TRANSITION MATRIX
Finally, related to open form is the transition matrix approach to music. A transition matrix builds on the open form idea and contains a series of small files that enable the game engine to analyze two cues and to select an appropriate precomposed transition. The cues must use markers to indicate possible places in the score where a transition may take place. As shown in chapter 3, iMUSE offered a series of commands that function similarly to those needed by the transition matrix, and although it remains proprietary software, these ideas have been incorporated into a variety of middleware and game engines. In these software tools, musical sequences contain decision points, or markers, within the tracks. These decision points mark places where changes or branches in the performance may occur based on a condition in the game in real time. When the sound driver reaches a decision point, it evaluates the conditions that have been set and determines the appropriate action. Actions do not take place unless the sound driver encounters a decision point and the correct condition is met. For instance, a command to jump within a sequence may have a marker point of "when we hit middle C." The music would play until arriving at middle C, and at that stage, the trigger would be executed. The composer, then, composed musical sequences, and then conditionalized those sequences, making decisions involving which segments should play continuously, change, be enabled or disabled, loop, converge, branch, jump, and so on.

This means that the composer must map out and anticipate all possible interactions between sequences at any marker point, and compose compatible transitions—an incredibly time-consuming process. Consider the following example that describes the event-driven music engine, consisting of the sequences or segments of music, and the control logic (the commands that control them):

> In Kesmai's *Multiplayer Battletech*, control logic determined the selection of segments within a game state and the selection of sets of segments at game state changes. Thus, the control logic was able to construct melodies and bass lines out of one to two measure segments following a musical pattern. At game state changes, a transition segment was played, and a whole different set of segments was selected. However, this transition segment was played only after the current set of segments finished playing so as not to interrupt the flow of the music. I selected game states and also tracked game state changes based on the player's relative health vs. the health of the opponent. Overall, I composed 220 one to two measure segments that could all be arranged algorithmically by the control logic. (Bernstein 1997)

The number of transitions may rapidly increase, however, for a larger game. Return, for instance, to our "room," room A, discussed previously. As the player moves about the room, there are six possible directions, and thus there could be at least six possible trigger-points or *events* within the room to signal a cue change. From this room (A), the player may have several options in terms of direction, each of which may require a new musical cue: Forward to multiple enemy fire (A to B), Back to a dangerous laboratory fire (A to C), Up to roof (A to F), down a trapdoor to underground (A to G), left to single enemy fire (A to D), right to the communications room (A to E), or exit to the menu (A to menu). Transitioning from A to any other sequence will require a multitude of potential transitional units. For example, if we have a sixteen-bar sequence A and the potential to move from A to B is to occur at the first downbeat of any bar, there must be sixteen possible transition units to B. With sixteen more to C and sixteen more to D, and so on, for just this one room, the composer needs 376 transitions, and sixteen bars is a very short duration—most cues need to be longer. What if there were thirty rooms in each level, each with a sixteen-bar sequence? That would be 11,280 transitional units needed, and if there were ten levels, there would be over one hundred thousand transitional units needed. Not only this, but the player (and thus the music) must also be able to return: B to A, C to A, and so on.

In addition to specific location-based trigger-points within a game (which are *interactive*), there may also, of course, at any time be event-based trigger points (based on an ongoing battle, for instance), or other run-time parameter triggers (sometimes referred to as RPCs or run-time parameter controls), which are the continuously evolving parameters such as timers, player health, ammunition, and so on (which are *adaptive*), and which may also require changes in the music. Therefore, in addition to the thousands of transitional segments from specific location-based triggers, there may also need to be transitions to RPC-based music.

Although some transitions can be reused effectively in various places, composers must still deal with a considerable amount of composition. So how can composers cope with such a problem? It would be possible to have fewer marker points, with the downside of increased time between transitions creating a lag. This may be fine in some situations, but in others, the transition may take too long to be effective. It would also be possible to create more repetitive music, meaning sequenced music whereby, say, one bar out of every four repeats—this would involve composing fewer transitional units, because some of the units could be reused, but we have now limited the construction of the cue in terms of what we can do musically, and may end up with a musically uninteresting clip. It is also possible to reuse music in other parts of the game, or other parts of the level—but this would, in a sense, defeat its original purpose and create a repetitive score.

A solution developed for *Anarchy Online* was to create a software tool, the SIM (Sample-based Interactive Music), to allow a combination of many small sequences into one long continuous track. Every musical sequence was organized with a list of possible following sequences or transitions. The composer had to enter the tempo and meter of each sequence in order to line up the beats. The game featured over 750 sequences in all, each of which had to be numbered and organized in relation to each other, and in relation to other layers, or groups of sequences that may represent a different part of the game and therefore be quite different in flavor. Sequences were played back randomly if the player stayed in one location, so that the layer (or song) never played the same way twice, and was one infinite piece of music.

> Each layer [group of sequences] can change into any other layer at any time. For example: The player moves from a forest and into a desert area. It is daytime. The "forest day" layer is currently playing. Once the player enters into the desert, the SIM tool will find out if the current sample [sequence] playing has a transition to a sample in the "desert day" layer. If it does, then this is the sample that will play next. If the sample has no transition to the "desert day" layer, the tool will find the shortest possible path to the "desert day" layer via other "forest day" samples.[9] (Lagim 2002)

Here then, open form is combined with a series of transitional segments that are conditionalized, similar to the Boulez piece described above.

Guy Whitmore (2004, p. 389) highlights another approach in regard to *No One Lives Forever* (Monolith, 2000). The game had various points of action and ambience. The composer wrote a thematic idea and then arranged it into "a variety of music states using subjectivity naming conventions that reflect their functionality (or intensity) in the overall score," such as "ambient" or "action." Each state was between one and three minutes in length, and these could then loop until a new state was needed, or to fade to silence. Each theme was then arranged into six substates to make up a musical set (silence, super ambient, ambient, suspense/sneak, action1 and action2). Any given state had to be able to modulate at any time to the other five states. The cue could wait until the next marker point, or simply fade out rapidly when a quick transition was needed. "However, the most satisfying transitions were the ones that built up to a more intense music state or resolved downward to a less intense music state (without missing a beat, so to speak)" (Whitmore 2004, pp. 387–415).

The transition matrix in *No One Lives Forever* kept track of the potential transitions between musical states. Transitional cues could be constructed and assigned as specific transitions. For the six states, there were thirty transitions (from one to five other states). Whitmore notes, however, that many transitions did not need transition segments, as they worked fine when hard cutting on an appropriate boundary. Marker points were set a maximum of eight seconds (four-bar marker points), although typically two bars were used. The marker types (Whitmore calls them "boundary types") were Immediate, Grid, Beat, Measure, and Segment, and each was used for a different situation—immediate or Grid worked for quick transitions in rhythmically ambiguous sections, whereas Beat and Measure markers suited music with a rhythmic pulse. "Segment boundaries allowed the currently playing melodic phrase or harmony to resolve before transitioning" (ibid.). With careful construction of the beginning of the state cues, this jump could be made much more easily. Some transitional cues could be reused, since many were organized in terms of moving from intense music to less intense music, so going from action$_1$ or action$_2$ to ambient could work with the same transitional segment. The music must also be constructed in such a way that is conducive to this type of dynamism, as Whitmore (ibid., pp. 387–388) notes:

> The key to composing music for any given music state is to give the music enough musical ebb and flow to keep things interesting while staying within the intensity range prescribed by the music state. For example, the "ambient" music state may rise and fall a bit in musical density but should not feel like it has moved up or down too dramatically. The goal is to maintain the musical state while holding interest. One way that the music sets in NOLF achieve this level of sustained interest is through instrument-level variation. Using variation on just a few instrument tracks of a given music state was very effective and didn't cut too deeply into the production schedule. Instrument-level variation is used in the lower intensity music states quite often. These music states start differently every time they're called up, giving the illusion of more music. In some cases, a four- to eight-measure repeating music state feels like three to five minutes of fresh music.

There is clearly evidence that a transition matrix approach can be very effective in a game, although the planning required means constraints on time that may be prohibitive.

CONCLUSION

Dynamic music offers many interesting challenges to the composer, from dealing with the unpredictable interaction between dialogue and sound effects, to having to introduce considerable variability into the music. Variability may take rather simple forms of changes in tempo, pitch, volume, or DSP. Variation may also take more complex forms, with algorithms for altering melodies or harmonies, songs structured in layering, "accumulative form" approaches,[10] variable sequences in open form, or a branching, conditionalized open form. To some extent, the effectiveness of these ideas is dependent on genre. Certain genres lend themselves well to certain dynamic styles of music: puzzle games, for instance, are perhaps better suited to layered approaches than first-person shooter games. Games that have longer levels, such as adventure games, can make effective use of open form. These approaches require new ways of thinking about music, and will require new software tools and teaching methods to accommodate them.

The many approaches to variability in music discussed in this chapter also raise many interesting questions regarding the future of Western music in general. Westerners are spending an increasing amount of time engaging with this malleable musical form. According to the Entertainment Software Association, the average adult spends seven and a half hours per week playing games, and gaming is increasingly taking the place of time spent with more traditional linear media forms (especially television).[11] With an increasing amount of time spent engaging with and hearing nonlinear games music, how will this impact our relationship to music, and to its communicative functions? Kramer (1981, p. 549), for instance, notes that "Phrases have, until recently, pervaded *all* Western music, even multiple and moment forms: phrases are the final remnant of linearity." But as shown, the music of games is not necessarily written in a phrase structure, it is more malleable, more indefinite. Kramer refers to nonlinear music in his discussion of "vertical time," noting, "I can say for certain that having written a number of nonlinear scores, I'll never think about music the same way again. In a way, it's freed my thinking about how music is put together. Even when listening to linear music, I sometimes think 'Hmmm ... this piece could just as easily start with this section instead of that one' or 'I bet they could've started that transition two measures earlier!,' etc. Music is malleable and only frozen when we record it" (ibid.).

Are we seeing the beginnings of not only a new form of music, but a new form of thought that may have far-reaching implications? Certainly looping and repetition have become standard since the development of tape—will video games usher in another more nonlinear approach to cultural forms? There are many examples of films that adopt visual elements from games (such as Corey Yuen's adaptation of Tecmo's video game, *DOA: Dead or Alive* in 2006), as well as other films adapted from games, along with the rise of *Machinima* (a filmmaking technique that uses games technology to make films in the virtual reality of a game engine). Many movies on DVD offer alternate endings or additional cuts, approaching a more nonlinear form. Anahid Kassabian (2003, p. 92) has discussed the possible influence of game audio on the mixing and production of film sound in what she calls the "evaporating segregation of sound, noise and music." Kassabian suggests that the soundscape of games has had an impact on film scores such as *The Matrix* (1999), where the distinction between sound design and underscore is greatly reduced. A similar disintegration between sound effects and music is occurring in hip-hop and electronic music where sound effects (or "nonmusical sound") regularly make appearances in songs. This raises the further possibility that game sound is influencing approaches to musical production in popular and cinematic music and that the consequences—or results—of nonlinearity in music extend beyond nonlinear media.[12] It could be suggested that if popular music artists continue to create music for games, we may soon see releases of albums geared toward nonlinear playback of these tracks, and other approaches, such as the variability described in this chapter.

CHAPTER **9**

CONCLUSION

As shown throughout the book, in addition to the nature of games and the requirements of game audio in its functions (commercial, anticipatory, structural, spatial, and so on), game sound can be seen as the product of a series of pressures from technological, economic, ideological, social, and cultural spheres. The first few chapters addressed some of these aspects within the historical context of games, with a particular focus on the technological constraints imposed by an emerging form, which have to a considerable extent now been overcome. Game composers and sound designers no longer rely on synthesis chips to create ambience, sound effects, dialogue, or music, but instead have at their disposal as many sounds and instruments as can be imagined. As such, game audio has grown beyond fulfilling functions to becoming an art form in its own right. Nevertheless, the nature of video games as nonlinear, participatory media continues to create many interesting challenges of a technological and aesthetic nature.

Chapter 5 discussed the processes of game audio's development, and it became clear that audio decisions are a series of negotiations with a team of people, who must work together on these challenges in order to create the best possible result from their individual audio assets. In particular, mixing is an area of games in which a constant negotiation between the aesthetic output and the functional processes of the sound is undertaken. Although such difficulties certainly exist in linear forms of audiovisual media, the additional challenge of unpredictable timings means that intermingling sound assets must constantly be judged in terms of priority in any given sequence of play, throughout the entire game.

The added commercial pressures placed on game composers by the influx of linear licensed music into the game development industry were discussed in chapter 6. This influx has meant that there has been an increased attention paid to promoting their craft as critical to the overall impact of a game. The incorporation of unplanned or replaceable licensed music is unlikely ever to replace specially composed music in games, since licensed music, unless very carefully planned, will often fail to fulfill the many functions required of sound in games (as shown in chapter 7). Licensed music also offers interesting possibilities in terms of potentially leading to new playback devices, user-generated playlists, and so on, which may create other cultural innovations in the near future.

Finally, chapter 8 explored some of the possible approaches to the nonlinear and participatory aspects of gaming that music in games seeks to address in a variety of ways. The requirements of gameplay for a variable playback environment has led to the incorporation of many interesting ideas drawn significantly from the avant-garde, including algorithmic generation, granular synthesis, and open form. Although these ideas continue to be mined, it seems likely that some approaches to this problem may also pass in the other direction—from games to contemporary musicians and composers. Certainly, we can expect to see some of these techniques turn up in popular music, particularly if user-generated tagged playlists become incorporated into gaming.

In a sense, this book has raised as many questions as it has provided answers. It should be noted that my focus has been on game audio's production, at the expense of its reception and its users. Kristine Jørgensen's (2008, p. 175) study of the reception of game sound (primarily, sound effects), has shown that "games suffered both as user-oriented game systems and as virtual worlds when sound was not present, which means that both the progression through the game and the sense of presence in the game environment were affected." Nevertheless, as she demonstrates in two games, this affect is genre-specific, and her limited focus (on only two games, on only male respondents, without dividing sound effects from music, and so on) makes the study largely inconclusive in discussing games as a whole. More research needs to be undertaken into how audio functions in games and other dynamic media.

Moreover, there are, as shown, several different ways in which the player is connected to, participates in, or interacts with the sound of a game, and several ways in which this sound acts internally or externally to the game's diegesis. How is the audio used, and how does the medium of games influence reception? When the player can become a causal agent in the audio's playback, how does this change their relationship to sound and to music? As the player is no longer a passive listener, but may be involved in invoking sound and music in the game, we must reevaluate theories of reception. Not only this, but audio in games is heard in highly repetitive atmospheres, and we must examine how this has affected its reception, and how it may influence future production and distribution of popular music or video games in light of its obvious recent popularity.

Claudia Gorbman (1987, p. 15) suggests that there is a "mutual implication" between image and audio in their reception. But when the timing of events is such that the audio (in the case of music, for instance) may not coincide with the same image with each play, what happens to this "mutual implication"? It is unlikely that music will be triggered at exactly the same times with each gameplay. With sound effects being randomized through granular synthesis, even these will be played back differently every time the game is played. Ambience may be set so that different ambient sounds are heard every time the player is in a location, and the user controls a number of sound effects within any given scene, altering the soundscape. In other words, the close synchronization of audio with any series of images does not exist in games. Analyses of music and the moving image such as those undertaken by, for instance, Philip Tagg (2000; using a semiotic approach with multiple reception tests) or Nicholas Cook (2004; using a variety of approaches), although valuable, have used a fixed text, which is the same every time it is played back. Without this fixedness, what becomes of the meaning? Are the meanings different every time, or do they carry similar meanings, despite different timings? If the latter is the case, then are the studies of the close synchronization of music and image redundant?

Consider, for instance, if, in a film, the director wants an off-screen (in Chion's terminology, *acousmatic*) dog barking to inform the audience that there is a dog nearby. The sound designer records a dog bark and it is inserted into the film's mix. The audience then hears the dog bark and recognizes that there is a dog nearby in the off-screen activity. Nevertheless, the audience brings their own meanings to that sound, which may be "my dog recently died and I am sad." In other words, the meaning is enriched by the connotation of the connotations. In terms of semiotic theory, I have elsewhere called this secondary level of signification *supplementary connotation* (Collins 2002, pp. 430–433). These are the unpredictable, individual, and often personal connotations associated with a text.

However, even this approach does not account for dynamic media such as games, in which the audience plays an active role in the construction of the (audio) "text." The traditional semiotic chain of communication from transmitter (the composer/sound designer) to channel (the sounds) to receiver (the audience) is disturbed in games by the interplay between the player and the audio. In some cases, the player becomes a cotransmitter, and therefore, just as the audio in games is nonlinear, it may be worth considering the communication chain as also nonlinear, perhaps in a more circular fashion in which the receiver plays a more active role (see figure 9.1).

Using the example of the dog barking, in this case, let us say that the player is in a driving game, and happens to take a curve too quickly just after the dog barks. The sound of the tires squealing is added to the transmission. In this case, the audience may interpret that supplementary connotation one level further, as

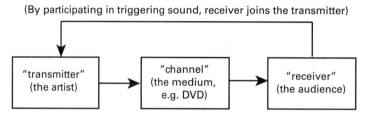

FIGURE 9.1
Participation's impact on the traditional transmitter-channel-receiver chain of events.

"my dog recently died when he was hit by a car and I am sad and I hate cars," moving the train of thought away from the dog and toward the car. The participatory nature of video games in other words potentially leads to the creation of additional or entirely new meanings other than those originally intended by the creators by not only changing the reception, but also changing the transmission. We might refer to these meanings as *participatory supplementary connotations*, as the original meaning (that there is a dog somewhere) is maintained, but, through our own experiences and through participation, is supplemented by additional meanings.

Furthermore, even the language and assumptions of linear media theories are inadequate for games. As discussed particularly in chapter 7, in game audio there is a breakdown of the traditional notions of author and text. When the music does not exist as a single linear track, there is no *musical text*, and the "author" is perhaps as much the player–listener, whose moves and involvement affect the playback of the audio, as the composer, who is responsible for composing them, and the audio integrator, who makes decisions regarding playback and incorporates sound elements into the gameplay. As mentioned above, sound effects may be created algorithmically by an amalgam of granules, and therefore be different with every play, further disturbing this notion of text. The idea of the game as one text or one complete work especially fails in the face of unscripted online games, localized games, and so on. As suggested, this reduction of text and authorial power may even have an impact on the future development of music in general. Artists may construct new approaches to songwriting, and listeners may play more of an active role through the generation of tagged playlists in which they control the placement of music in a game. What happens to the reception of music when the well-known and well-used structural popular forms developed since the days of Tin Pan Alley disintegrate? And what happens to reception when players may consciously articulate connotations by inserting mood-based tags into their music playlists?

Moreover, since with games there is no record of playback—games are different every time, particularly, as noted, with online games—there is no set text from which we can work (unless we do a video screen capture, and then treat it as a linear media form). Indeed, since not only games, but every game *play* and game *player* is different, what methods can we use to determine how players hear, use, and interpret game audio? I can provide no answers at this time, but this is clearly an area that needs significantly more research, particularly in light of the increasing role that dynamic media forms are having in our daily lives.

Of course, there is also the issue of rhythm-action and other music or audio-based games, and how these affect the reception of the audio. Music has recently taken on somewhat of a primary role in certain styles of games, driving the structure of games in some cases. The power of the composers in some games companies is notable (if rare). As Nintendo composer Hip Tanaka illustrated: "When it comes to music, I didn't discuss it with anybody. They allowed me to be in charge of the game's music. I even insisted that game designers change certain graphical concepts in the maps from my point of view" (cited in Brandon 2002). As discussed, recent games like *Rez*, *Electroplankton*, and *Lumines*, as well as the popularity of rhythm-action games, suggest areas where the composition of music in games can be taken much further, so that games are built around music, rather than the other way around.

New interface devices, such as the Nintendo DS stylus, or new multitouch screens, in which images (and potentially sounds) can be moved about on a screen by hand, suggest that a participatory element to audio's consumption will become a standard in which users may physically manipulate the playback of the audio that they want to hear. Moreover, the rise of dynamic audio in theme parks, museums, educational tools, appliances, toys, art installations, and other areas in our lives suggests that even outside of video games, this cultural form is having a significant impact on the ways in which sound is produced, mediated, and consumed.

Notes

1   Introduction

1. While some prefer to distinguish video games (that is, console games) from computer games (played on PC or Mac), I combine them here for brevity's sake. As I define them, all video games contain a controller or input device of some kind (a joystick, a keyboard, a stylus, a games controller), a processing unit (a CPU), and a visual interface (with the exception of some audio-only games). Many games are distributed on some form of media, although digital downloads and mobile games are quickly making the idea of a CD, a DVD, or cartridge obsolete.

2. At times it was not possible to obtain the original games, and so the games had to be run on emulators, which mimic the original game engine on a home computer. The trouble with this method is that elements can be inaccurate, as I found with one emulator that ran the audio at about half a semitone off.

3. Or at least, is intended to be played back in a specific order. The presentation of movies on DVD offers nonlinear playback options by choosing which scene to play, although most viewers would find it difficult to follow a movie that is not played back in the intended order.

2   Push Start Button: The Rise of Video Games

1. Kline, Dyer-Witherford, and de Peuter (2003) explore the earlier links between the hacker culture and scientists at military-funded research centers as the initiators of early games, but none of these were commercialized (nor, to my knowledge, did they have sound), and so are not of concern here.

2. For a time in the 1930s the fashion was for the machines to be much quieter, when they became known as the silent bells. For further details, see Ken Durham's "History of Slot Machines" (1996): http://www.gameroomantiques.com/HistorySlot.htm.

3. As research into recent gambling machines suggests: "A particular piece of music ... can send out a signal that a person has won on the machine, both to the player and to others in the vicinity.... The music can create the illusion that winning is more common than losing, for you do not hear the sound of losing" (Griffiths and Parke 2005). Although today's machines are more elaborate and cunning in their use of music, even a ringing bell to attract onlookers to a winning machine would have the same enticing effect.

4. From an early advertising flyer, available at http://marvin3m.com/arcade/cspace.

5. For an excellent online museum of arcade flyers, see the Arcade Flyer Archive at http://www.arcadeflyers.com/.

6. See http://www.arcadeflyers.com/?page=flyer&id=4376&image=2.

7. See http://www.arcadeflyers.com/?page=flyer&id=4376&image=2 and http://www.arcadeflyers.com?page=flyer&id=1290&image=1.

8. In *The Text Book of Video Game Logic* (Kush N' Stuff Amusement Electronics Inc., 1976, p. 46). It is interesting to note that there is no mention of the potential for *music* generation in the text.

9. "Nondiegetic" refers to sound that does not take place within the diegesis (narrative space) of the game. The distinctions between the various levels of diegesis and sound are discussed in chapter 7.

10. A few companies built their own chips, such as Atari, who created the Pokey, the "Potentiometer and Keyboard Integrated Circuit," responsible for controlling the paddle or joystick and keyboard (pots and keys) as well as audio on Atari machines. The four-channel Pokey chip was also used in the Atari 5200, the Atari XE, and various Atari 8-bit computers. Each channel was square-wave and had a three-octave frequency register and control register (setting the distortion and its volume).

11. For further examination of the use of cover songs and licensed material in games, see chapter 6.

12. A variety of different types of speech chips were used, with various compression methods including ADPCM, PCM and linear predictive coding (LPC). See box 2.1, "Synthesis," and box 2.2, "Sampling."

13. There were a few other advances, such as the Curtis CEM3394 (used in Sequential Circuits 6-Trak and Max, and the Akai AX73), introduced in 1984, but used in only a handful of games. It had only one voice per chip, but it had selectable pulse, triangle, and saw-tooth wave forms, rather than the typically square waves of other PSG chips. Most games that used the chip had several—up to six—copies of the chip on board, such as *Chicken Shift* (Bally, 1984).

14. According to The Old Computers Museum. See http://www.old-computers.com/museum/computer.asp?c=878&st=2.

15. More accurately, the waveforms were approximated, rather than completely sine wave, square wave, and so on.

16. Although "advanced" is subjective, in the context of the drive toward higher fidelity and realism (see chapter 7), it is an adequate description.

17. There were a variety of reasons for the "fall" of the industry in the early to mid-1980s, including oversaturation of the market and poor investment choices at Atari. See Kent 2001 for further details.

18. Using an 11-bit divider, capable of a range of about 55 Hz to 12 KHz.

19. Capable of a range of about 27 Hz to 56 KHz. The triangle channel also had no volume or envelope control.

20. Also using a 4-bit frequency divider and capable of a range of about 29 Hz to 447 KHz.

21. The origin of the term *port* to refer to cross-platform releases is unknown; however, I suspect it may come from *game port*, the name of the interface device hardware on old PCs.

22. Earlier platform and adventure games tended to be quite formulaic in having a "good world" (overworld) and an underground "evil world" (underworld), as well as battle scenes with significant enemies (bosses) at the end of each level.

23. In 1988, Access Software developed a PWM technique for using a normal 3″ PC speaker to play relatively realistic digital audio samples, without the addition of a soundcard. Using Realsound, as it became known, it was possible to create 6-bit digitized samples, commonly used for sound effects or for title music in games. More important, it could do this using a minimal amount of the processor's power. Realsound was used in a few popular games, such as *Mean Streets* (Similar Games, 1989) and *Space Racer* (Loriciels, 1988), but failed to catch on, as many PCs of the time came with small tweeter speakers, rather than the original 3″ PC speaker, and there was no need for Realsound technology when soundcards became popular.

24. There were four releases of Mockingboard: Mockingboard "A," the base card, which added six-voice music and sound synthesis. The Mockingboard "B" worked with the "A" by adding speech synthesis capabilities via the Votrax SC-01 Speech Synthesizer or the SSI-263 speech synthesizer. The Mockingboard "C" was essentially an "A" and "B" packaged together. The later Mockingboard "D" had the same capabilities as the "C," but attached to the Apple IIc via the serial port.

25. The ring modulation option, producing nonharmonic overtones, allowed the combining of information from two channels (the triangle plus a second waveform), used commonly for sound effects like bells, chimes, and gongs. The registers designed for modulation, however, were rarely used, since software could simulate them, without sacrificing the triangle form, although "for novice programmers they provided a way to create vibrato or filter sweeps without having to write much code." Bob Yannes, cited in Varga 1996: http://www.landley.net/history/mirror/commodore/yannes.html.

26. Creator Bob Yannes lamented, "The filter is the worst part of SID because I could not create high-gain op-amps in NMOS, which were essential to a resonant filter. In addition, the resistance of the (field effect transistors) varied considerably with processing, so different lots of SID chips had different cut-off frequency characteristics. I knew it wouldn't work very well, but it was better than nothing and I didn't have time to make it better." Cited in Varga 1996.

27. Martin Galway on the *Short Circuit* theme: http://www.remix64.com/interview_martin_galway .html.

28. The code can be seen by using the *Ransid* disassembler program.

29. See *Sid-In* magazine: http://digilander.libero.it/ice00/tsid/sidin/index.html.

30. Interview with Martin Galway, at http://www.remix64.com/interview_martin_galway.html.

31. As Martin Galway commented on his use of Ben Dalglish's music for *Arkanoid*, "I'm glad you spotted *Cobra* on the Spectrum, whose tune I was in love with and HAD to use somewhere else! I figured no-one would complain if I used it a year later on the C64." *Sid Tune Information List* (STIL v3.4), http://www.prg.dtu.dk/~theis/stil/html/text/Galway_Martin.htm.

32. Rob Hubbard interview, http://www.freenetpages.co.uk/hp/tcworh/int_6581.htm.

33. Constraints, notes Prendergast, were not so much technological, but rather a matter of cost, the lack of orchestras in theaters, and the fact that conductors—responsible for the music—would often see precomposed music as an infringement on their domain and boycott it. Cue sheets and later photoplay music books were published to assist the pianist with rapid modulations. See, e.g., Rapée 1924 or Zamecnik 1913. This is discussed at length in Altman 2004, pp. 258–269.

34. William Gibbons (2008, forthcoming) notes that all of the songs for the NES release of *Captain Comic* (Color Dreams, 1989) appear to be taken from Denes Agay's *More Easy Classics to Moderns* (New York: Amsco, 1960).

35. See, e.g., Théberge 1997 (pp. 59–60), who acknowledges the influence of computers, but not the games.

3 INSERT QUARTER TO CONTINUE: 16-BIT AND THE DEATH OF THE ARCADE

1. Nintendo Entertainment Corp., "Inside the System," http://www.nintendo.com/systemsclassic ?type=nes.

2. "The owner of the copyright in a popular game such as *Pac-Man* may be as jealous of its method and pattern of play as he is about the particular colors and shapes of the game's 'gobbler' and 'ghost monsters'" (Hemnes 1982, p. 172).

3. F.C.J. No. 1100 (T.D.). *Video Game Law Blog*, http://davis.ca/community/blogs/video_games/ archive/1982/12/09/634.aspx. Moreover, as Théberge (1997, p. 76) indicates, during the time period there was no copyright available for individual sounds or synthesizer patches.

4. *Vending Times*, cited in http://www.popmatters.com/pm/features/article/8752/a-final-arewell-to-arcades. Although there have been sporadic temporary resurgences, and the coin-op industry argues that if one includes all coin-ops, the business is fairly stable, Konami's recent decision to close its American operations is a strong signal that the era of the video game arcade has changed, if not ended.

5. For a more detailed tutorial on FM synthesis, see *Computer Music*'s guide at http://www .computermusic.co.uk/tutorial/fm/fm1.asp.

6. Another form of compression known as adaptive differential pulse code modulation (ADPCM) was also used in speech chips, a significant advantage over PCM for games owing to their high compression ratios, such as the OKI Electric Industry Co.'s OKI 6295 chip, used in *Pit Fighter* (Atari, 1990).

7. Sheff goes into detail about what he describes as Nintendo's "straightjacket" licensing. See Sheff 1993, p. 356. This is also discussed by Kline, Dyer-Witherford, and de Peuter 2003.

8. There were three models of the Sega Genesis released, each one becoming more affordable. Released in 1991, the Sega CD, a CD-ROM add on allowed for much better audio quality (adding extra channels and capable of full motion video playback), and an additional Motorola 68000 processor. Despite these advances, the system was priced out of the market for many users.

9. From Sega's *Sonic Central* website, http://www.sega.com/sonic/globalsonic/post_sonicteam .php?article=nakamura.

10. *VGM Tool* allows a user to decompress and dump the code from a game audio file (VGM) to a text file.

11. Paragraph adapted from the *Sega Genesis Technical Manual*, found at http://www.smspower .org/maxim/docs/ym2612/index.html.

12. ADT, or *automatic double tracking*, was originally developed on tape recorders as a way to strengthen voice or instrument sounds by doubling up with an identical track, with very slight delay.

13. According to the Old Computer Museum, http://www.old-computers.com/MUSEUM/computer .asp?c=837.

14. The wavetable synthesizer stored samples in a compressed format known as bit rate reduction, at a ratio of 32:9, in order to not overtax the system memory. This worked well for many instruments and sound effects, though vocal samples still sounded scratchy.

15. Some games were released on both systems, of course, and these typically had very similar sounding music.

16. Some of these movie tie-ins were also released on the Genesis.

17. Of course, as on the NES there were exceptions, including *Super Metroid* (Nintendo, 1994), which maintained the sparse ambient textural audio lacking a definite structure that *Metroid* had shown on the NES.

18. The Commodore FM SFX Sound Expander, for instance, had been made in 1985 using a YM3526 chip.

19. See Eric Wing, "The History of PC Game MIDI": http://www.queststudios.com/quest/midi.html.

20. Sierra's game composers have set up a page where guests can listen to a game clip on various soundcards. See http://queststudios.com/digital/compare2005/compare2005.html.

21. Lyndsay Williams, "The History of Sound Cards and Digital Audio on PCs from 1980–89." Http://research.microsoft.com/users/lyn/soundcardhistory.ppt.

22. This information comes from the composers at Sierra, at http://www.queststudios.com/quest/ midi.html.

23. For the full MIDI specifications, see http://www.borg.com/~jglatt/tech/midispec.htm.

24. There were four significant MIDI-based 16-bit iMUSE adventure games: The Secret of Monkey Island 2: LeChuck's Revenge (1991), Sam & Max Hit the Road (1993), Indiana Jones and the Fate of Atlantis (1992), and The Day of the Tentacle (1993). All of the games were co-composed by Clint Bajakian, Peter McConnell, and Michael Land, the creators of the iMUSE system.

25. See the articles collected at the *Scumm Bar*: http://www.scummbar.com/games/index.php?game =2&sub=media&todo=6.

26. For instance, Darius Zendeh's Sound System, used in *R-Type* and *Katakis* games, Aegis' Sonix, or EA's Deluxe Music.

27. For samples, see Mahoney's website, http://www.ejeson.se/mahoney/index_download.php.

28. Eric Wing, "The History of PC Game MIDI": http://www.queststudios.com/quest/midi.html.

29. "Improvements" are, of course, subjective, as many fans prefer the older sound chip feel to game audio. Improvements, then, are considered in comparison with standards and aesthetics set by non-computer-generated audio.

4   PRESS RESET: VIDEO GAME MUSIC COMES OF AGE

1. 1992's hit *Mortal Kombat* (Midway), for instance, relied on a simple DAC, an OKI 6295 voice chip and an old YM2151, as did *Legend of Silkroad* (Unico, 1999), while *Prehistoric Isle 2* (Yumekobo/SNK, 1999) used a "prehistoric" YM2610. The major coin-op companies, however, did develop some significantly improved sound for their important releases. The late 1990s saw a lot of subwoofers added to racing games, such as *Time Crisis II* (Namco, 1998), *Ferrari F355 Challenge* (Sega, 1999), and *Hydro Thunder* (Midway, 1999). Wavetable synthesis became a standard part of Taito's arcade games (notably the Ensoniq ES5505, used in, for instance, *Bubble Bobble* (1994). The chip had thirty-two digital audio channels (8- or 16-bit PCM) with separate envelope generators and digital filters, and a 44.1 kHz sample rate. Similar chips were used by Namco (with their C352, first released in 1993 with the game *Ridge Racer*, although it had slightly inferior sampling), Konami (with their KO54539), Sega (with their Yamaha SCSP, also used in the Saturn), and the QSound chip, used by Capcom in the arcade hit *Super Street Fighter 2* (1993), among others. Recent games have seen surround sound with projector screens (*House of the Dead 4*, Sega, 2005), with air blast and vibrate features, and licensed music (*Road Rebel*, Roxor Games, 2006, for instance, features nine tracks from Fat Wreck Chords).

2. *The 7th Guest* was also the first to use General MIDI. See Bedigian 2006, "GZ Interviews Game Audio Revolutionist 'The Fat Man,'" *Gamezone*: http://pc.gamezone.com/news/08_08_03_06_24PM.htm.

3. QSound, or Q3D, is one popular 3D positional audio algorithm, used by Electronic Arts, Activision, Sega, and others. Later versions have added support for DirectSound 3D, a component of Microsoft's DirectX software.

4. See also the full specs on the MIDI Manufacturer's Association website, http://www.midi.org/about-midi/dls/dlsspec.shtml.

5. A first-person 3D shooter or FPS is a first-person point-of-view game in which, typically, the player must point and shoot with a handheld weapon at enemies on-screen.

6. Puzzle games require the player to solve a series of increasingly difficult puzzles. Adventure games typically incorporate puzzles into a quest narrative.

7. "Robyn Miller Interview," *Myst Obsession* (2006): http://www.mystobsession.com/?page=Robyn%20Miller%20Interview.

8. Sales statistics according to a press release by Electronic Arts, "Open for Business" (April 1, 2006): http://thesims2.ea.com/news/detail.php?id=659.

9. Truecolor generally refers to 24 or 32-bit graphics technology, allowing for a very high number of colours and shades.

10. A tube-shooter is a shooting game that typically gives players a single axis of movement around the circumference of a "tunnel" or "tube-like" shape.

11. The PC release of the same game featured a software synth, Yamaha's YXG-100.

12. See Nintendo's sales reports, available at http://www.nintendo.co.jp/n10/news/050126e.pdf.

13. One person lamented, "Come on! In the days of CDs, only a moron would decide to use a format that should have died with the 80s." See http://www4.dealtime.com/xPR-Nintendo-Nintendo-64~RD-1241707.

14. Sega today continues to develop games, but has not announced any new plans to release another console.

15. Surround sound was simulated using Dolby Pro-Logic II, in 5.1, for instance.

16. It had 256 2D voices, or 64 voices using 3D positional audio, with five DSP units.

17. For a copy of the flyer, see http://www.atarihq.com/dedicated/touchme.php.

18. It had six stereo channels from a TI 76489 PSG and a Yamaha YM 2612 FM chip.

19. *Nintendo Annual Report* (2005):
    http://www.nintendo.com/corp/report/NintendoAnnualReport2005.pdf.

20. Channels 3 and 4 could also operate as 4-bit DACs to play samples.

21. "The Audio Advance: GBA Development for the Masses": http://belogic.com/gba.

22. See the Nintendo site, http://www.nintendo.com/techspecgba.

23. Wave options for pulse wave were 12.5 percent, 25 percent, 50 percent, 75 percent. The 4-bit envelope function allowed for fade-ins or fade-outs.

24. There are other forms of arguably "online games," such as downloadable episodic content, but for the sake of brevity I will focus on these two forms here.

25. For an excellent overview of the casual games market, see the *IGDA Casual Games Whitepaper*, at http://www.igda.org/casual/IGDA_CasualGames_Whitepaper_2005.pdf.

26. I am indebted to the IAsig's report on Internet audio formats for this section, notably "Interactive Audio on the Web," published at http://www.iasig.org/pubs/wawg-rpt.pdf.

27. See the *Warbears* homepage, http://www.warbears.com/missions.php?id=2.

28. The main percussive rhythm upon which the loop is based does change in a few key places.

29. Although even these are being sold as high-end items for gamers. Empower Technologies, for instance, sells a PowerPlay 5.1 Media Chair which can work with Xbox and PlayStation consoles, and includes a "tactile transducer" for players to feel as well as hear the effects. HotSeat Chassis, Inc. sells a similar immersive home surround sound racing system.

30. *Middleware* is software typically generated by third-party specialists to connect various applications with the game engine and offer cross-platform programming solutions. Audio examples are discussed below. Generally, middleware is licensed on a per-title basis, and can cost in the tens of thousands of dollars per title, per platform.

5 GAME AUDIO TODAY: TECHNOLOGY, PROCESS, AND AESTHETIC

1. Ranked in terms of annual revenue figures, average aggregated review scores, number of releases, and anonymous developer surveys regarding milestone payments, pay and perks, and producer quality. The full "2006 Top 20 Publishers" listing, including statistics and analysis is available in the October 2006 issue of *Game Developer* magazine.

2. Games design is a complex process that is outside the scope of this book. There are many ways to produce a design document, and many excellent resources on games design and development, including Richard Rouse's *Game Design Theory and Practice* (2005), which provides sample design documents and further details on each stage of the document writing process.

3. *Foley* is the term used for recording sound effects in the studio using a variety of props. It is often specifically used for the everyday natural sounds, rather than special effects. In nearly

all games studios, the foley artist is also the sound designer (who is also often the audio programmer).

4. "The 'temp track,' a temporary mock-up of a film's soundtrack, is assembled from pre-existing music prior to the real, commissioned score being composed" (Sadoff 2006, p. 1).

5. Audio boot camp, Game Developer's Conference, San Francisco, Calif., 2007. Others have divided emotions in different ways—see for instance mood music libraries or photoplay music books.

6. Keynote talk presented in the audio tutorials track day at Game Developer's Conference 2007.

7. *Automated dialogue replacement*, or ADR, is voice recording performed in a studio after the visual film scene has been shot. This was originally done as a last resort to replace poor production sound, but is now used more often than not.

8. As was seen, for example, in *Biometal* in chapter 3, which had different soundtracks for European/North American and Asian markets.

9. In a talk given at Game Audio Boot Camp, Game Developer's Conference 2007, San Francisco, March 6, 2007.

6 Synergy in Game Audio: Film, Popular Music, and Intellectual Property

1. Entertainment Software Association, "Top 10 Facts," http://www.theesa.com/facts/top_10_facts .php.

2. As cited on "Computer and Video Game Market Sales": http://forum.pcvsconsole.com/folder .php?fid=23.

3. Available at *BusinessWeek Online*: http://www.businessweek.com/innovate/content/jun2006/ id20060623_163211.htm.

4. In 2004, the number was only twelve, with fifty-two games selling more than 500,000. Kerr 2006, p. 45.

5. Although there are attempts, with software like *Torque* or Microsoft's *XNA*, to make at least casual gaming more available to an independent market.

6. According to *Screen Digest* research, as cited at "Profitability in video game industry" (February 26, 2007): http://compsci.ca/blog/profitability-in-video-game-industry.

7. Ibid.

8. Kerr (2006, p. 68) gives the example of Infogrames' purchase of Shiny for $47 million in 2002 to obtain access to the *Matrix* film licensing.

9. Thanks to Dan at the Arcade Flyer Archive for scanning the originals for me. See http://www .arcadeflyers.com/?page=flyer&id=1290&image=1.

10. It is worth noting that there are two important areas that I do not discuss here: games as subjects of popular music (the aforementioned "Pac-Man Fever," etc.), and games or game sounds as instruments or samples in popular music (from chiptunes to the experiments of artists like Alec Empire and Beck): in these instances, the main sales or marketing "object" is the music, whereas my focus here will be on those associations where the game is the primary component.

11. The DICE awards are the Design, Innovate, Create, Entertain convention awards, sponsored by the Academy of Interactive Arts and Sciences (AIAS) game-development association.

12. Bands promoting games in advertising began as early as 1982, when Activision hired the Tubes to write the theme song for *Megamania*, and featured in the television commercial.

13. There seems to be some debate as to what exactly was contributed outside of "The Dark" by May, but the game does not include details. Bits from "Resurrection" were used, but most of the tracks ended up on the sequel, *Resurrection: Rise 2*.

14. As with other games discussed here, there are many more examples than what I present. Another example was Psykosonik's soundtrack for the SNES game, *X-Kaliber 2097* (Activision, 1994). Part of the Wax Trax!/TVT roster, Psykosonik enjoyed moderate success with a few dance hits in the early 1990s, and subsequently wrote the music to *X-Kaliber* before falling into obscurity. Negativland's Chris Grigg was quite well known as a Commodore 64 composer, and the band's Mark Holser also at one time programmed games music for Epyx in the 1980s.

15. There are also increasing numbers of Hollywood composers who are trying their hand at games, including Danny Elfman (*Fable*, Lionhead, 2004), and Howard Shore (*Soul of the Ultimate Nation*, Webzen, 2007). As Radical Entertainment's sound director Rob Bridgett points out, however, these composers do not necessarily do all the work. In the case of *Fable*, Elfman provided a theme that was worked on by the in-house composers. Bill Brown cited in Bridgett 2005.

16. Cited at http://www.runningdream.com/news.htm, under January 2006.

7 GAMEPLAY, GENRE, AND THE FUNCTIONS OF GAME AUDIO

1. Industry categories have been critiqued for being too reliant on representational characteristics, rather than on interactivity. See, e.g., Apperley 2006. Genre distinctions also change over time. A look back at *SNES Force*, a UK magazine from the mid-1990s, divides the genres into eight categories: arcade, adventure/RPG, beat-'em-up, platform, puzzle, shoot-'em-up, sports/racing, and sims/strategy. *SNES Force* 1/9 (February 1994). Platform games have almost disappeared altogether from today's consoles, however.

2. See Galloway 2006 (p. 5) for an alternate division of diegesis through distinguishing what he calls the "operator action" (that enacted by the player) and "machine action" (enacted by the machine), so that "locating a power-up in *Super Mario Bros* is an operator act, but the power-up actually boosting the player character's health is a machine act."

3. And could be subdivided further, for instance, as Michel Chion (1994) has elaborated in his discussion of the diegetic–nondiegetic divide; Gorbman's "metadiegetic" subjective sound categories (1987, p. 450), and so on. Although the use of the division of diegetic–nondiegetic is called into question in contemporary film studies because of its inability to deal with these other categories of sound, I do not wish to further complicate the issue here. My point is that the relationship of the audio to the player and to their character in games is different from that of film because of the participatory nature of games.

4. Cut-scene cinematics require "a dramatic score to grab a player's attention and motivate them to make it through the next level to see the next movie. These offerings often serve as a reward to the player, where they are able to watch the on-screen action and inwardly pride themselves for making it happen" (Marks 2002, p. 190).

5. Stockburger provides a fairly extensive analysis of what he terms the "spatialising functions in the game environment," focusing on what he has called the "dynamic acousmatic function," which, he elaborates, is distinguished from film by the "kinaesthetic control over the acousmatisation and visualisation of sound objects in the game environment" See Stockburger 2003: http://www.audiogames.net/pics/upload/gameenvironment.htm.

6. However, the active involvement of the player with a game also has other repercussions that can lessen the immersive quality, such as the player's fumbling with the controller, for instance. Even after playing a game for several hours, for example, I find that I forget what function some of the buttons have, and this can cause the immersive effects of the game to recede.

7. Others have provided similar divisions, such as Brown and Cairns (2004), who categorize immersion into "engagement," "engrossment," and "total immersion."

8. It is perhaps ironic, then, that of the top five of the "Top 100 Games Ever," only one is from a recent generation, and three of the top five are from much older (16-bit) technology. This seems to suggest, then, that realism is not entirely relevant, at least in comparison to gameplay and narrative, except perhaps as temporary novelty. The top five are (in descending order): *The Legend of Zelda* (Nintendo, 1992), *Super Metroid* (Nintendo, 1993), *Resident Evil 4* (Capcom, 2005), *Chrono Trigger* (Nintendo, 1995), and *The Legend of Zelda: Ocarina of Time* (1998). IGN (2006): http://top100.ign.com/2006.

9. Nintendo DS headphones: "Outstanding sound quality will make your games come alive," http://www.toysrus.com/sm-nintendo-ds-headphones-black--pi-2453563.html. Creative Sound Blaster Live!: "With Sound Blaster Live! 24-bit ... make your games come alive," http://www.gamepc.com/shop/product.asp?catalog_name=GamePC+Online+Products&category_name=Sound+Card&product_id=SBLIVE71&cookie%5Ftest=1. Creative speakers: "make your games come alive with life-like sound," http://www.discount-alienware-computers.com.

10. "The emerging hierarchy between essential sounds and mere noise grew in authority throughout the 1930s. Concurrently, it became the norm not to match visual and acoustic 'scale,' not to locate the microphone with the camera, not to respect the acoustics of the space of production, and not to offer a perceptually based 'coherent point of audition' from which the spectator could identify" (Lastra 2000, p. 188).

11. See, e.g., their website: http://www.eastwestsamples.com/details.php?cd_index=1009.

8 COMPOSITIONAL APPROACHES TO DYNAMIC GAME MUSIC

1. From the LucasArts press release, "Indy Game Features Euphoria Technology" (April 27, 2006): http://www.indianajones.com/videogames/news/news20060427.html.

2. The composers for the game were Morten Sørlie, Tor Linløkken, and Lagim.

3. Moreover, techniques were developed in which, with slight adjustments in playing (that is, using staccato, tremolo, and so on), the piece's affect could be altered (Altman 2004, p. 263).

4. Fay, Selfon, and Fay (2004) provide detail and examples from the composition. I use the "Gravity Ride" track for this discussion. The game is part of the XP Plus package offered by Microsoft.

5. The layout of my transcription is borrowed from Garcia 2005, though the blocks of bars are basically laid out in much the same fashion as sequencing software. The passage of time is followed from left to right, with each block representing one bar of music. Each vertical layer in the stack of blocks represents a new instrument sound.

6. See Spicer 2004, who argues that a similar "accumulative" form gained considerable use in popular music in the 1970s, particularly after the introduction of electronic instruments.

7. Glassner (2004, p. 240) suggests the term *resequencing* for a narrative in which the order of presentation of parts can be reordered.

8. An "X" means the moment is "neutral"; it gives and receives no *Einschübe*. If the arrow has a figure two above it, it means "next-but-one moment" or "last-but-one moment." A plus and minus sign above the arrow means that the moment being referred to is to be played twice, first with the *Einschub* and then without it. See Smalley 1974.

9. There are certain obvious drawbacks to this system. Since the music samples are set to change only at certain points during playback, it takes a few seconds to change into a different layer. As long as the music is playing within the same layer, everything is fine. This is especially evident in combat music. In certain cases, the music will keep playing a few seconds after the enemy has been killed, or if the player has been killed, the combat music will keep going for a few seconds before changing into the "death" layer.

10. See Spicer 2004 (p. 33) where he defines accumulative form and claims that the "technique of building up a groove gradually from its constituent parts is often the defining feature of smaller formal units within larger compositions."

11. See the Entertainment Software Association's website: http://www.theesa.com/facts/gamer_data .php.

12. There are of course other reasons for this sound–music disintegration. Recent technology has made this far easier than in the past, for instance. I would speculate that one of the most significant contributing factor to this idea is the changing role of the sound effects editor to sound designer in the last few decades and the subsequent more creative uses of nonmusical sound in film.

GLOSSARY

ADAPTIVE AUDIO   refers to sound that occurs in the game environment, reacting to gameplay, rather than responding directly to the user. An example is *Super Mario Bros.* (Nintendo, 1985), in which the music plays at a steady tempo until the time begins to run out, at which point the tempo doubles.

ADDITIVE SYNTHESIS   (sometimes referred to as Fourier synthesis, as it is based on Fourier's theorem that all sound waves are made up of sine waves), refers to the creation of a sound wave by adding together simpler sound waves (typically sine waves).

ADPCM   *Adaptive Differential PCM* (also known as adaptive delta PCM), is essentially a method of compressing a PCM sample. The difference between two adjacent sample values is quantified, reducing the pitch or raising the pitch slightly, to reduce the amount of data required. ADPCM uses only 4 bits per sample, therefore requiring only one quarter of the space of a 16-bit PCM sample. This works well for lower frequencies, but at higher frequencies can lead to distortion. PCM and ADPCM are now subclasses of the Microsoft waveform, WAV, although Windows system hardware does not understand ADPCM, and so it must be decompressed before playing as a PCM sample.

ADR   Automatic Dialogue Recording: post-production audio re-recording of an actor's lines in the studio, as opposed to production recording.

AI   Artificial intelligence comprises the routines or algorithms that control actions in a game. AI engines typically control the physics and actions of non-playing characters and environments, although there is also a desire among game audio personnel to create audio AI engines that can intelligently respond to the game parameters.

ARCADE GAME   A stand-alone game unit, typically in a cabinet style, but also found as countertops or sit-in ride games in public spaces, generally coin-operated and therefore also known as a *coin-op.*

BIT   A bit, derived from binary digit, is the smallest unit of information in computer language, a one (1) or zero (0) (also sometimes referred to as "on or off," or "white or black"). In referring to processors, the number of bits indicates how much data a computer's main processor can manipulate simultaneously. For instance, an 8-bit computer can process 8 bits of data at the same time. Bits can also be used to describe sound fidelity or resolution. Bit depth is used to describe the number of bits available in a byte. Higher bit depths result in better quality, but larger file sizes. 8 bits can represent 2^8 (binary being base 2), or 256 variations in a byte. When recording sound, 256 divisions are not very accurate, since the amplitude of a wave is rounded up or down to fit the nearest available point of resolution. This process, known as quantization, distorts the sound or adds noise. CD quality sound is considered 16-bit, although often the CDs are recorded in 24-bit and converted to 16-bit before release.

CHIPTUNES   popular music recorded with "retro" sound chips, typically from the early 8-bit era. Also known, or with subgenres known, as *bithop*, and *micromusic*.

CONSOLE   Game hardware connected to a television set.

CONTROLLER   The peripheral user interface with which the user interacts with the game.

DACs   Digital-to-analog converters involve the re-creation of a sound wave from sample data (binary code) to an analog current (an electrical pressure sound-wave). DACs have bit depths and sample rates. The higher the bit rate and sample rate, the "better" the resulting sound. DACs most often work through pulse code modulation (see below).

DIEGETIC   Diegetic sounds (*source music* or *real sounds*) are sounds that occur in the diegesis (the narrative space, or character's space). Nondiegetic sound refers to "background" music and sound effects.

DSP   Digital signal processing/processor: refers to the processing of a signal (sound) digitally, including using filters and effects.

DYNAMIC AUDIO   Any audio designed to be changeable, encompassing both inter-active and adaptive audio. Dynamic audio, therefore, is sound that reacts to changes in the gameplay environment and/or in response to a user.

ENGINE   The software or code that controls a game and enables it to function.

FREQUENCY MODULATION   (FM) synthesis: FM uses a modulating (usually sine) wave signal to change the pitch of another wave (known as the carrier). Each FM sound needs at least two signal generators (oscillators), one of which is the carrier wave and one of which is the modulating wave. Many FM chips used four or six oscillators for each sound, or instrument. An oscillator could also be fed back on itself, modulating its original sound.

GENERATOR   An oscillator is capable of either making an independent tone by it-self, or of being paired up cooperatively with its neighbor in a pairing known as a generator. To create realistic musical sounds two sorts of generators are needed: (1) oscillators to produce the basic waveform, and (2) envelope generators to change the waveforms as the notes age.

GRANULAR SYNTHESIS   A relatively new form of synthesis that is based on the principle of microsound. Hundreds—perhaps thousands—of small (10–50 millisecond) granules or grains of sound are mixed together to create an amorphous soundscape that can be filtered through effects or treated with envelope generators to create (often variable) sound effects and musical tones.

INTERACTIVE AUDIO   Sound events occurring in reaction to gameplay, which can respond to the player directly. In other words, if for instance a player presses a button, the character on screen swings his or her sword and makes a "swooshing" noise. Pressing the button again will cause a recurrence of this sound. The "swoosh" is an interactive sound effect.

LINEAR ARITHMETIC (OR LA) SYNTHESIS   See Wavetable synthesis.

LOCALIZATION   The process of adapting a game's dialogue (or other elements, which is referred to as blending) to cultures and languages other than the one for which the game was originally designed.

MIDDLEWARE   A third-party supplementary software package that enables a programmer to build part of a game or assets for a game.

MIDI   Musical instrument digital interface: A musical standard by which instruments can be connected to each other, as well as a series of codes (data) to control musical playback.

MMO   Massively multiplayer online games: Online games in which many players participate.

OSCILLATOR   An electric signal that generates a repeating shape, or wave form. Sine waves are the most common form of oscillator.

PCM   Pulse code modulation (otherwise known as raw, or AI2 synthesis): Analog sound converted into digital sound by sampling an analog waveform. The data is stored in binary, which is then decoded and played back as it was originally recorded. The downside of this method is the amount of space required to store the samples: as a result, most PCM samples in early games are limited to sounds with a short envelope, such as percussion. 8-bit PCM samples commonly have an audible hiss owing to the resolution problems.

PLATFORM   The hardware and/or the operating system on which a game is played. For instance, PlayStation is a platform, as is Microsoft Windows.

PLATFORM GAME   A two-dimensional game that requires the player to jump about on platforms of various levels.

POLYNOMIAL COUNTERS   also known as linear-feedback shift registers (LFSR): A type of binary counter that uses a pseudo-random way of counting, rather than the normal binary incremental/decremental sequences. A number is divided down from the system clock, meaning many pitches are not in tune with others, making it difficult to program melodies.

PORT   A copy of a game for a platform other than the one for which it was originally designed.

PSG   Programmable sound generators: silicon sound chips designed for audio applications that generate sound based on the user's input. These specifications are usually coded in assembly language to engage the oscillators. Instrument sounds are typically created with a waveform (tone generator) and envelope generator.

PULSE WAVES   Pulse waves contain only odd harmonics, and are rectangular waveforms with "on" and "off" slopes, known as the duty cycle. When the duty cycle is of equal length in its "on" and "off" period, it is known as a square wave. Changing the duty cycle options (changing the ratio of the "on" to "off" of the waveform) alters the harmonics. At 50 percent (square), the waveform is quite smooth, but with adjustments can be "fat," or thin and "raspy". Square waves are often referred to as "hollow" sounding.

PWM   *Pulse Width Modulation* works by generating variable-width pulses to represent the amplitude of an analog input signal (sample). The PWM method can attain higher volume and achieve a range of interesting timbres (such as a pseudo-chorus or phasing sound), but the samples are low quality (4-bit). On the Commodore 64, the noise channel could double as a simple PWM sampler. PWM was used for sampling short sounds like percussion, and to simulate a low-frequency oscillator (LFO) to the volume (creating a tremolo effect, as heard on *Parallax*).

REDBOOK   Standard (uncompressed) CD audio.

SAMPLE RATE   (also known as sample frequency): A sample is a measurement of amplitude. A sample contains the information of the amplitude value of a waveform measured over a period of time. The sample rate is the number of times the original sound is sampled (measured) per second. A CD-quality sample rate of 44.1 KHz means that 44,100 samples per second were recorded. If the sample rate is too low, a distortion known as aliasing will occur, and will be audible when the sample is converted back to analog by a digital-to-analog converter. Analog-to-digital converters will typically have an anti-aliasing filter, which removes harmonics above the highest frequency that the sample rate can accommodate.

SUBTRACTIVE SYNTHESIS   Starts with a wave form created by an oscillator, uses a filter to attenuate or subtract specific frequencies, and then passes this through an amplifier to control the envelope and amplitude of the final resulting sound. Subtractive synthesis was common in analog synthesisers, and is often referred to as *analog synthesis* for this reason. Most PSGs were subtractive synthesis chips, and many arcades and home consoles used subtractive synthesis chips, such as the General Instruments AY-8910 series.

UI User interface: The controls and connection points between the game and the user, referring to both the hardware (joystick, keyboard, etc.) and the software (clickable icons, etc.).

WAVETABLE SYNTHESIS Uses preset digital samples of instruments (often combined with basic waveforms of subtractive synths). It is therefore much more realistic sounding than FM synthesis, but is much more expensive as it requires the soundcard to contain its own RAM or ROM. The Roland MT-32 MIDI soundcard used a form of wavetable synthesis known as *Linear Arithmetic*, or LA synthesis. Essentially, what the human ear recognizes most about any particular sound is the attack transient. LA based synthesisers used this idea to reduce the amount of space required by the sound by combining the attack transients of a sample with simple subtractive synthesis waveforms. This was known as cross modulation.

WHITE NOISE Sound that contains every frequency within the range of human hearing in equal amounts. In games, it is commonly used for laser sounds, wind, surf, or percussion sounds. Pink noise is a variant of white noise. Pink noise is white noise that has been filtered to reduce the volume at each octave. It is commonly used for rain or percussion sounds in games, sounding a bit like white noise with more bass.

References

Altman, Rick (2001). "Cinema and Popular Song: The Lost Tradition." In *Soundtrack Available: Essays on Film and Popular Music*, edited by Pamela Robertson Wojcik and Arthur Knight, 19–30. Durham, N.C.: Duke University Press.

Altman, Rick (2004). *Silent Film Sound*. New York: Columbia University Press.

Apperley, Thomas H. (2006). "Genre and Game Studies: Toward a Critical Approach to Video Game Genres." *Simulation and Gaming* 37, no. 1: 6–23.

Arrasvuori, Juha (2006). "Playing and Making Music: Exploring the Similarities between Video Games and Music Making Software." Ph.D. diss., University of Tampere.

Bajakian, Clint, David Battino, Keith Charley, Rob Cairns, Alain Georges, Mark Griskey, Danny Jochelson, Rob Rampley, and Linda Law (2006). "Group Report: What Is Interactive Audio? And What Should It Be?" Paper presented at the annual Interactive Music Conference Project Bar-B-Q, Texas: http://www.projectbarbq.com/bbq03/bbq03r5.htm.

Bajakian, Clint (2007). "Music: Design Production and Implementation." Paper presented at the annual Game Developers' Conference, San Francisco, March 4–9, 2007.

Battino, David, and Kelli Richards (2005). *The Art of Digital Music*. New York: Backbeat Books.

Bedigian, Louis (2006). "GZ Interviews Game Audio Revolutionist 'The Fat Man.'" *Gamezone*: http://pc.gamezone.com/news/08_08_03_06_24PM.htm.

Behrman, David (1966). "The Question of Order in New Music Henri Pousseur." *Perspectives of New Music* 5, no. 1: 93–111.

Belton, John (1992). "1950s Magnetic Sound: The Frozen Revolution." In *Sound Theory, Sound Practice*, edited by Rick Altman, 154–170. New York: Routledge.

Belton, John (1999). "Awkward Transitions: Hitchcock's *Blackmail* and the Dynamics of Early Film Sound." *Musical Quarterly* 83, no. 2: 227–246.

Berardini, César (2004). "EA Pumps Up the Volume with Rhino Records." *TeamXbox* (June): http://news.teamxbox.com/xbox/6067/EA-Pumps-Up-The-Volume-With-Rhino-Records.

Berg, Charles Merrell (1973). "An Investigation of the Motives for and Realization of Music to Accompany the American Silent Film, 1896–1927." Ph.D. diss., University of Iowa.

Bernstein, Daniel (1997). "Creating an Interactive Audio Environment." *Gamasutra*: http://www.gamasutra.com/features/19971114/bernstein_01.htm.

Bevilacqua, Joe (1999). "Celebrity Voice Actors: The New Sound of Animation." *Animation World Magazine* 4, no. 1: http://www.awn.com/mag/issue4.01/4.01pages/bevilacquaceleb.php3.

Booth, Jason (2004). "A DirectMusic Case Study for *Asheron's Call 2: The Fallen Kings*." In *DirectX 9 Audio Exposed: Interactive Audio Development*, edited by Todd M. Fay, Scott Selfon, and Todor J. Fay. Plano, Texas: Wordware Publishing.

Bosco, Clyde (1991). *Nintendo Adventure Books: Double Trouble*. New York: Archway/Pocketbooks.

Brandon, Alexander (2002). "Shooting from the Hip: An Interview with Hip Tanaka." *Gamasutra*: http://www.gamasutra.com/features/20020925/brandon_01.htm.

Brandon, Alexander (2005). *Audio for Games: Planning, Process and Production*. Berkeley, Calif.: New Riders.

Bridgett, Rob (2005). "Hollywood Sound." *Gamasutra*: http://www.gamasutra.com/features/20050916/bridgett_03.shtml#3.

Bridgett, Rob (2006). "Establishing an Aesthetic in Next Generation Sound Design." *Gamasutra*: http://www.gamasutra.com/features/20060621/bridgett_01.shtml.

Bridgett, Rob (2007). "Sound Design and Mixing Using a Post-Production Audio Model." Paper presented at the Game Developer's Conference, San Francisco, March 2007.

Bridgett, Rob (2008). "Dynamic Range: Subtlety and Silence in Video Game Sound." In *From Pac-Man to Pop Music: Interactive Audio in Games and*, edited by Karen Collins, 127–134. Aldershot: Ashgate.

Brightman, James (2007). "Denis Dyack's Utopian Video Game Future." *GameDaily* (April 5): http://biz.gamedaily.com/industry/feature/?id=15712&page=3.

Brown, E., and P. Cairns (2004). "A Grounded Investigation of Game Immersion." In *CHI 2004, Proceedings of the ACM Conference on Human Factors in Computing*: 1297–1300. Vienna, Austria ACM Press.

Brown, Royal S. (1994). *Overtones and Undertones: Reading Film Music*. Berkeley: University of California Press.

Bush, Tracy W., Scott Gershin, Martin H. Klein, Adam Boyd, and Sarju Shah (2007). "The Importance of Audio in Gaming: Investing in Next Generation Sound." Paper presented at the annual Game Developer's Conference, San Francisco, March 4–9, 2007.

Cameron, Andy (1995). "Dissimulations: Illusions of Interactivity." *Millennium Film Journal* 28: 33–47.

Campbell-Kelly, Martin (2004). *From Airline Reservations to Sonic the Hedgehog: A History of the Software Industry*. Cambridge, Mass.: MIT Press.

Canham, Mark (2004). "The Driv3r Soundtrack: Be Good, Be Bad, Be Something New?" *Music4games* (September 6): http://music4games.net/Features_Display.aspx?id=78.

Carlsson, Anders (2008). "Chip Music: Low Tech Data Music Sharing." In *From Pac-Man to Pop Music: Interactive Audio in Games and New Media*, edited by Karen Collins. Aldershot: Ashgate.

Carr, Neil (2002a). "An Interview with Dave Warhol." *Remix64*: http://www.remix64.com/interview_david_warhol.html.

Carr, Neil (2002b). "An Interview with Mark Cooksey." *Remix64*: http://www.remix64.com/interview_mark_cooksey.html.

Chandler, Rafael (2005). "Organizing and Formatting Game Dialogue." *Gamasutra* (Nov. 18): http://www.gamasutra.com/features/20051118/chandler_02.shtml.

Charne, Jim (2006). "Fair Treatment of Music and Composers in the Games Industry—A Personal Perspective." *GameDaily* (February 14): http://biz.gamedaily.com/industry/myturn/?id=11862.

Chion, Michel (1994). *AudioVision*. New York: Columbia University Press.

Cohen, Annabel J. (1999). "Functions of Music in Multimedia: A Cognitive Approach." In *Music, Mind, and Science*, edited by S. W. Yi, 40–68. Seoul: Seoul University Press.

Cohen, Annabel J. (2001). "Music as a Source of Emotion in Film." In *Music and Emotion: Theory and Research*, edited by Patrick N. Juslin and John A. Sloboda, 249–279. Oxford: Oxford University Press.

Collins, Karen (2002). "The Future Is Happening Already: Industrial Music, Dystopia, and the Aesthetic of the Machine." Ph.D. diss., University of Liverpool.

Collins, Karen (2006a). "Flat Twos and the Musical Aesthetic of the Atari VCS." *Popular Musicology Online* (issue 1, Musicological Critiques): http://www.popular-musicology-online.com.

Collins, Karen (2006b). "Loops and Bloops: Music on the Commodore 64." *Soundscapes: Journal of Media Culture* 8 (February): http://www.icce.rug.nl/~soundscapes/VOLUME08/Loops_and_bloops.shtml.

Collins, Karen (2007). "An Introduction to the Participatory and Non-Linear Aspects of Video Games Audio." In *Essays on Sound and Vision*, edited by Stan Hawkins and John Richardson. Helsinki: Helsinki University Press, 2007.

"Commodore Aims at Video Games" (1983). *New York Times*, April 12.

Comolli, Jean-Louis (1986). "Technique and Ideology: Camera, Perspective, Depth of Field." In *Narrative, Apparatus, Ideology*, edited by Philip Rosen, 421–443. New York: Columbia University Press.

Connick, Jack (1986). "... And Then There Was Apple." *Call-A.P.P.L.E.* (October).

Cook, Nicholas (2004). *Analysing Musical Multimedia*. Oxford: Oxford University Press.

Cox, Alan (1994). "Multi-User Dungeons." *Interactive Fantasy 2*: 15–20. Available at http://www.mud
.co.uk/richard/oarchive.htm.

Dack, John (2004). "Notes on the Realization of Scambi." Available at http://www.scambi.mdx.ac.uk/
documents.html.

D'Arcy, Keith (2004). "Music Licensing for Videogames: How Popular Music and Artists Can Make
Games Pop." Paper presented at the annual Game Developer's Conference, San Francisco.

Davis, Richard (1999). *Complete Guide to Film Scoring*. Boston: Berklee Press.

Demaria, Russell, and Johnny L. Wilson (2002). *High Score! The Illustrated History of Electronic
Games*. Berkeley, Calif.: McGraw-Hill.

Demers, Joanna (2006). "Dancing Machines: *Dance Dance Revolution*: Cybernetic Dance, and Musical
Taste." *Popular Music* 25, no. 3: 401–414.

Dolby.com (n.d.). "Interview with Richard Dekkard, Owner, HammerJaw Audio and Media Services
Company." Http://www.dolby.com/consumer/games/interview_08.html.

Drescher, Peter (2006). "Could Mobile Game Audio BE More Annoying?!" *O'Reilly Digital Media*
(April): http://digitalmedia.oreilly.com/2006/04/26/could-mobile-game-audio-be-more-annoying.html.

Droney, Maureen (2004). "Chronicling Riddick: Simultaneous Sound Design for Film, Games, Anime."
Mix (August 1): http://mixonline.com/mag/audio_chronicling_riddick.

Durham, Ken (1996). "History of Slot Machines." *GameRoomAntiques.com*: http://www
.gameroomantiques.com/HistorySlot.htm.

Eidsvik, Charles (1988–1989). "Machines of the Invisible: Changes in Film Technology in the Age of
Video." *Film Quarterly* 42, no. 2: 18–23.

Electric Artists (n.d.). "Video Games of Note." White paper originally published on their website: http://
www.electricartists.com.

Ermi, Laura, and Frans Mäyrä (2005). "Fundamental Components of the Gameplay Experience: Analysing Immersion." Paper presented at the Digital Games Research Association conference.

Fay, Todd M., Scott Selfon, and Todor J. Fay (2004). *DirectX 9 Audio Exposed: Interactive Audio Development*. Plano, Texas: Wordware Publishing.

Ferrari, Michelle, and Stephen Ives (2005). "Slots: Las Vegas Gamblers Lose Some $5 Billion a Year at
the Slot Machines Alone." In *Las Vegas: An Unconventional History*. Bulfinch. Available at http://www
.pbs.org/wgbh/amex/lasvegas/sfeature/sf_book_03.html.

Fish, Elliot (2005). "The Secret of Monkey Island." *PC Powerplay Magazine* 108 (January): 94–97.
Available at http://www.scummbar.com/games/media/mi12/RonGInterview122604184612.pdf.

Folmann, Troels (2006). "*Tomb Raider Legend*: Scoring a Next-Generation Soundtrack." Paper presented at the annual Game Developer's Conference, San Jose, Calif., March 20–24.

Fornäs, Johan (1998). "Filling Voids Along the Byway: Identification and Interpretation in the Swedish
Forms of Karaoke." In *Karaoke Around the World*, edited by Tōru Mitsui and Shūhei Hosokawa, 118–
138. New York: Routledge.

Galloway, Alexander R. (2006). *Gaming: Essays on Algorithmic Culture*. Minneapolis: University of
Minnesota Press.

Game Localization Network (2005). "Game Localization." Http://www.gamelocalization.net/
localization_game.html.

Garcia, Luis-Manuel (2005). "On and On: Repetition as Process and Pleasure in Electronic Dance Music." *Music Theory Online* 11, no. 4: http://www.societymusictheory.org/mto/issues/mto.05.11.4/toc .11.4.html.

Geuens, Jean-Pierre (2000). *Film Production Theory*. New York: State University of New York Press.

Gibbons, William (forthcoming). "Blip, Bloop, Bach? Some Uses of Classical Music on the Nintendo Entertainment System."

Glassner, Andrew (2004). *Interactive Storytelling: Techniques for 21st Century Fiction*. Wellesley, Mass.: AK Peters.

Gorbman, Claudia (1987). *Unheard Melodies: Narrative Film Music*. Bloomington: Indiana University Press.

Grau, Oliver (2003). *Virtual Art: From Illusion to Immersion*. Cambridge, Mass.: MIT Press.

Greenspan, Charlotte (2004). "Irving Berlin in Hollywood: The Art of Plugging a Song in Film." *American Music* 22, no. 1: 40–49.

Griffiths, Mark, and Jonathan Parke (2005). "The Psychology of Music in Gambling Environments: An Observational Research Note." *Journal of Gambling Issues* 13: http://www.camh.net/egambling/ issue13/jgi_13_griffiths_2.html.

Grigg, Chris, Guy Whitmore, Pat Azzarello, Jonathan Pilon, Fabien Noel, Scott Snyder, Pierre Lemieux, Peter Drescher, Tracy Bush, Alain Georges, Peter Otto, Oren Williams, Matt Tullis, Jim Rippie, and David Battino (2006). "Group Report: Providing a High Level of Mixing Aesthetics in Interactive Audio and Games." Paper developed at the Annual Interactive Music Conference Project Bar-B-Q, Texas.

Hanson, Robert (2007). "Locked and Loaded: Crafting the Sounds for *Halo 3* with Thousands of Dialog Lines, an Evil Alien Armada, and a Cast of Superhuman Soldiers." *Mix* (March): 29.

Harbinson, William G. (1989). "Performer Indeterminacy and Boulez' Third Sonata." *Tempo* 169: 16–20.

Harlin, Jesse (2007). "Aural Fixation: Does It Sound Next Gen?" *Game Developer* (February): 47.

Hays, Tom (1998). "Direct Music for the Masses." *Game Developer* (September). Available at http:// www.gamasutra.com/features/sound_and_music/19981106/directmusic_01.htm.

Hedges, Stephen A. (1978). "Dice Music in the Eighteenth Century." *Music and Letters* 59, no. 2: 180–187.

Hemnes, Thomas M. S. (1982). "The Adaptation of Copyright Law to Video Games." *University of Pennsylvania Law Review* 131, no. 1: 171–233.

Henein, Michael (2007). "Sound Integration: The Next Revolution Will Be Played." *Mix* (March): 32.

Hoffert, Paul (2007). *Music for New Media: Composing for Videogames, Websites, Presentation, and Other Interactive Media*. Boston: Berklee Press.

Huang, Eugene (2007). "GDC: Next-gen Audio Will Rely on MIDI, Says Sony." *GamePro.com*: http:// www.gamepro.com/news.cfm?article_id=106508.

IGN (2006). "Readers' Choice 2006: The Top 100 Games Ever." Http://top100.ign.com/2006.

Jørgenson, Kristine (2008). "Left in the Dark: Playing Computer Games with the Sound Turned Off." In *From Pac-Man to Pop Music: Interactive Audio in Games and New Media*, edited by Karen Collins, 163–176. Aldershot: Ashgate.

Juul, Jesper (2006). *Half Real: Video Games between Real Rules and Fictional Worlds*. Cambridge, Mass.: MIT Press.

Kalning, Kristin (2007). "If *Second Life* Isn't a Game, What Is It?" *MSNBC* (March 12): http://www .msnbc.msn.com/id/17538999.

Kassabian, Anahid (2003). "The Sound of a New Film Form." In *Popular Music and Film*, edited by Ian Inglis, 91–101. London: Wallflower.

Katz, Mark (2004). *Capturing Sound*: *How Technology Has Changed Music*. Berkeley: University of California Press.

Kent, Steven L. (2001). *The Ultimate History of Video Games: The Story Behind the Craze That Touched Our Lives and Changed the World*. New York: Random House, 2001.

Kerr, Aphra (2006). *The Business and Culture of Digital Games: Gamework/Gameplay*. London: Sage.

Kline, Stephen, Nick Dyer-Witherford, and Greig de Peuter (2003). *Digital Play: The Interaction of Technology, Culture and Marketing*. Montreal: McGill University Press.

Kolodny, Lora (2006). "Global Video Game Market Set to Explode" *GameDAILY* (June 23). Available at *BusinessWeek Online*: http://www.businessweek.com/innovate/content/jun2006/id20060623_163211 .htm.

Kompanek, Sonny (2004). *From Score to Screen: Sequencer, Scores and Second Thoughts: The New Film Scoring Process*. New York: Schirmer Trade Books.

Kondo, Koji (2007). "Painting an Interactive Musical Landscape." Paper presented at the annual Game Developer's Conference, San Francisco, March 4–9.

Kozloff, Sarah (1988). *Invisible Storytellers: Voice-over Narration in American Fiction Film*. Berkeley: University of California Press.

Kozloff, Sarah (2000). *Overhearing Film Dialogue*. Berkeley: University of California Press.

Kramer, Jonathan D. (1978). "Moment Form in Twentieth Century Music." *Musical Quarterly* 64, no. 2: 177–194.

Kramer, Jonathan D. (1981). "New Temporalities in Music." *Critical Inquiry* 7, no. 3: 539–556.

Kramer, Jonathan D. (1988). *The Time of Music*. New York: Schirmer Books.

Kush N' Stuff Amusement Electronics, Inc. (1976). *The Text Book of Video Game Logic*. Campbell, Calif.: Kush N' Stuff Amusement Electronics, Inc.

Kutay, Steven (2006). "Bigger Than Big: The Game Audio Explosion." *GameDev.Net*: http://www .gamedev.net/reference/music/features/biggerthanbig.

Lagim, Bjørn Arve (2002). "The Music of Anarchy Online: Creating Music for MMOGs." *Gamasutra* (Sept. 16): http://www.gamasutra.com/resource_guide/20020916/lagim.

Land, Michael Z., and Peter N. McConnell (1994). Method and Apparatus for Dynamically Composing Music and Sound Effect Using a Computer Entertainment System. US Patent No. 5,315,057. May 24, 1994.

Langston, Peter (1986). "(201) 644-2332 or Eedie and Eddie on the Wire: An Experiment in Music Generation." Morristown, N.J.: Bell Communications Research.

Langston, Peter (1989). "Six Techniques for Algorithmic Music Composition." Paper presented at the 15th International Computer Music Conference (ICMC), Columbus, Ohio, November 2–5.

Lastra, James (2000). *Sound Technology and the American Cinema: Perception, Representation, Modernity*. New York: Columbia University Press.

Law, Linda (2003). "Introducing the Interactive XMF Audio File Format." *Gamasutra* (May 28). Http:// www.gamasutra.com.

Lehrman, Paul D. (2007). "The Noise in the Box: Audio for Videogames, Part 2." *Mix* (March).

Linkola, Joonas (1997). "Monkey Island 2: LeChuck's Revenge." Http://www.adventureclassicgaming .com/index.php/site/reviews/37.

Lissa, Zofia (1965). *Ästhetik der Filmmusik*. Berlin: Henscherverlag.

Macan, Edward (1997). *Rocking the Classics: English Progressive Rock and the Counterculture*. Oxford: Oxford University Press.

MacDonald, Mark (2005). "The Legend of Zelda." *Electronic Gaming Monthly.* Http://www.1up.com/do/feature?pager.offset=5&cId=3140040.

Manninen, Tomi Kujanpää, Laura Vallius, Tuomo Korva, and Pekko Koskinen (2006). "Game Production Process: A Preliminary Study." LudoCraft/ELIAS project, Oulun lääninhallitus Interreg III A Karjala (February 28): http://ludocraft.oulu.fi/elias/dokumentit/game_production_process.pdf.

Manovich, Lev (2001). *The Language of New Media.* Cambridge, Mass.: MIT Press.

Manvell, Roger, and John Huntley (1975). *The Technique of Film Music.* New York: Focal Press.

Marino, Gerard (2006). "*God of War*: Sound and Music Production." Presentation at the annual Game Developer's Conference, San Jose, Calif., March 20–24.

Marks, Aaron (2002). *The Complete Guide to Game Audio: For Composers, Musicians, Sound Designers, and Game Developers.* Lawrence, Kansas: CMP Books.

Martin, Josh (1983). "Sound in Video Games: How Do They Make It? How Do We Use It?" *Video Games Player*: http://gamesmuseum.pixesthesia.com/texts/sound.txt.

Mendez, Santiago (2005). "The Dig Museum: Exclusive Interview with Michael Land." Http://dig.mixnmojo.com/museum/interview_land.html.

Middleton, Richard (1996). "Over and Over: Notes towards a Politics of Repetition: Surveying the Ground, Charting Some Routes." Paper presented at the Grounding Music conference, Berlin, May.

Miller, Mark (1999). "3D Audio." *Gamasutra*: http://www.gamasutra.com/features/19991102/gameaudiosupp/3daudio.htm.

Morton, Scott B. (2005). "Enhancing the Impact of Music in Drama-Oriented Games." *Gamasutra* (January 24): http://www.gamasutra.com/features/20050124/morton_01.shtml.

Murch, Walter (2000). "Stretching Sound to Help the Mind." *New York Times* (October 1): http://www.filmsound.org/murch/stretching.htm.

Murray, Janet H. (2005). "The Last Word on Ludology v. Narratology in Game Studies." Paper delivered at the Digital Games Research Association conference, Vancouver, Canada (June 17): http://www.lcc.gatech.edu/~murray/digra05/lastword.pdf.

Nokia Corporation (2005). "From Beeps to Soundscapes: Designing Mobile Game Audio." Http://sw.nokia.com/id/e2b3d80a-5ea7-453b-978e-1814310b4639/From_Beeps_To_Soundscapes_Designing_Mobile_Game_Audio_v1_0_en.pdf.

Oldenbourg, Nannette Drake (2005). "A Conversation with Walter Murch." *Transom Review* 5, no. 1: http://www.transom.org/guests/review/200504.review.murch3.html.

Oxford, Nadia (2005). "Trials and Tribulations: Video Games Many Visits to the Courts." Http://www.1up.com/do/feature?cId=3146206.

Paul, Leonard (2008). "An Introduction to Granular Synthesis in Next-Generation Games." In *From Pac-Man to Pop Music: Interactive Audio in Games and New Media*, edited by Karen Collins. Aldershot: Ashgate.

Peterson, Ivars (2001). "Mozart's Melody Machine." *MAA Online* (August 27): http://www.maa.org/mathland/mathtrek_8_21_01.html.

Pimentel, Sergio (2006a). "Music Acquisition for Games." Paper presented at the annual Game Developer's Conference, San Jose, Calif., March 20–24.

Pimentel, Sergio (2006b). "Wipeout Pure Interview with Sergio Pimentel, Music Licensing Manager—Sony Computer Entertainment Europe." *Music4Games* (February): http://music4games.net/Features_Display.aspx?id=4.

Poole, Steven (2000). *Trigger Happy: Video Games and the Entertainment Revolution.* New York: Arcade Publishing.

Pouladi, Ali (2004). "An Interview with Ben Dalglish." *Lemon 64*: http://www.lemon64.com/interviews/ben_dalglish.php.

Powers, Ann (2007). "Nine Inch Nails Creates a World from 'Year Zero.'" *Los Angeles Times* (April 17).

Prendergast, Roy (1977). *A Neglected Art: A Critical Study of Music in Films*. New York: New York University Press.

Prince, Bobby (2006). "Tricks and Techniques for Sound Design." Paper presented at the annual Game Developer's Conference, San Jose, Calif., March 20–24.

Prince, Stephen (1996). "True Lies: Perceptual Realism, Digital Images, and Film Theory." *Film Quarterly* 49, no. 3: 27–37.

Rapée, Erno (1924). *Motion Picture Moods for Pianists and Organists*. New York: G. Schirmer. (Reprinted in 1974 by the Arno Press.)

Righter, Dennis, and Rebecca Mercuri (1985). "The Yamaha DX-7 Synthesizer: A New Tool for Teachers." In *Proceedings from the 5th Symposium on Small Computers in the Arts*. Philadelphia: IEEE Computer Society.

"Robyn Miller Interview" (2006). *Myst Obsession*: http://www.mystobsession.com/?page=Robyn%20Miller%20Interview.

Rollings, Andrew, and Ernest Adams (2003). *Andrew Rollings and Ernest Adams on Game Design*. Indianapolis: New Riders Publishing.

Rona, Jeff (2000). *The Reel World: Scoring for Pictures*. San Francisco: Miller Freeman.

Rouse, Richard (2005). *Game Design Theory and Practice*, second edition. Plano, Texas: Wordware.

Sadoff, Ronald H. (2006). "The Role of the Music Editor and the 'Temp Track' as Blueprint for the Score, Source Music, and Scource Music of Films." *Popular Music* 25, no. 2: 165–183.

Salen, Katie, and Eric Zimmerman (2003). *Rules of Play: Game Design Fundamentals*. Cambridge, Mass.: MIT Press.

Salt, Barry (1985). *Film Style and Technology: History and Analysis*. London: Starword.

Sanger, George (2003). *The Fat Man on Game Audio: Tasty Morsels of Sonic Goodness*. Berkeley, Calif.: New Riders.

Schadt, Toby (2007). "Postmortem on Tony Hawk's Downhill Jam for Wii 'Not Your Typical Grind.'" *Game Developer* 14, no. 1 (January): 30–32.

ScoreKeeper (2007). "ScoreKeeper with Composer John Debney about Scoring *LAIR* for PlayStation 3, Maybe Iron Man, and More!!" (March 6): http://www.aintitcool.com/node/31783.

Selfon, Scott (2005). "Variation." In *DirectX 9 Audio Exposed: Interactive Audio Development*, edited by Todd M. Fay, Scott Selfon, and Todor J. Fay, 41–53. Plano, Texas: Wordware Publishing.

Selfon, Scott (2006). "Audio Boot Camp." Paper presented at the annual Game Developer's Conference, San Jose, Calif., March 20–24.

Shah, Sarju (2006). "Next Gen Audio: Metal Gear Solid 4." *Gamespot*: http://www.gamespot.com/features/6147812/index.html.

Sheff, David (1993). *Game Over: How Nintendo Zapped an American Industry, Captured Your Dollars, and Enslaved Your Children*. New York: Random House.

Shinkle, Eugénie (2005). "Feel It, Don't Think: The Significance of Affect in the Study of Digital Games." Paper presented at the 2005 Digital Games Research Association conference.

Slocum, Paul (2003). "Atari 2600 Music and Sound Programming Guide." Http://qotile.net/files/2600_music_guide.txt.

Smalley, Roger (1974). "Momente: Material for the Listener and Composer." *Musical Times* 115, no. 1571: 23–28.

Smith, Jeff (1998). *The Sounds of Commerce: Marketing Popular Film Music*. New York: Columbia University Press.

Spicer, Mark (2004). "(Ac)cumulative Form in Popular Music." *Twentieth Century Music* 1, no. 1: 29–64.

Stockburger, Axel (2003). "The Game Environment from an Auditive Perspective." *AudioGames.net*: http://www.audiogames.net/pics/upload/gameenvironment.htm.

Stolberg, Eckhard (2003). "VCS Workshop." Http://home.arcor.de/estolberg/texts/freqform.txt.

Sweet, Michael (2004). "Using Audio as a Game Feedback Device." In *Game Design Workshop: Designing, Prototyping, and Playtesting Games*, edited by Tracy Fullerton, Christopher Swain, and Steven Hoffman, 307–310. Burlington, Mass.: CMP Books.

Tagg, Philip (2000). *Kojak: Fifty Seconds of Television Music*. New York: Mass Media Music Scholars' Press.

Tessler, Holly (2008). "The New MTV? Electronic Arts and 'Playing' Music." In *From Pac-Man to Pop Music: Interactive Audio in Games and New Media*, edited by Karen Collins, 13–26. Aldershot: Ashgate.

Thayer, Alexander, and Beth E. Kolko (2004). "Localization of Digital Games: The Process of Blending for the Global Games Market." *Technical Communication* 51, no. 4: 477–488.

Théberge, Paul (1997). *Any Sound You Can Imagine: Making Music/Consuming Technology*. Middletown, Conn.: Wesleyan University Press.

Totilo, Stephen (2006). "Think 'Nintendogs' Was Strange? Try Making Interactive Music with Plankton." MTV.com: http://www.mtv.com/games/video_games/news/story.jhtml?id=1520528.

Trenkamp, Anne (1976). "The Concept of 'Alea' in Boulez's 'Constellation-Miroir.'" *Music and Letters* 57, no. 1: 1–10.

Varga, Andreas (1996). "Interview with Bob Yannes." Http://www.landley.net/history/mirror/commodore/yannes.html.

Wallis, Alistair (2007). "Playing Catch Up: Zombies Ate My Neighbors' Mike Ebert." *Game Career Guide* (January 11): http://www.gamasutra.com/proto_edu/industry_news/12360/playing_catch_up_zombies_ate_my_neighbors_mike_ebert.php.

Warwick, Rich (1998). "Avoiding a DirectSound 3D Disaster." *Game Developer Magazine* (January): http://gamasutra.com/features/sound_and_music/19980417/directsound3d_disaster_01.htm.

Weske, Jörg (2000). "Digital Sound and Music in Computer Games." Http://www.tu-chemnitz.de/phil/hypertexte/gamesound/pcsound-main.html.

Whitmore, Guy (2003). "Design with Music in Mind: A Guide to Adaptive Audio for Game Designers." *Gamasutra* (May 28): http://www.gamasutra.com/resource_guide/20030528/whitmore_pfv.htm.

Whitmore, Guy (2004). "Adaptive Audio Now! A Spy's Score: A Case Study for *No One Lives Forever*." In *DirectX 9 Audio Exposed: Interactive Audio Development*, edited by Todd M. Fay, Scott Selfon, and Todor J. Fay, 387–416. Plano, Texas: Wordware Publishing.

Whalen, Zach (2004). "Play Along: An Approach to Videogame Music." *Game Studies* 4, no. 1: http://gamestudies.org/0401/whalen.

Wing, Eric (n.d.). "The History of PC Game MIDI." Http://www.queststudios.com/quest/midi.html.

Wolf, Mark J. P. (2002). "Genre and the Video Game." In *The Medium of the Video Game*, edited by Mark J. P. Wolf, 113–134. Austin: University of Texas Press.

Zamecnik, J. S. (1913). *Sam Fox Moving Picture Music*. Cleveland, Ohio: Sam Fox Publishing.

Zizza, Keith (2000). "Your Audio Design Document: Important Items to Consider in Audio Design, Production, and Support." *Gamasutra* (July 26): http://www.gamasutra.com/features/20000726/zizza_pfv.htm.

Zölzer, Udo, Xavier Amatriain, and Daniel Arfib (2002). *DAFX–Digital Audio Effects*. Mississauga: John Wiley and Sons Canada.

INDEX